The Lobbying and Advocacy Handbook
for Nonprofit Organizations

SECOND EDITION

The Lobbying and Advocacy Handbook

FOR NONPROFIT ORGANIZATIONS

SHAPING PUBLIC POLICY AT THE STATE AND LOCAL LEVEL

SECOND EDITION

Marcia Avner

FIELDSTONE
ALLIANCE

SAINT PAUL
MINNESOTA

We thank The David and Lucile Packard Foundation
for support of this publication.

Fieldstone Alliance
An imprint of Turner Publishing Company

445 Park Avenue, 9th Floor
New York, NY 10022

200 4th Avenue North, Suite 950
Nashville, TN 37219

www.turnerpublishing.com
www.fieldstonealliance.com

Fieldstone Alliance is committed to strengthening the performance of the nonprofit sector. Through the synergy of its consulting, training, publishing, and research and demonstration projects, Fieldstone Alliance provides solutions to issues facing nonprofits, funders, and the communities they serve. Fieldstone Alliance was formerly Wilder Publishing and Wilder Consulting departments of the Amherst H. Wilder Foundation. If you would like more information about our services, please contact Fieldstone Alliance, (651)556-4500.

Edited by Vincent Hyman and Christina Roth
Designed by Kirsten Nielsen and Mike Penticost
Cover designed by Rebecca Andrews and Gina Binkley

Manufactured in the United States of America

First printing, July 2013

Library of Congress Cataloging-in-Publication Data

Avner, Marcia, 1943-
 The lobbying and advocacy handbook for nonprofit organizations : shaping public policy at the state and local level / Marcia Avner.
-- Second edition.
   pages cm
 ISBN 978-1-63026-449-9
1. Lobbying--United States--Handbooks, manuals, etc. 2. Lobbying--Law and legislation--United States--Handbooks, manuals, etc. I. Title.
JK1118.A95 2013
659.2--dc23
                              2013013944

Dedication

This book is dedicated to the achievements of nonprofit organizations in shaping public policy—past, present, and future.

It is also dedicated to you, the staff and board members, who work tirelessly to accomplish your nonprofit's mission, and to faculty and students everywhere who rely on this book to guide a sector-wide understanding of the power of advocacy and lobbying.

Thank you for all that you do to position nonprofit organizations to be intentional, systematic, and strategic in advancing policy priorities. The experience and expertise of nonprofits is essential to a fully informed policy dialogue. Your leadership and your efforts to engage the people you serve in the decisions that impact their lives and communities strengthen our democracy.

This is work worth doing well. Plan, organize, advocate! Make a difference!

About the Author

MARCIA AVNER is a consultant whose national practice includes advocacy planning and strategy; issue-campaign design, organizing, lobbying, and media training; curriculum development; and facilitation. She works with nonprofits, foundations, and academic centers on initiatives to advance advocacy and increase activism. The unifying thread in Avner's work is a deep commitment to advancing advocacy in the nonprofit sector and the broader community.

Avner is a faculty member and Coordinator of the Nonprofit Concentration in the Masters in Advocacy and Political Leadership Program (MAPL) at the University of Minnesota-Duluth. She teaches courses in the relationships between government and nonprofits, nonprofit advocacy and organizing, and the role of art in social-change movements. MAPL is a program that integrates theory and practice as it prepares individuals to work in organizing, advocacy, and political leadership.

She is a senior Fellow at the Minnesota Council of Nonprofits (MCN), where she was Public Policy Director from 1996 to 2010. MCN is a statewide association of nonprofits with over 2,000 member organizations. At MCN, Avner's work encompassed advocacy strategy, program design, and leadership of the Council's policy research, analysis, training, civic engagement, and lobbying initiatives.

Avner has authored *The Lobbying and Advocacy Handbook for Nonprofit Organizations: Shaping Public Policy at the State and Local Level* in its first edition (2002), and *The Board Member's Guide to Lobbying and Advocacy* (2004). For Northwest Area Foundation, she wrote *Advancing Public Policy Strategies for Poverty Reduction: An Invitation to Foundations* (2009). In 2009, she also wrote the advocacy chapter for the third edition of the *Jossey-Bass Handbook on Nonprofit Leadership and Management.* She authored the handbook *Advocate for Impact: Policy Guide for State and Local United Ways* for United Way Worldwide in 2010.

Prior to her work with MCN and MAPL, Avner served as Communications Director for U.S. Senator Paul Wellstone, Deputy Mayor of St Paul, Executive Director of The Minnesota Project, Assistant Commissioner of Energy for the State of Minnesota, and Legislative Director with the Minnesota Public Interest Research Group.

Avner serves on numerous community and nonprofit boards, including Wellstone Action! and the Wellstone Action Fund, United Family Medicine, and Jewish Family Service. She recently completed board service with the Center for Lobbying in the Public Interest and the Nonprofit Information Networking Association, which publishes *The Nonprofit Quarterly*. She volunteers with the Center for Victims of Torture.

About the Contributors

JOSH WISE is a founding partner of Sinderbrand Wise Strategies, a consultancy dedicated to working with electoral and advocacy campaigns to connect the right message to the right group of people in order to maximize their efforts. He is the Executive Director of the Minnesota Fair Trade Coalition and previously worked with the Service Employees International Union (SEIU) and with Minnesota Citizens for the Arts. While at SEIU, Wise co-founded and still directs the Twin Cities Labor Chorus, uniting his passions of music and social justice. His work reflects a strong belief in the power of advocacy and organizing to create a better world for all. In addition to his professional work, he serves on the St Paul Regional Labor Federation Labor Community Action Committee and on the organizing committee of the Minneapolis Battle of the Jug Bands, which raises funds for nonprofits in the West Bank neighborhood of Minneapolis. Wise contributed the social media and other communications components of this book.

JEFF NARABROOK is a the Voter Outreach Director in the Office of the Secretary of State in Minnesota. In his previous work at the Minnesota Council of Nonprofits, he provided leadership to the Minnesota Participation Project, MCN's program that builds capacity among nonprofit organizations for engaging their constituencies and communities in civic participation. He led MCN's 2009–2010 outreach and education efforts on the 2010 Census and participated in MCN's work on redistricting and election-reform efforts. He also managed public policy web communications, wrote and distributed e-newsletters, and created GIS maps. Narabrook contributed the chapter on Civic Engagement to this edition of the Handbook.

JEANNIE FOX is the Deputy Director of Public Policy at the Minnesota Council of Nonprofits. She is responsible for direct and grassroots lobbying and advocacy efforts on behalf of the nonprofit sector in Minnesota. Fox is a frequent speaker and trainer to nonprofits, increasing their capacity to do advocacy and civic-engagement work. She has developed extensive training curricula for MCN-sponsored training series in Minnesota as well as custom policy institutes in various states, including Michigan, Illinois, Colorado and Florida. Jeannie is also an adjunct faculty member of the University of Minnesota-Duluth, Masters in Advocacy and Political Leadership department, and at the Hubert H. Humphrey School of Public Affairs at the University of Minnesota. She chairs the Board of the Immigrant Law Center of Minnesota and is a Legislative Fellow in the Department of State's Legislative Fellows Program. Fox contributed additions on administrative advocacy and work with the Executive branch of government to the text and worksheets in this Handbook.

SUSIE BROWN is the second Public Policy Director in the history of the Minnesota Council of Nonprofits. Prior to her role at MCN, she served as executive director of Child Care WORKS, a policy organization working toward building a quality, affordable child-care system for all of Minnesota's families. Prior to that role, she served as Public Policy Director for The Family Partnership, Minneapolis, and in several roles with Planned Parenthood in Connecticut and Vermont, including Public Affairs Director and Director of Planned Parenthood's 501(c)4 Vermont Action Fund. She has been adjunct faculty and practitioner in residence at the Hamline School of Business, teaching nonprofit management and public policy in the Masters of Nonprofit Management Program. Brown contributed information about ballot measures and public policy committees to this Handbook.

About the Case Study Contributors

PATTI WHITNEY-WISE is Executive Director of Partners for a Hunger-Free Oregon and its policy body, Oregon Hunger Task Force. She helped Oregon become the only state in the country to reduce hunger, as measured in the 2005 USDA report. She is an author of "Act to End Hunger: 40 Ways in 5 Years to Make a Difference." Whitney-Wise's 32 years of experience include multi-state outreach on federal programs for the Children's Rights Group and addressing poverty issues as the Executive Director for the California Council of Churches. She has recently partnered with Oregon First Lady Cylvia Hayes to incorporate her "Ending Hunger" plan into Hayes's new prosperity initiative.

KENZA HADJ-MOUSSA is Communications and Development Director for the Minnesota Coalition for the Homeless. She previously worked for the Minnesota Department of Human Services and St. Stephens Human Services. Hadj-Moussa serves on the board of Our Saviours Community Services and the Social Change Fund Committee of the Headwaters Foundation. She holds an M.A. in Advocacy and Political Leadership from the University of Minnesota-Duluth.

Contents

Foreword

"Never doubt that a small group of thoughtful,
committed citizens can change the world.
Indeed, it's the only thing that ever has."
— *Margaret Mead*

Legislative advocacy by nonprofit organizations has been a defining aspect of U.S. social progress for the last 50 years. Organized citizen voices (sometimes criticized as "pressure groups") have been essential contributors to the passage of landmark pieces of legislation, from the Civil Rights Act of 1964 to the Clean Air Act of 1970 and the Americans with Disabilities Act of 1990—and made similar impacts at the state, county, and city level on any number of issues. Americans have learned that, if you want to fight (or support) City Hall, you are far more effective when you do it with others, have a clear agenda, and have a lobbying plan.

This instrumental role of "people power," using the power of numbers combined with a savvy knowledge of legislative processes, media, and persuasion, goes at least as far back as the formation of the United States. Beginning in 1791, the First Amendment guaranteed the "right of the people peaceably to assemble, and to petition the Government for a redress of grievances," anticipating important roles for citizens beyond simply electing representatives, and this is now an essential complementary voice in democracies worldwide.

While nonprofits may be best known for the activities of sponsoring arts and culture, providing health and human services, forming schools and universities, underlying each of these activities is the belief that citizens in a democracy have a right (and for many a natural desire) to be involved in collective efforts that are larger than friends and family but smaller than the state. It is also true that the nonprofit sector's active democracy role inevitably leads to tension with government, resulting in regulation and some restrictions, and in some countries outright suppression and police action.

Even as the democratic role of nonprofit organizations is a permanent fixture on the political landscape, the methods and vehicles are constantly evolving. From Internet advocacy, social media, and new organizational forms to changes in regulations and disclosure requirements, the last 10 years have seen both an increase in nonprofit advocacy and a major shift in the way it is done—making this new edition of the Handbook a necessity.

Many important fields of the U.S. nonprofit sector have their origins in an intense period of activism and direct public and legislative advocacy but now have a greatly reduced presence in public decision making after becoming institutionalized with public contracts, full-time paid staff, well organized fundraisers, and websites. This is true for many organizations across the domestic-violence movement, neighborhood organizing, education reform, environmental protection, civil rights, HIV/AIDS, disability access, etc. While the highest point of activism and public attention of early years may not be possible to sustain over the long run, it should not be abandoned since "eternal vigilance is the price of liberty." It is regrettable that only about a third of nonprofits are actively engaged in public policy, even though the issue and people they work with are deeply affected by government decisions every day—and sometimes the very existence of their organization is dependent on continued government funding.

Fortunately, there is a growing partnership among longtime advocates and new leaders joining the sector who agree that there is no good reason for nonprofits to be bystanders, not have a public policy committee or participate in the decisions affecting their field. That is a leadership responsibility, and to do otherwise ignores a key aspect of how the modern world functions. In this book, Marcia Avner presents a critical guide and skill set for leaders of organizations. I have seen that board members and managers of nonprofit organizations are constantly drilled in every aspect of the basics of financial management, IRS reporting, HR, performance measurement, good governance, and so on. Public policy advocacy needs to be seen in that same light as an essential competency if nonprofit organizations are to achieve their potential.

If I had my way, every interview for a new nonprofit executive director, CEO, board chair, or senior manager would include the questions "What do you think should be on this organization's public policy agenda? How would you go about making that happen?" For the second question, the pages that follow offer the best guide there is.

Jon Pratt
Executive Director, Minnesota Council of Nonprofits

This is the 2nd Edition of *The Lobbying and Advocacy Handbook for Nonprofit Orga-*

Acknowledgments

nizations. The initial version of this book and the new edition have been shaped by many advocates who have been my teachers, colleagues, and inspiration. This work has always depended on the insights, experience, and expertise of leaders in the field:

David Arons, co-founder, Center for Lobbying in the Public Interest, author and advocate
Gary Bass, The Bauman Foundation
Patricia Bauman, The Bauman Foundation
Depaak Bhargava, Center for Community Change
Jeff Blodgett, founder, Wellstone Action
C. Scott Cooper, RE-AMP Network
Dan Cramer, Grassroots Solutions
Gary Cunningham, Northwest Area Foundation
Suzanne Koeplinger, Minnesota Indian Women's Resource Center
Dan McGrath, TakeAction Minnesota
Nan Madden, Minnesota Budget Project, Minnesota Council of Nonprofits
Javier Morillo-Alicea, SEIU
Erik Peterson, Wellstone Action, Teacher, Organizer
George Pillsbury, Nonprofit VOTE
Jon Pratt, Minnesota Council of Nonprofits; Masters in Advocacy and Political Leadership
Miles Rapoport, Demos
Robert Richman, Grassroots Solutions
Mark Ritchie, Secretary of State, Minnesota
Sheila Smith, Minnesota Citizens for the Arts
Bob Smucker, founder, Center for Lobbying in the Public Interest
Bob Tracy, Minnesota Council on Foundations
The late Sen. Paul and Sheila Wellstone
Christina Wessel, Minnesota Budget Project, Minnesota Council of Nonprofits

Special thanks to the colleagues who contributed to this new edition of the Handbook. Josh Wise is himself a nonprofit leader, musician, and social-media strategist who has added new dimensions to a work that initially mentioned only MySpace and the websites at large organizations. (In 2002, it was impossible to anticipate Twitter, Facebook, texting, and the as-yet-unknown advances in moving messages.) Jeff Narabrook serves as a national leader in encouraging nonprofits to ensure that civic engagement is an ongoing component of their work. He has developed materials, training, and messages that have supported hundreds of nonprofits in doing nonpartisan voter engagement well. Jeannie Fox is a master trainer and experienced advocate who knows how to sustain work with administrative and legislative bodies. She has been effective in promoting and protecting the nonprofit sector in many arenas of change. Susie Brown, who succeeds me as the Public Policy Director at the Minnesota Council of Nonprofits, has led effective advocacy campaigns throughout her career. She unites the nonprofits in Minnesota around shared interests and opportunities. Jon Pratt has provided the Foreword for this edition of the Handbook, and he has been committed to the creation and expansion of the Handbook throughout the many years that we have worked together. His enthusiasm for expanding the field is key to sector advocacy.

My students have been drivers of the updates and revisions in this edition. Special thanks to all those in the Masters in Advocacy in Political Leadership at the University of Minnesota-Duluth and to the first cohort in the Minnesota Council of Nonprofits Advocacy Institute.

Vince Hyman, the editor at Fieldstone Alliance who worked with the first edition of this book, helped me to understand how to design this book to reach its intended audiences and to be a useful tool for advocacy planning, skill building, and issue-campaign design. Christina Roth at Turner Publishing has guided this new edition and moved it into the marketplace of nonprofit resources.

Thanks to my son, Caleb Janssen, who tossed me into the field of advocacy in 1972. I am forever grateful.

Wyman Spano, my husband and best friend, has also been my mentor. He reminds me every day of how important it is to support nonprofit leaders in being "people of the process." Now, more than ever, nonprofits need to be trusted resources to political leaders. His work and mine are joined in doing all that we can to encourage individuals to lead the way with knowledge, skills, and integrity.

Foundations that understand the importance of nonprofit advocacy have supported the development of this book in its initial and updated forms. The McKnight Foundation, the Minneapolis Foundation, the Northwest Area Foundation, the Packard Foundation, and the St Paul Foundation have been leaders in recognizing that people and communities need to have a voice in the issues that shape their quality of life.

My grandmother, Mania Zaludkowski, often said, "You don't ask, you don't get." Therefore, advocate!

Why Engage in Advocacy? Why Lobby?

Nonprofit organizations can and should lobby.

It isn't difficult.

It isn't mysterious.

It isn't expensive.

And it *is* a proper role for nonprofits.

The Essential Role of Nonprofits in Shaping Public Policy: Why Lobby?

Lobbying builds public policies that improve people's lives and the places where they live. It enriches a nonprofit's ability to fulfill its mission.

Nonprofits do a lot to promote the interests of their communities. Your organization most likely already does some advocacy work. You may be raising awareness of the value of literacy or fighting for livable wages or encouraging recycling. Perhaps you advocate for victims in the criminal-justice system or urge social-service programs to incorporate arts into their programs. Think of lobbying as a specific and critical component of that general advocacy you already do for the people and ideas that matter to you.

Through nonprofit organizations, people are able to join together to nurture the values and provide programs and services that strengthen their communities. The first philanthropic organizations gained legal status in the United States shortly before the Civil War. Since then, nonprofits have served a wide range of societal goals in arts, education, environment, social services, human services, health care, social justice, and economic security.

It is through working in nonprofits that we have one of our best opportunities to shape the social contract—the choices we make about how we will connect to one another. Nonprofits, community-based organizations, voluntary associations, and charities have been excellent vehicles for people to engage in the life of their communities. Nonprofits animate people to do together what they cannot do separately. And now more than ever, the people involved in nonprofits understand that their role is not only to deliver programs and services but also to engage in public discussions about the governmental policies that shape our local, state, and federal priorities.

Lobbying is exciting and rewarding work! This is your organization's opportunity to provide leadership in shaping and sustaining public policies that reflect your values and priorities. It may be your best way of guaranteeing that you can carry out services and programs in a supportive environment and that your community works on long-term and lasting solutions to the problems you address.

Consider some of the positive changes brought about by nonprofit lobbying:

- Nonprofit organizations that work to eradicate poverty have led many states to pass earned-income-tax-credit legislation. These measures ensure that people who work have a better chance of maintaining income levels that will support themselves and their families.

- Affordable housing, child care, and improved transportation options have received increased funding because of nonprofit lobbyists who have worked to move people off of welfare and out of poverty.

- Arts organizations have been effective lobbyists for public art projects: murals, sculpture gardens in public spaces, and art as a required component of publicly funded building projects.

- At the national and state level, nonprofit lobbying has played a key role in legislation to protect clean air, safe water, and waste reduction.

This book will guide the work of nonprofit boards, staff, volunteers, and constituencies as they move into public policy arenas and lobby on issues essential to the well-being of their communities and the people they serve.

Nonprofit lobbying in the public interest makes a difference. Try it!

Lobby because it makes a difference

Without the experience and expertise of nonprofits, the public debate will never be fully informed. And without nonprofits doing direct and grassroots lobbying, many people will never make their voices heard in the centers of power in this country. Nonprofit lobbying fosters citizen action; it is an essential act in a democracy.

Who This Book Is For

This book is for boards and staffs of nonprofit organizations that aim to build their capacity and effectiveness in state and local public policy advocacy. It will also serve volunteers and supporters who participate in advocacy and care about the effectiveness of the organization's lobbying efforts.

Planning and implementation strategies included here are designed to serve all nonprofits, large or small, rookies or veterans in public policy work. If your organization is very small, you may wish to follow recommended shortcuts in the planning process. If your organization has significant experience in advocacy, you may want to choose the sections that will strengthen your work, filling in gaps in your capacity or actions by ensuring that you have internal systems to support your advocacy work or expanding the role of board members in your lobbying efforts. Keep in mind that the process of creating an advocacy agenda and carrying it out is one that, in general terms, applies to almost all organizations.

The information in this book will be useful to all community-based organizations, but it is specifically intended for 501(c)(3) charities. If your organization has been designated with 501(c)(4) or any other IRS status, the rules that govern your ability to lobby or engage in political activity will be different from the information provided in Chapter 4: Nonprofit Lobbying and the Law. National organizations, including the Alliance for Justice, National Council of Nonprofit Organizations, and Independent Sector, will help you to understand the unique tax laws that govern your activity. Information about these and other resources is included in Appendix B.

Note that this book does not constitute legal advice. If your organization has legal questions about lobbying and other advocacy efforts, consult an attorney.

The key concepts in this text are for everyone. Choose the components that suit your needs and interests, plan to adapt what you learn here to your unique situation, and lobby strategically!

Think nonprofits can't lobby?

While nonprofits are not allowed to engage in political activity, they are allowed and encouraged to lobby. Get all the details in Chapter 4.

How to Use This Book

The Lobbying and Advocacy Handbook for Nonprofit Organizations is a planning guide and resource for nonprofit organizations that want to be an effective voice on the issues that matter to them. It will support you as you mobilize others to be their own best voice. Working with this guide, you will build your capacity to shape the policies that touch people's lives. You will be better able to serve the public interest.

This step-by-step guide focuses on lobbying at the state level, with an emphasis on influencing state legislatures.

Advocacy makes a $37.5 million difference for affordable housing

Contributed by Kenza Hadj-Moussa, Minnesota Coalition for the Homeless

In 2011, nonprofit leaders formed the Homes for All coalition. The economy was fragile and human services budgets were being cut. Political gridlock shut down the state government for nearly a month. Homelessness had reached a record high.

On May 8, 2012, the Minnesota Legislature passed a bonding bill that invested a record $37.5 million in affordable-housing development. The bill was passed with broad political and geographic support. It was approved by a Republican-controlled legislature and Democratic governor.

Three factors drove the success of this campaign: unified advocacy, a clear goal, and coordinated leverage among nonprofit networks.

1. Unified Advocacy

The economic and political climate challenged complementary allies to take a unified approach to advocacy. Homes for All united homeless and housing advocates around a shared legislative agenda and campaign strategy.

Co-chaired by the Minnesota Coalition for the Homeless and Metropolitan Consortium of Community Developers, steering committee members included: Hearth Connection, Heading Home Minnesota, Catholic Charities, Lutheran Social Services, Twin Cities Habitat for Humanity, and Minnesota Housing Partnership.

Collectively, these organizations represented a united, broad constituency base including: private-housing developers, rural and urban social services, faith advocates, business leaders, foundation officers, and community development agencies.

2. Clear, Specific, Achievable Goal

In 2012, Homes for All launched a campaign to support a clear, specific, and achievable goal: pass $40 million in bonds for affordable housing. Leaders decided that the coalition would hold firm to the same message: $40 million for housing.

The clear, precise, repeated advocacy made affordable housing a key issue in the bonding bill.

The bill was widely supported by legislators and nonprofit organizations because it provided a broad boost to the housing sector as a whole. Instead of earmarking funding for specific projects, the legislation allowed development funds to be awarded through a competitive state grant process.

3. Leveraged Networks

Homes for All used their expansive network, an asset of the nonprofit community, to leverage their people-power. The coalition mobilized front-line staff, donors, volunteers, board members, and service participants in the effort. The core Homes for All team supported each other's organizations to execute lobby days, letters-to-the-editor drives, and postcard campaigns.

Citizen lobbyists were equipped with basic data and came with personal stories about homelessness in their areas and descriptions of what housing could be developed with the funding.

Short-Term Outcomes

In late 2012, Minnesota Housing awarded $37.5 million to dozens of nonprofit and private developers to build or rehab over 3,100 affordable housing units across the state. Projects included fifty-five units for homeless veterans at Fort Snelling and housing for victims of domestic violence at the Tubman Center.

Long-Term Impact

In 2013, the Homes for All coalition shifted to focus on a $100 million campaign to stabilize families, prevent homelessness, and create workforce housing. Homes for All emerged with a stronger campaign. The coalition started educating legislative candidates and building relationships months before Election Day. During the summer, legislative ambassadors were recruited in districts across the state to be lead constituent advocates.

Highly coordinated policy, communications, and field teams were developed, mirroring the structure of an electoral campaign.

Homes for All has continued to use successful advocacy techniques to lead public policy work grounded in a shared commitment, clear direction, and process to leverage networks. Nonprofits have the expertise, the community standing, and the strength of organized constituencies to truly make a difference in all of our communities.

This text also shows your nonprofit how to use the strategies outlined here to have an impact on county and city governments. While the focus is on legislative bodies at the state and local level, plans for influencing the executive branch and the media are included.

Using this book, you will have the ability to

- Understand your nonprofit's role in shaping state and local public policy

- Assess the benefits of lobbying as a way to fulfill your organization's mission, service, and program goals

- Incorporate strategic lobbying efforts into your organization's culture and work plan

- Establish the infrastructure (systems, staffing, and resources) to support your lobbying efforts

- Choose issue priorities and strategies for initiating, supporting, or defeating bills

- Develop skills to ensure that your lobbying efforts are effective

- Build and mobilize supporters for your efforts

- Influence the executive branch of government to support your policy positions

- Use the media to build awareness of and support for your positions

- Learn how to comply with federal and state regulations and reporting requirements that govern nonprofit advocacy

As you proceed to build your capacity and skills for advocacy, keep in mind that grassroots organizing, media advocacy, and lobbying serve your mission most effectively if you commit to long-term and ongoing work. Understand that effective advocacy is an on-going cycle of planning, engaging people, advancing issues, and building an ever growing base of supporters and sustained involvement in shaping public policy. Building advocacy as a sustained component of your mission-based work requires following the steps reflected in this cycle. Build capacity and impact cycle after cycle and keep your organization engaged in this leadership work.

If lobbying is new to you and members of your organization, use this book as a tool to support your decision making. For the person or team steering the organization's entrée to the world of lobbying, this book gives the basic tools to plan and carry out both short-term and long-term policy initiatives. The guide will help experienced organizations and lobbyists reinvigorate their efforts, review some tried-and-true strategies, and see some new ways to approach lobbying. Finally, the resources identified

Lobbying in D.C.

A note about lobbying at the national level: This guide focuses on legislative activity at the state and local level. Nevertheless, many of the planning steps and principles apply to national activity. For specific guidance on national lobbying, consider resources offered by national organizations, especially Independent Sector, Center for Lobbying in the Public Interest at the National Council of Nonprofits, and the Alliance for Justice. Bob Smucker's *The Nonprofit Lobbying Guide* is an excellent starting point for groups wanting to have an impact on congressional decisions. Information about these resources is included in Appendix B.

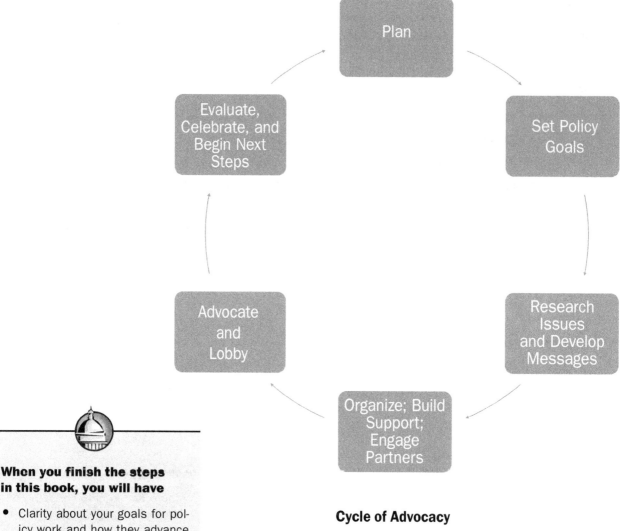

Cycle of Advocacy

**When you finish the steps
in this book, you will have**

- Clarity about your goals for policy work and how they advance your mission

- A detailed strategic plan for your public policy work

- The organizational infrastructure to support your lobbying efforts

- Skills in lobbying the legislative and administrative branches, building and mobilizing grassroots support for your issues, and gaining media support for your positions on issues

- Resources for future reference and further development

throughout the text provide connections to groups whose experience and expertise can support your organization's public policy initiatives.

What's Ahead

There are four chapters in this book, designed around key steps in the development of an advocacy plan for your organization. A series of worksheets help guide you and your organization through the steps to a plan of action. Sample worksheets, embedded in the guide, illustrate the process.

Blank worksheets are found in Appendix E; you may reproduce them as needed to facilitate your planning. Worksheets are also available online to purchasers of this book. To use the online worksheets, visit http://www.turnerpublishing.com/lobbying-and-advocacy-handbook-worksheets.

Chapter 1: *Get Ready!:* **Develop a Plan for Advocacy and Lobbying** helps you "plan your plan," setting the stage for your organization's decision to engage in public policy efforts. This chapter leads you from launching the organizational discussion about public policy through outlining a planning process.

Chapter 2: *Go!:* **Implement Your Advocacy and Lobbying Plan** has two parts. The first directs the planning team through the planning process. It includes a self-assessment tool to help you figure out your baseline capacity. Examples and worksheets provide models and a systematic way for the planning team to record decisions. Your planning team will develop a strategic public policy work plan for the organization to adopt. The second part moves your organization into the action mode. This part contains two sections. First, it guides you in setting up internal systems and structures to facilitate your lobbying activity. Then it guides you through specific legislative lobbying skills to initiate, support, or defeat a bill. It also helps you understand how to use the media to strengthen your public policy impact.

Chapter 3: Sustaining the Cycle of Advocacy: Expanding Impact through Civic Engagement explains how your ongoing advocacy work will be strongest if you adopt a cyclical (rather than linear) model of change. Doing so not only helps insulate your organization from economic and political misfortunes but also allows you to create favorable conditions to advance your issues.

Chapter 4: Nonprofits and the Law explains ways in which the federal government encourages nonprofit lobbying and discusses limits on lobbying expenditures and systems for accounting for lobbying activity. This chapter also includes information about state-level registration and reporting and how to learn about your state's requirements.

Appendices include directions for responding to a crisis or an opportunity (Appendix A); lists of resources for nonprofit lobbying (Appendix B); a guide to legislative processes (Appendix C); an annotated package of samples from a nonprofit (Appendix D); all the blank worksheets (Appendix E); and, finally, a guide to evaluating advocacy (Appendix F).

Ten reasons to lobby for your cause

1. **YOU can make a difference.** In Toledo, Ohio, a single mother struggling to raise her son without the help of a workable child-support system put an ad in a local newspaper to see if there were others who wanted to work for change. There were. Over time, they built the Association for Child Support Enforcement, which has helped change child-support laws across the country.

2. **People working together can make a difference.** Mothers Against Drunk Driving convinced dozens of states to toughen up their drunk-driving laws. As a result, the numbers of drunk-driving deaths are lower nationwide.

3. **People can change laws.** History is full of people and groups that fought great odds to make great changes: child-labor laws, public schools, clean-air and -water laws, Social Security. These changes weren't easy to achieve. They all took the active involvement—the lobbying—of thousands of people who felt something needed to be changed.

4. **Lobbying is a democratic tradition.** The act of telling our policy makers how to write and change our laws is at the very heart of our democratic system. It is an alternative to what has occurred in many other countries: tyranny or revolution. Lobbying has helped keep America's democracy evolving over more than two centuries.

5. **Lobbying helps find real solutions.** People thinking creatively and asking their elected officials for support can generate innovative solutions that overcome the root causes of a problem. Through such work, abused children have found rapid placement in safe homes, and restaurants have been able to donate excess food to food shelves.

6. **Lobbying is easy.** Lobbying isn't some mysterious rite that takes years to master. You can learn how to lobby—whom to call, when, what to say—in minutes. There are a few simple reporting rules that your nonprofit organization needs to follow, but they aren't complicated.

7. **Policy makers need your expertise.** Few institutions are closer to the real problems of people than nonprofits and community groups. Every professional lobbyist will tell you that personal stories are powerful tools for change. People and policy makers can learn from your story.

8. **Lobbying helps people.** Everything that goes into a lobbying campaign—the research, the strategy planning, the phone calls and visits—will help fulfill your goal whether it be finding a cure for cancer, beautifying the local park, or some other cause that helps people.

9. **The views of local nonprofits are important.** Because local governments often decide how to spend federal and state money, local nonprofits have even more responsibility to tell local policy makers what is needed and what will work. Your lobbying can have an immediate, concrete impact on people in need.

10. **Lobbying advances your cause and builds public trust.** Building public trust is essential to nonprofit organizations and lobbying helps you to gain it by increasing your organization's visibility. Just as raising funds and recruiting volunteers are important to achieving your organization's mission, so is lobbying.

Adapted from "Ten Reasons to Lobby for Your Cause" by the Center for Lobbying in the Public Interest, now a part of the National Council of Nonprofits. Used with permission.

CHAPTER ONE

Get Ready!
Develop a Plan for Advocacy and Lobbying

Nonprofits increase their likelihood of impacting public policy when they are intentional and prepared. Your organization can design a public policy lobbying effort that serves its mission well. To do so, you will engage in a planning process that answers two key questions:

1. What are our public policy goals on the issues that affect the people we serve?

2. How will our organization carry out our lobbying work?

This chapter prepares you to create a planning process that will answer these questions. It covers ways to get an organizational commitment to public policy participation and maps an eight-step planning process. When you finish this chapter, you will have a plan for advocating in the public interest that includes your work in organizing, lobbying, and media advocacy. In Chapter 3, you will have the opportunity to add one more component to your work, civic engagement. The full cycle of advocacy can and should include work to engage your constituencies in many forms of citizen engagement, including election activity. While being fully nonpartisan, you can strengthen the impact of your organizing and increase elected officials' accountability to their constituents, by educating voters on the process and mobilizing them to vote. Be prepared to incorporate this work into your organization's advocacy plan.

Many nonprofit organizations get drawn into lobbying efforts because of a pressing need to respond to a particular legislative proposal. This is not a bad way to start, and you can use what you learn in such crisis lobbying to plan for strategic, sustainable public policy involvement. Planning will ensure that you will be ready to respond to emerging issues and that you will be positioned to provide leadership in shaping policy. Your involvement will be consistent and purposeful.

While planning should be structured to suit your organization's unique need and specific timeline, some basic steps are generally helpful:

- Launch the discussion. One person can begin the conversation that inspires your nonprofit to understand how lobbying helps fulfill your mission. Interest your organization in considering how advocacy and lobbying makes good sense because it will further your cause.

- Get key leaders' approval to create a public policy plan. Get formal agreement that the organization will design a public policy component as part of its overall work plan. Secure their commitment so planning will be structured and timely.

- Select the public policy planning team and establish a clear set of responsibilities for team members.

- Outline the planning process.

- Begin!

Instructions for accomplishing each of these steps follow.

Launch the Discussion

Your organization may be starting from one of a variety of levels of involvement:

- This may be your first exploratory look at how public policy work could help further your mission.

- You may have been catapulted into public policy work by a threat to your funding or programs. Now you want to back up and think about strategies for long-term policy involvement.

- Yours may be one of many groups that lobby frequently but in a reactive, crisis-oriented mode. It is time, you suspect, to stabilize that effort and operate from a position of strength.

Regardless of your starting point, someone needs to urge the organization to see well-designed public policy advocacy as an opportunity to fulfill your mission and build on your accomplishments. Anyone—YOU, an individual, or a small group—can take a leadership position and begin the discussion. Convince your organization to join the public policy dialogue. Core arguments might include these convincing points:

"This is work worth doing well. Let's figure out a way to target our efforts to make a difference on our key issues. And let's be ready to move into this work with a strategic and sustainable effort."

"I think that if we want to further our mission, meet the needs of our clients and other stakeholders, and change systems that aren't working for the communities we care about, we have to be a voice in the public policy debate."

"We have an opportunity to make a difference on issues that affect our mission. It is our responsibility to use the information we have to inform the public debate and to give our constituencies a chance to be a strong voice for issues that matter to them."

"Providing services and programs isn't enough. We need to lobby for the policies and resources that will solve problems and sustain our efforts to build strong communities and improve people's lives."

"Proactive is better than reactive. Planning matters."

"When we organize our supporters to work for policy changes that further our work, we create a powerful voice in the community. This is leadership work!"

"If we plan to build public policy advocacy into our core work, we will be making the best use of our experience and expertise and serve as a resource to decision makers and opinion shapers who are working with the issues we know well."

"Sometimes the best service that we can provide to our community is to give people an opportunity to work together and have a voice in the decisions that impact their lives."

You know the needs that will convince your organization to embrace public policy as a part of its work. Frame your argument and imbue it with your passion. The next step tells you how to frame the argument. You'll have to provide the passion!

When you face a crisis . . .

If you are surprised by a crisis or an opportunity and need to act quickly on a public policy issue, turn to Appendix A: Rapid Responses to Crises or Opportunities, page 163. Once the immediate policy effort is under control, return to this part of the text for support in building policy work into your overall work plan for the long term.

Get Approval to Develop a Public Policy Plan

You—or whoever is the lead proponent for advocacy and lobbying—will need to meet with the key leaders in your organization to make your case for adding public policy to your organizational agenda. Prepare by framing the arguments as follows:

1. State your mission.

2. Identify how policy work will further your mission. Which state or local policies and funding decisions will solve (or compound) the problems faced by your clients or community? Which policies will strengthen your organization's ability to provide essential programs and services?

3. Specify what your organization could contribute to the debate on the issues you

identify. Your nonprofit no doubt has information and insights without which the public policy debate is not fully informed.

4. For extra impact, identify the consequences of failing to get involved.

5. Show that policy work energizes supporters and builds relationships with decision makers and community partners. It may also engage your members and supporters in exciting new ways. People want your organization to be relevant and to weigh in on issues where you have an interest.

Once you have framed the reasons why lobbying is important to your group's work, raise the issue with your organization's leaders, especially its executive director and board chair. These are the people who set your nonprofit's decision-making agenda. They can determine what additional information, if any, is needed before they seek full support for a planning process. When these key leaders understand the relationship of lobbying to mission, they will be willing to secure board and staff support for this effort and to encourage the participation of those who will do the planning.

In some organizations, the lead advocate can take a well-framed argument straight to the board for approval. In others, he or she may need to take steps to solidify organizational agreement to make public policy a priority. Organizations have used one or more of the following options to get organizational commitment for lobbying. Choose approaches that suit your organization and be creative!

- Discuss the merits of lobbying with the organization's key leaders.

- Meet with other nonprofit lobbyists or executive directors and board members who can speak from experience about the benefits of lobbying.

- Provide leaders with information from state and national groups that support nonprofit lobbying, such as Independent Sector, the National Council of Nonprofits or your own state's nonprofit association, and the Alliance for Justice. (See information in Appendix B: Resources for Nonprofit Lobbying, page 171.)

- Invite your organization's decision makers to participate in nonprofit lobbying training. Many state associations of nonprofits (identified in Appendix B) offer basic training in the how, what, and why of nonprofit advocacy.

- Be sure that leaders know that nonprofits are allowed to lobby—the federal and state laws are quite clear about this—and that lobbying is, in fact, encouraged. There are clear and easy-to-meet guidelines that your nonprofit can follow for lobbying within the limits of the law. (See Chapter 4: Nonprofit Lobbying and the Law.)

- Provide clear expectations about time and resource commitments. Nonprofits can lobby with minimal commitments of staff time and money. Your approach can be as basic or elaborate as needed to fulfill your mission and balance your workload. Nonprofits that dedicate three hours a month to public policy work have shown clear results!

- Prepare a board resolution that would authorize the planning process.

- Offer a sample step-by-step planning process that the organization could adopt and adapt to meet your specific needs. (See Outline the Planning Process in this chapter.)

- Write a charge to the planning team. The worksheets in this book can serve as the guides to the process the team will follow and the format for a plan. Set deadlines that are realistic—but carry momentum—for planning and action.

- Volunteer to help coordinate or support the effort.

Test your own lobbying skills as you persuade your target audience that public policy advocacy is the route to take. Convince your audience that advocacy is in the best interest of the communities you serve. Then seek commitment. Remember that you are NOT asking the board of directors to commit to a specific policy plan at this point. You are asking them to

- Authorize the executive director to proceed with development of a public policy plan for the organization.

- Agree to review the planning process that will be proposed before the actual planning takes place.

- Review, alter, or commit to the plan and budget developed as a result of the process being launched here.

Select the Planning Team

Once your board authorizes the development of a public policy plan, it is wise for the director and board to delegate the planning to a working team. The *public policy planning team* should represent the interests of leaders and stakeholders who will inform your policy work and who will be critical to the adoption and implementation of the plan. Keep the team manageable; three to five people can do this planning with focus and momentum.

Consider including

- The board chair or a board director with an interest in policy work and the ability to inspire thoughtful board review of plans to be proposed.

- The executive director or a staff person with high-level responsibility for the organization's strategic plan and work plans.

- Someone—board member, staff member, volunteer—who understands policy issues and arenas of influence. This person will help shape your organization's strategy for impacting issues that matter to your mission.

- A staff member or volunteer who will be the *planning coordinator*, shepherding this process through its various phases and facilitating communication with larger groups of stakeholders along the way.

- Someone willing and skilled at *recording* the process.

A few terms you need to know:

Public Policy

Public Policy is the combination of goals, laws, and rules set by public officials that determine how government meets needs, solves problems, raises resources, and prioritizes public spending. Public policy is formally set by elected officials at the federal, state, and local levels through the legislative process. Informally, think of public policy as the set of decisions that our elected representatives makes about how we in this society will care for one another, our communities, and the land.

Advocacy

Advocacy involves embracing and promoting a cause. It is an effort to increase awareness about an issue and make the case for changes that are needed. Advocacy may or may not include a call for actual changes in the law. In public policy work, "advocacy" is the overarching term that encompasses many types of activity and persuasion: conducting policy research and analysis to understand problems and shape policy solutions; promoting key ideas about what is needed in society; collecting, creating, and disseminating information about a policy issue; organizing support for issue campaigns; taking a position on a specific policy proposal and lobbying on it; building alliances and coalitions to support causes; mobilizing supporters; promoting favorable media coverage of your issue or position; generating media to move your messages; and countless other ways in which nonprofits advance causes.

For example, when a nonprofit works to end smoking in public buildings, it advocates in many ways: aggregates research about the health impact of nicotine products, publicizes the personal and public costs of health problems related to smoking, argues that everyone has a right to breathe clean air, and organizes a coalition of health-related organizations to form a statewide Smoke Free Coalition.

Lobbying

Lobbying is one specific form of advocacy. It is that component of advocacy that focuses on supporting or opposing a specific law that is being proposed. For example, the nonprofit that wants smoke-free environments and its allies in the Smoke Free Coalition are lobbying when they propose a specific legislative proposal (e.g. a bill, an ordinance) or urge elected officials to vote for or against a specific piece of legislation. The Smoke Free group isn't lobbying when it promotes the general idea that a smoke-free environment is a public-health imperative. It IS lobbying when it urges decision makers to pass a specific bill that, for instance, would prohibit smoking in public buildings and parks. Once the nonprofit asks a decision maker to vote "for" or "against" something, the organization is lobbying. Lobbying requires the "ask."

Organizing

Organizing is an essential component of nonprofit advocacy. It involves people and organizations in coming together to advocate for policies that are important to them and to their community. For many people, nonprofits that organize constituencies to support or oppose an issue create a pathway for people who want to play a meaningful role in the life of their community. An organizing component of an advocacy effort builds a strong base of support for your long-term goals, your ongoing advocacy work, and timely issues campaigns. Organizing builds collective power and positions nonprofits to be an effective force for change. Components of organizing include identifying people and organizations that share your values and policy goals or are persuaded to do so when they are educated about the issue. Organizers do outreach, engage people in discussions about their interests and aspirations, involve people in the development of issues and advocacy strategies, support leadership development among their constituencies, and mobilize supporters to take action.

Media Advocacy

Media advocacy is the component of this work that allows your nonprofit to reach its specific audiences through the mediums that appeal to them. Nonprofit advocacy and organizing have changed significantly over the past decades because of technology advances. The component of advocacy allows for broader reach and greater innovation than ever before, and effective advocates develop media advocacy strategies that are core to their policy work. Nonprofits serve as a resource to journalists and work to get coverage in media venues to inform target audiences about their issues. One target for nonprofit advocates continues to be traditional media: print newspapers, radio, and television. Newer media venues that nonprofits rely on and either create or court include Internet-based media: online newspapers, blogs, websites, and countless forms of social media from Facebook and YouTube to Twitter and beyond. In an age when we see videos and listen to the news at newspaper sites, read the news and enjoy podcasts at radio station websites, and look to blogs for information and commentary, nonprofits can maximize creative options for telling their stories and promoting their messages. Advocates build awareness and understanding about their issues and promote their positions on issues, by using all forms of media to reach their own committed and potential supporters, the general public, opinion shapers, and elected and appointed officials. Nonprofits also need to be media savvy—prepared to respond to media coverage of their issues in timely, responsible, and dynamic ways.

Arenas of Influence

Arenas of influence are where public policy is decided. They include the legislative branch of government, including Congress, state legislatures, county commissions, city councils, metropolitan governments, school boards and other regional or local entities. The administrative branch is equally important. Here changes are made through executive order, through changes in administrative rules, policies, and procedures, and through the use of the veto power by elected executives: the president, governor, or mayor. Some policy decisions are eventually made in the courts, and nonprofits do engage in litigation. Your organization's planning involves targeting the arenas where your issues will be decided and where your involvement can make a difference.

Advocacy Triangle

A Framework for Approaching Public Policy

As your nonprofit develops its public policy plan, it is useful to have a basic framework for thinking about the core components of effective advocacy. This triangle serves as a visual reminder that, once your organization develops its mission-related policy goals, once it identifies the issues for near- and long-term work, there are three key advocacy strategies to employ: organizing, lobbying, and media advocacy.

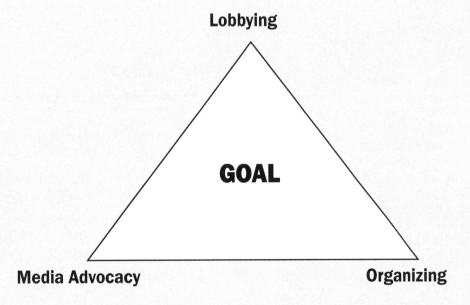

Invite people who *want* to do this planning and who are well respected by the larger stakeholder groups in the organization. A planning team whose members are committed to mission, have good communication skills, and hold honest discussions with one another will have productive and positive outcomes.

Outline the Planning Process

The steps set forth here—or an adapted version that suits your circumstances—can serve as the charge to the planning team. *Preplanning* includes forming the planning team. Once this is accomplished, the actual steps in developing a work plan for your nonprofit's public policy work can be accomplished in six meetings that cover eight planning steps. These steps are discussed in detail and with guiding worksheets in Chapter 2, but they are outlined here so you can tailor them as you create your own process.

If your organization is small, or your board members are not in close geographic proximity, or you are just plain impatient, a few shortcuts are suggested throughout the planning process. Most organizations will be able to accomplish the steps in this process with only six meetings. And you are encouraged to adapt this process to your organization's situation and personality.

Worksheet samples: one organization, GREAT!, serves as a model

The worksheet samples in this book illustrate the planning stages of a fictional nonprofit, one based on a composite of several organizations with which the author has worked. The Gloriously Responsive Employment Advancement Training! (GREAT!) organization provides workforce development programs. Its mission is to support people with barriers to employment to move out of poverty and into jobs that provide a career path and livable wages. GREAT! is probably very different from your nonprofit. These illustrations are intended only to suggest how documentation of the planning process might look.

Preplanning: Team Logistics and Startup

In the preplanning stage you will

1. Name the planning team.

2. Identify the team's planning coordinator who will call meetings and serve as facilitator.

3. Name the recorder who will capture key points of discussion and decisions and who will write up the plan.

4. Review the planning steps outlined here and discussed fully in Chapter 2.

5. Set a schedule of meetings and deadlines for completing each stage of planning. Keep in mind that preplanning should begin well before a legislative session or the crucial stages of local government decision making. Adapt your calendar to your state and local legislative timelines.

The Preplanning Checklist, page 205, is a convenient place to record team members, meeting times, and the formal charge of the planning team. A sample is on page 35.

Eight Planning Steps in Six Meetings

Following are the eight planning steps, set up to be accomplished in six meetings as outlined below. Use this format, or modify it to fit your charge, the size of your organization, and the probable complexity of your plan.

First meeting

Planning Step 1: Prepare the Planning Team. Provide basic orientation for the planning process. This includes a "public policy readiness inventory" that will help you to understand your organization's current capacity for doing public policy work. The inventory is included in Worksheet 1 on page 207.

Planning Step 2: Articulate Vision and Goals. In this step, you create a picture of where you'll go with public policy work, and some goals that will help you get there.

Second meeting

Planning Step 3: Establish Criteria and Identify Issues. In this step, you decide the specific issues you'll tackle.

Third meeting

Planning Step 4: Target Arenas of Influence. In this step, you'll determine which legislative or administrative bodies will be deciding on your issues. You'll begin to learn about those groups.

Fourth meeting

Planning Step 5: Choose Strategies and Tactics. In this step, you'll select the strategies you'll use and begin to develop some tactics to accomplish them.

Planning Step 6: Design Organizational Infrastructure. In this step, you work out decision making, staff commitments, and resource allocations for your public policy work.

Fifth meeting

Planning Step 7: Create Your Work Plan. This is the time to tie all your strategies and tactics into a work plan with specific actions and target dates.

Sixth meeting

Planning Step 8: Present the Work Plan. This is the time to show the plan to key decision makers in your organization and secure their commitment to move forward.

Shortcuts in the process

Organizations that have few employees or wish to proceed more rapidly can condense the eight planning steps and six meetings recommended in this book into two full meetings of the planning committee. To do so, the planning committee should combine the scheduled meetings and delegate to staff additional responsibilities for developing the plan as directed below.

For Planning Step 1, the staff member coordinating the planning process should prepare a succinct written document that presents

1. The charge to the planning team
2. A schedule and expectations for each step of the planning process
3. A completed Public Policy Readiness Inventory for planning committee members to review

These draft documents should be routed to the planning committee members for review and comment. Then the planning committee convenes for its first meeting. During this meeting, members should have the discussions covered in Planning Steps 2 and 3. This includes

1. Articulating visions and goals for the organization's public policy work
2. Deciding the specific issues that the organization will address in its public policy agenda

Staff can then complete Planning Steps 4, 5, and 6. This includes an analysis of

1. Arenas of influence
2. Strategies for policy initiatives
3. Development of a proposal for the organization's internal structures for carrying out lobbying activities

The draft documents of this analysis should be sent to planning committee members for ideas and reactions. All members of the committee should review and comment on the drafts.

Finally, the committee should meet for a second time to debate and agree to key strategies and organizational infrastructure commitments. The staff will have integrated these into a proposed work plan for the committee to rely on as a starting point for discussion.

At the end of this discussion, staff should have adequate direction to shape an advanced draft of a work plan, submit it to committee members in written form for their review and comment, and finalize a plan to present to the board and staff for adoption.

Summary: You're *Ready!*

At this point, you have built the case for public policy advocacy in your organization, persuaded the organization to commit to a planning process, selected a team, and sketched out the process. Now it is time to create your plan.

PREPLANNING CHECKLIST

After completing this checklist, circulate it to all members of the planning team prior to the first meeting.

1. **Identify members of the planning team for GREAT!: Glorious Responsive Employment Advancement Team. (This fictional nonprofit will be used throughout to illustrate the way in which the worksheets in this book may be used.)**

   `Executive director`

   `Communications director`

   `Board chair`

   `Board member with policy experience`

   `Volunteer with grassroots organizing experience`

2. **Set a schedule of meetings.**

   `All meetings will be held at GREAT! in the small conference room. Sandwiches and beverages will be provided.`

   Meeting 1: **1/15**   `5—9 PM`

   Meeting 2: **1/29**   `5—9 PM`

   Meeting 3: **2/12**   `5—9 PM`

   Meeting 4: **3/1** `(Note: Sat. meeting-full agenda)` `10 AM—5 PM`

   Meeting 5: **3/22** `(Note: Sat. meeting—work plan)` `10 AM—3 PM`
   `An additional meeting will be scheduled if needed.`

   Meeting 6: **4/16**   `6 PM Board Meeting Presentation!`

3. **Write the "charge" or "job description" for the planning team.**

   `The team will develop goals, a strategy, and a work plan that will guide GREAT! in lobbying at the state and local levels on issues that help us to meet our organizational mission: "To support people with barriers to employment in moving out of poverty and into jobs that provide a career path and livable wage." In the planning process, the team will follow the planning steps in The Lobbying and Advocacy Handbook for Nonprofit Organizations.`

(continued)

GREAT!'s stakeholders will be consulted as appropriate to ensure that they add their ideas, priorities, and expertise to the planning process.

The communications director will serve as the planning coordinator of the process, including setting up meetings and reminding participants of schedules. She will staff the team, including preparing packets of information for team members to read and review prior to each meeting so that everyone is prepared to use meeting time to move forward with the work. She will document the process and all decisions, including the final work plan. The executive director will facilitate the discussions.

The team will complete its work in six meetings, devote the needed time to interim research and reading, and deliver a proposed work plan to the board at its April meeting.

You're ready. Now get set. It's time to design your lobbying plan. Use this eight-step planning process, once step at a time. Agendas are provided for six planning meetings that constitute a thorough, thoughtful, and energetic process. Worksheets for each planning step provide a ready vehicle for recording your decisions. When you have completed the six meetings and eight steps described here, you will have a public policy work plan for your organization to adopt and implement.

The eight planning steps are

> Step 1: Launch the planning team
>
> Step 2: Articulate your vision and goals for your policy work
>
> Step 3: Develop your policy agenda: Establish criteria and identify issues
>
> Step 4: Target arenas of influence where issues are decided
>
> Step 5: Choose strategies and tactics for effective advocacy
>
> Step 6: Design the organizational structure that you need

Step 7: Create your plan

Step 8: Finalize your organizational approval of the plan and begin the work

Let the planning begin!

Planning Step 1: Create a Planning Process and a Planning Team

Preparations can be accomplished in one four-hour meeting. In the preplanning step, you appointed one member of the planning team to be the team's planning coordinator and facilitator of the entire process. His or her role is to

- Coordinate the meeting dates, times, and places for the planning process

- Ensure that the agenda is clear and everyone understands what is to be accomplished in each meeting

- Keep the discussion moving while providing all participants with the opportunity to have ideas heard

- Be sure that someone records key points of discussion and decisions (worksheets will help with this process)

- Maintain any records of the planning process

- Be sure the plan proposed by the team is presented to the organization for discussion and approval

The planning coordinator has a key role to play. In addition to being the steward of the process, the planning coordinator keeps the team focused on the big picture: engaging in public policy work so that the organization can be more effective at meeting its mission. Select the person with the passion and skills best suited for the task.

At least one week prior to the meeting, the planning coordinator should send each member a packet containing the following:

- List of team participants with contact information (phone, fax, e-mail).

- Agenda for the first meeting, including date, time, and location.

- The charge to the planning team. This may have been incorporated into a board resolution or the organization's overall strategic plan.

- The list of steps and projected schedule for the planning process as developed earlier. (See the Preplanning Checklist, page 205.)

- List of key terms from Chapter 1 of this book.

- This book so that all participants can read the background information and tackle the worksheets; or a copy of Worksheet 1: Public Policy Readiness Inventory, page 207.

Here is a sample agenda for the first part of your first meeting. Specific instructions for each substep are included. (A summary of the agenda for the first meeting appears in the box on this page.)

1. **Make introductions.** Ask each person to provide an introduction that answers these questions: What's your specific interest in being part of the planning process? Why do you see public policy and lobbying as a priority? What stakeholder groups' interests do you represent?

2. **Review the charge to the planning team.** Whether or not planning team members participated in preliminary discussions of the planning process, it will be helpful to read and discuss the charge to the team. Make sure everyone shares the same basic expectations and sense of purpose.

3. **Discuss the planning process.** This can be accomplished easily with a brief review of the six proposed meetings and their suggested agendas. Review the schedule of meetings if it has been set, or use this time to schedule the remaining meetings. The planning coordinator should discuss key ground rules for the process, such as everyone has a chance to participate, honesty is expected, meetings will begin and end on time, and other guidelines that suit your organization's culture.

4. **Review key terms.** This is as simple as referring team members to the terms used in Chapter 1 on page 30 for review and handy reference.

5. **Complete the Public Policy Readiness Inventory.** Complete Worksheet 1: Public Policy Readiness Inventory on page 207 to get a baseline inventory of your organization's public policy readiness. The team members should fill this out together, discuss individual's perceptions about where the organization stands, and reach consensus about current levels of readiness. You can revisit the assessment tool at the end of the planning process and as you implement plans. Returning to this baseline inventory and updating your status will help everyone involved appreciate progress. A completed sample of this worksheet can be found on page 62. (Note: Throughout this book, samples of completed worksheets for the fictional nonprofit GREAT! will appear at the end of the chapter to give you a sense of how an organization might use the worksheets.)

Upon completing Worksheet 1, you have completed Step 1. The team shares an understanding of how you will proceed with fulfilling your charge to create a work plan for the organization's public policy work. The organizational self-assessment helps

Agenda—Meeting 1

Preparation: Be sure each member has received a packet containing team membership roster, meeting agenda, meeting schedule, list of key terms, Preplanning Checklist, and Worksheet 1: Public Policy Readiness Inventory.

Planning Step 1: Prepare the Planning Team

1. Make introductions.
2. Review the charge to the planning team.
3. Discuss the planning process as outlined in Chapter 2.
4. Review key terms.
5. As a group, complete Worksheet 1: Public Policy Readiness Inventory.

BREAK (15 minutes)

Planning Step 2: Articulate Vision and Goals

6. Review your organization's mission and reaffirm that your public policy work will enhance your ability to meet your mission.
7. Develop your vision for public policy work.
8. Develop the broad policy goals for your work.

Homework: Each member should gather a list of potential public policy issues to be discussed in the next meeting.

you to look at where you are in your readiness for public policy work. The questions suggest some components of planning that will ensure that you are well prepared to lobby effectively. Take a break and reconvene to complete Step 2.

Planning Step 2: Articulate Policy Vision and Goals

Step 2, covered in the second part of your first team meeting, provides an opportunity for inspiration and reflection. The planning team is ready to imagine what a strong and effective policy effort would accomplish and how it would enhance your ability to fulfill your organization's mission. The planning coordinator can guide the discussion as follows:

1. Review the organization's mission. Always go back to mission! Have a written copy of the mission for each participant. Read it out loud. Underscore how important it is to shape a public policy work plan that furthers your mission in significant ways. Write the mission statement on Worksheet 2: Mission, Vision, and Goals on page 213.

2. Brainstorm a list of ways in which public policy advocacy and lobbying can further the mission. Capture all ideas.

3. From the list, create a written statement of your vision for the organization's public policy advocacy work. (The sidebar Two Approaches to Public Policy: Initiate and Respond, on page 40, can help you envision your approach to public policy.) A vision expresses what your organization will look like in three to five years with a strong and effective public policy component in place. How will the people you serve be helped by your public policy efforts? How will your mission be advanced by your public policy work? How will you increase your ability to provide programs or services? How will you create new opportunities for people to get involved in work that supports your organization and its mission?

4. After you've created a vision, you can identify your organization's public policy goals. Identifying broad goals early in this process will make later decision steps manageable. Typical goals include

   - Specific changes in policies or funding for programs

   - Increased opportunities for people to participate effectively in the policy decisions that shape their lives

   - Strong ongoing and positive relationships with policy shapers

   - Working alliances with other nonprofits and other sectors on issues of shared interest

Planning shortcut

If you are using the "shortcut" option for your planning process, begin your first meeting with Planning Steps 2 and 3. Staff should have all of the preparation described in Planning Step 1 ready for the planning team to have as background material.

Two approaches to public policy: initiate and respond

As you envision your future policy work, think about a dual path: your nonprofit can *initiate* new ideas and *respond* to existing proposals that you support or oppose.

Take the initiative: Introduce a new legislative idea. Your organization—your staff, board, constituents, and stakeholders—is likely to know more about your issues and the community's needs in your program and service areas than most public officials. Without your involvement, the public policy debate is not fully informed. You have an instrumental role in developing and advocating for new and improved policies that will address problems and promote the general welfare.

Given your experience and expertise, your organization can take a proactive leadership role. Work with legislators to promote solutions that you know will work. Offer new ideas for policy and programs. Provide positive alternatives to weak budget proposals or unfair tax policies. Develop an idea, support it with solid information and stories about how your idea will make a difference, and then lobby until your idea becomes law.

Be responsive: Lobby to support an idea proposed by others or to stop a bad idea from becoming law. You know the issues, the affected populations or places, and many of the stakeholder groups relevant to your mission, so you have an important role to play in responding to legislative ideas. Your support can make a strategic difference in whether or not legislation now "in play" passes. You can oppose an idea by pointing out its harmful consequences and by offering alternative solutions to a problem.

In either case, your organization should have a voice, and it should encourage the people you serve to be their own best voice about how proposed legislation will affect them. Become responsive by being vigilant about

- Monitoring legislative activity
- Identifying proposals that will affect your work as soon as they are introduced
- Alerting people to proposals that will touch their lives
- Coordinating efforts to inform and persuade decision makers to develop policies and funding streams that will address your organization's concerns responsibly

Specific techniques for initiating and responding are covered in Chapter 3.

- Capacity within your organization to do effective public policy work over the long term
- Enhanced positioning of your organization as a valuable resource in the community

Enter your vision statement and goals on Worksheet 2: Mission, Vision, and Goals on page 213. A sample is on page 69.

Summary of Planning Steps 1 and 2

At the end of your first meeting, you have completed the first two steps of your planning process. You have assessed your current public policy readiness and stated your vision and goals. It is essential to continuously tie the vision and development of your public policy work to your organization's mission. As you conclude your discussion of vision and goals, urge planning team members to read ahead to the plans for discussing issue priorities. Ask the team to do preliminary "scouting" about issues that relate to your vision and goals. Staff members may be in a strong position to prepare short briefing papers about the status of issues that they are aware of and that you might want to include in your next discussions.

Now you are ready to move to the next step in the planning process. Allow up to four hours for this second meeting of the planning team.

Planning Step 3: Develop a Policy Agenda: Establish Criteria and Identify Issues

In Planning Step 2, you set broad public policy goals. Review what you recorded in Worksheet 2: Mission, Vision, and Goals. In Step 3 of this process, you will select more-specific issues to tackle.

You can usually complete Step 3 in one four-hour meeting. Here is an agenda for that meeting. (A summary of the agenda for the second meeting appears in the box on this page.)

Establish Criteria

Before you select issues, you need to create governing criteria for your public policy issues. These criteria will help you decide which issues to pick. The criteria become increasingly important as you become more active. Public-interest topics and new legislative agendas can crop up overnight, and you need to be prepared with firm guidelines to help you decide which battles to choose.

As in the first meeting of your planning team, review the mission and vision and then discuss the criteria that should govern your organization's decisions about issue selection. Keep the criteria simple, mission-focused, and limited in number. The criteria should express your organization's mission and deepest values. Invite all ideas and then agree on the criteria that are most essential. Enter your recommended criteria on Worksheet 3: Criteria for Selecting Issues on page 215. A sample worksheet is on page 70.

Agenda—Meeting 2

Preparation: Each team member should prepare a list of potential public policy issues.

Planning Step 3: Establish Criteria and Identify Issues

1. Review the mission, vision, and goal statements discussed at the first meeting.
2. Establish criteria for setting issue priorities.
3. Identify issues that are important to your organization and the people you serve.
4. For each issue, identify specific policy objectives and hoped-for outcomes of the lobbying effort.
5. Rank issues for your public policy agenda.

Homework: Make sure each participant reads Appendix C: Legislative Process (page 179). Assign one or more people to research state and local processes and to outline them for the planning team.

When reviewing sample Worksheet 3, note that GREAT!'s criteria would support making child-care accessibility and affordability a priority. The organization would have no doubts about engaging in lobbying when proposed legislation would cut the child-care services essential to its clients' ability to get and hold jobs. On the other hand, the criteria would probably screen out lobbying on the issue of state aid for K-12 education. While an important social issue, it is not close enough to GREAT!'s core mission and areas of expertise.

Identify Issues

With criteria set, you can begin to identify issues that are important to your organization and the people you serve. This is often the most exciting component of planning. You will be deciding where you will use your time, talents, and energy to make a difference!

To identify your specific public policy issue priorities, the planning team will need to build a list of key issues that affect your mission and goals. Consider three types of issues:

1. Issues already in discussion in public policy arenas

2. Issues anticipated to be on the agenda of state or local decision makers

3. Issues you want to initiate in the public policy debate

In this first step of identifying issues, research can be both formal and informal. In smaller organizations, the planning team alone may be able to name the majority of issues. Larger organizations with multiple programs may need to start a process that solicits issues from program directors, staff, clients, other advocacy groups, and other key stakeholders. Use a process that fits your size, budget, and broad goals.

Based on how wide-ranging you choose to be in identifying possible issues for your agenda, planning team members will need to list

- Issues that you know about from media coverage and general knowledge.

- Issues that coalitions or allied organizations have identified as priorities. This may require meetings with the executive director, lobbyist, or other key leaders from the relevant coalitions or organizations.

- Issues that elected officials who represent your district or who take a leadership role in your field identify as key legislative items. This will require meetings with targeted legislators for state-level activity and county, city, or other officials if your work will focus on local government.

- Issues that grow out of your organization's experience and expertise that are not being addressed but need attention.

Once you have identified a basic list of issues, do a preliminary assessment of fit with mission, goals, and criteria. Use Worksheet 4: Identify Issues on page 217 to record your analysis. A sample is on page 71. Remember that issue selection is an ongoing process. As a planning team, you are providing initial suggestions and testing a process for the development of your issue agenda.

Set Objectives and Priorities

At this point in the planning process, the team will need to use the criteria to decide which issues to pursue. Ask, "Based on our goals and criteria, and on how much attention the issue is getting, how does each of our issues rank in importance?" Return to Worksheet 4 to rank the importance of each issue. Consider how closely each issue matches your criteria. Also consider how likely it is that the issue will actually be addressed by decision makers. (Is it a "live" issue?) Your top priorities should be those issues most important to your mission, vision, goals, and criteria that will have a chance to progress in policy debates. Choose to initiate issues that are likely to be taken seriously and acted on by legislators. Prepare to respond to those "hot" items that are in debate and have significant implications for your work and for the people you serve.

Once you have decided on the issues you will pursue, you must determine your lobbying objectives and positions on each issue by answering the following questions:

1. On this issue, what is our public policy objective? What change or new initiative do we want to see in place?

   For example, GREAT! wants to see adequate and effectively targeted state support for workforce training. One of its policy objectives is a coordinated state system for workforce training.

2. To achieve the policy objective and attain the desired change, what specific position will we take on this issue? Do we agree with a current proposal for legislation, or do we want to offer an alternative proposal?

GREAT!'s position is to support a current bill, HF 554, that would provide funding and other assistance to coordinate workforce training across the state.

Many organizations will do both a long-term and a short-term policy issue agenda. To document your decisions about issues for your policy agenda, use separate copies of Worksheet 5 for immediate and long-term agendas.

A short-term issue is one that can be addressed and resolved in the very near future. These issues are often uncontroversial. Sometimes they are issues that have to be addressed quickly because of their very nature, such as budget appropriations. A short-term agenda item for GREAT! might be to stop another group's proposal to cut current funding for workforce development programs. GREAT! would move into rapid action to encourage legislators to defeat that measure. This issue would have to be addressed in the short term—during the same legislative session in which it was proposed and the budget was being set.

A long-term issue is usually one that requires extensive education and requires you to build support for your position over time. Sometimes it is an issue that requires that you attain your objectives incrementally rather than in one single step. For GREAT!, a long-term issue might be integration of state and federal workforce-development programs. This could be initiated with a proposal to synchronize one aspect of the programs, perhaps the reporting requirements that federal and state agencies have. It could build over time to a more significant coordinated effort to share program goals and jointly fund projects.

Worksheet 5: Issues, Objectives, and Positions on page 219 will guide you in this process. On this worksheet, you have the opportunity to state your specific position on the issue. A sample is on page 72.

Summary of Planning Step 3

At the end of this third step in the planning process, you have reached a major point of accomplishment. You have determined

- Criteria for issue selection

- An issue agenda for immediate and long-term policy work

- Positions and objectives for your lobbying efforts

Planning shortcut

For organizations using a short-cut to the planning process, staff should prepare all of the information developed in Planning Steps 4, 5, and 6. These materials can be sent to planning committee members prior to their second meeting and discussed before they complete Steps 7 and 8.

As a result of this work, you are beginning to get a more concrete sense of just where your vision will take you. At your planning team's next meeting, you will tackle Planning Step 4: Target Arenas of Influence. In this step, you will learn about the state and local legislative bodies and administrative agencies where your issues will be decided.

Planning Step 4: Target Arenas of Influence Where Issues Are Decided

Three arenas where you can influence public policy are described in this step: the legislature, the executive or administrative branch of government, and the courtroom. This book focuses primarily on ways you can influence the legislative branch of government at the state and local levels. However, never overlook the importance of direct contact with the people responsible for implementing laws—the administrators in the executive branch. Also keep in mind the media. They can get an issue "on the radar screen" for decision makers. And, of course, some battles can only be won in the courtroom.

With careful preparation, you can accomplish this step in one four-hour meeting. This meeting can be a lot of fun, including a guest speaker and presentations on various forms of government. A discussion of the agenda for the third meeting follows. (See the box on this page for a summary of the agenda for the third meeting.)

Review Arenas of Influence

Your organization will be working to influence government decision makers in one of three arenas of influence. These are the legislative, executive, and judicial branches of government.

Legislative branch

Often the most effective action is shaping public policy through legislative lobbying. Legislatures create laws that impact all dimensions of human activity. Legislatures determine how government will collect revenues and how it will spend its resources.

Use the legislative arena to influence the funding priorities and appropriations decisions of your state or local government. For example, health-care advocates lobby at federal and state legislative arenas for funds to guarantee that children whose families don't have adequate health coverage still get the necessary immunizations.

Use the legislative arena to shape broad policies. For example, human-rights advocates have advocated at state legislative arenas for policies to protect workers from harassment in the workplace.

Use the legislative arena to pass laws that set the standards for acceptable social behavior and establish consequences for violations of those standards. For example, groups concerned about drunk driving have lobbied state legislatures to set standards for what level of alcohol in a person's blood constitutes drunkenness and stiff penalties for those convicted of driving while intoxicated.

Agenda—Meeting 3

Preparation: Make sure each participant reads Appendix C: Legislative Process (page 179). Assign one or more people to research state and local processes and to outline them for the planning team.

Planning Step 4: Target Arenas of Influence

1. Review the possible arenas of influence where your issues might be decided.
2. Identify a primary arena of influence for each of your issue priorities.
3. Learn more about the state and local legislative arenas where your organization works, with a special emphasis on those where your key issues are likely to be decided. Learn about the process and the people in these arenas of influence.
   Suggestion: Invite a guest speaker—legislative staff, an experienced lobbyist, or an elected official—to present an overview of the state and local processes where you expect to lobby.
4. Determine what additional steps team members will take before your next meeting to build your knowledge of how your targeted arenas of influence are structured and operate. Assign readings. Consider scheduling an additional meeting for a tour of your state capitol, county office, or city hall as part of the planning process.
5. Develop a plan for educating others in the organization about your arenas of influence.

Homework: Assign members to gather information about each arena of influence in which you are working. Assign one member to review Chapter 3 to guide choices to be made in the next meeting about direct lobbying and grassroots lobbying tactics.

Executive branch: elected officials and administrative agencies

Some issues can be addressed most effectively in the executive branch of government. A governor or mayor can act with executive authority to effect change on some policy issues. For instance, a governor has emergency powers and can mobilize public-safety or crisis responses. Executive leaders appoint administrative officials, propose policies and budgets, and have significant influence in negotiations over policy issues and fiscal decisions that involve controversy. Nonprofits benefit from serving as a trusted resource to executives and their key staff.

Administrative agencies carry out the programs and policies set in place by the legislative and executive decision makers. They implement policies with rules, program design, and contracts with nonprofits and other entities. Your state, county, and city have agencies and program managers who have oversight responsibility for the policies, programs and budgets that are related to your policy issues and work. They also serve as key advisors to the executive and legislative branch. Effective advocacy involves being known and trusted by administrators and executive leaders and staff. Your organization can have an important impact by advocating to those who prepare budgets, propose policies, and analyze the impact of policies proposed in the legislative branch.

Courts

For some long-debated and complex issues, the courts are the proper arena for influence. Nonprofits use litigation to meet their objectives when legislative bodies have no authority to act or refuse to act; when federal, state, and local legislative decisions are contradictory; and when there is reason to believe that laws have been violated. For example, nonprofits have initiated litigation against utility companies to force them to comply with environmental-quality standards when those utilities were violating existing laws. Another example: smoke-free coalitions and states have challenged the tobacco industry through individual and class-action litigation. Legal action was the best path for compelling the industry to pay states and victims for health problems related to smoking. Keep in mind that litigation is more costly than lobbying.

Multiple arenas

Sometimes you will want to work in multiple arenas for change. In parallel actions, states have curbed sales of tobacco to minors, controlled advertising practices, and taxed tobacco through legislative initiatives. On a campaign as broad in scope as tobacco control, such multiple strategies are essential. Your organization should assess where decisions will be made about your issue and how you can have an impact in one or more of those arenas.

Identify Arenas

Usually, the arenas in which you must work are fairly apparent. Return to Worksheet 5: Issues, Objectives, and Positions to review your policy issues. List them again on Worksheet 6: Identify Arenas of Influence, page 221, noting each issue, the arena or arenas in which action must be taken, and what actions your organization has already taken. A sample is on page 74.

Learn the Lawmaking Process

For planning purposes, study the overview of the legislative process included in Appendix C: Legislative Process, page 179. Then work with local experts and materials produced by your state and local governments to understand how the process works in your area. For this third meeting of the planning team, ask members to read Appendix C before you meet to discuss arenas. Also provide members with information about your own legislative process. Information is always available from your legislative information offices, from civic organizations such as the League of Women Voters, and at state legislative websites. The basic information presented in Appendix C will serve as background for getting up to speed on your state (or county or city) process.

In this third meeting of your organization's public policy planning team, consider inviting a guest speaker who knows your state or local process well. Ask a legislator, legislative staff member, city or county manager, or an experienced lobbyist to spend an hour outlining how the process works in your arena of influence. Ask the speaker to include a case study of how one idea moved through the process. Expand the length of the meeting if you choose to cover multiple arenas. Including a speaker may extend the meeting, but it is likely to be informative and energizing as you learn from "inside players" about how the process works.

Focus on learning the informal rules of the process as well as the formal steps you will need to take. For example, an informal rule is that the media often cover the first hour of a hearing. Therefore, you want to be sure that your witnesses sign up to testify early in the hearing. You will learn such informal rules from the "real stories" of guest speakers who have been involved in the legislative process.

Finally, you can begin to compile what you are learning by filling in Worksheet 7: The Legislative Arena on page 223. Do this as a group effort so that you review what you know and identify gaps that need to be filled. Most organizations will need to conduct a minor amount of research, using materials provided by legislative information services or local government information offices to complete this worksheet. Invite members of the team to volunteer to seek out the information that you are unable to fill out at the meeting. Your answers to Worksheet 7 become a part of your organization's public policy guide; of course, some dates will need to be changed annually. Because this worksheet is self-explanatory, no sample is provided.

Understand the legal mandates that govern your arenas of influence

This is a background step that will be useful for your organization's advocacy efforts. A member of the planning team should retrieve and review the legal mandates that govern the arenas of influence in which you will be advocating. This person becomes your expert and helps others to know the "rules of the game." This person should

- Review the state constitution, county charter, or city charter as fits your goals. What is the form of government described? What are the legal duties and responsibilities of elected officials and key administrators?

- Review official rules published by the legislative body that govern the process.

- Serve as the resource person on these legal mandates.

You may also rely on governmental websites and official offices—including those of the secretary of state, attorney general, county attorney, charter commission, and others—to have information about the jurisdictional mandates for each level of government. From time to time, you will need to know such things as whether a governor or mayor can address your issue through executive order without your having to become involved in the legislative process. You may need to know what is required to raise a tax, override a veto, or propose a ballot initiative. Those who know the rules can be most strategic in shaping policy plans.

Understand the legal mandates that govern your arenas of influence

Increasingly, the vast majority of information about a unit of government may be obtained online. Be familiar with the website of your targeted arena of influence. Make sure that you know where to access relevant information on the site. Often units of government and policy makers offer e-mail newsletters, schedules, alerts, and records of action. Some will have a public presence on social media as well. Subscribe to information resources that provide the information and updates that you will need about the governmental body.

Know the People of the Process

In addition to knowing the process for lawmaking, you must understand the people of the process. They are the decision makers who have the power to decide about your issues and who control the timing and tone of the debate. They include legislative leaders and staff, executive branch officials and staff, and others in the public-affairs community: lobbyists, political analysts, media, researchers, policy analysts, and engaged citizens. Remember that those who oppose you are also "people of the process" and need to be included in your assessment of all the important players surrounding your issue. Review the section The People of the Process in Appendix C: Legislative Guide. Then gather information from others with experience in arenas of influence and fill in Worksheet 8: The People of the Process on page 229. You can assign the worksheet to one or more members of the team to be completed before the third meeting. Or you can take part of the meeting to complete the worksheet as a group, depending on the time you have available.

Worksheet 8 will become part of your record for your policy guide. Naturally, names will have to be changed annually as new officials take office and new administrators are appointed. No sample of Worksheet 8 is provided, as the questions are self-explanatory.

While you are learning about the legislative process, take the opportunity to learn about the political and fiscal landscape of your area. Which political parties have power in state-level executive and legislative positions? Have there been changes in political power in recent elections? What is the fiscal landscape? Does the city, county, or state have a budget surplus or deficit? Why? Also learn about the political culture of the arena of influence. What are the values that dominate the landscape? What are the ideological frameworks of elected officials from different parties or areas of the state or district? What is the general political will on the issues that you champion? What are the "hot button" items that dominate political dialogue? How open is the process: i.e., are residents and community organizations welcome to participate in the process?

Your team is near the end of its third meeting and the completion of Planning Step 4. You have been learning about arenas of influence, identifying the gaps in your knowledge, and assigning individual team members to seek out information, fill in worksheets, and share what they find by the next team meeting.

Lobbying and learning about it can and should be fun! With that in mind, create an interesting field trip for your team. Schedule a two- to three-hour visit to your state capitol, county office, or city hall. Consider inviting not just the planning team but any other key stakeholders whom you'll want to involve in future advocacy efforts. The sidebar Treasure hunt at the capitol or city hall on page 50 describes an enjoyable way to get acquainted with the place where you'll be lobbying and the people there.

Develop a Plan for Educating Others in Your Organization

Once you have completed the team's discussion and work assignments for Planning Step 4, you will need a means for sharing the information with others in your non-profit. Keep a list of the ways in which you will compile and distribute the information. Some good ways to educate your colleagues include the following:

- Compile a policy notebook for all key staff and board members. Include the worksheets compiled in the planning process and any basic information that you have acquired about the arenas of influence and people of the process. Maintain this notebook in electronic format as a work in progress, ready for updates and new segments over time.

- Keep an e-mail list of key staff and board members for interim and ongoing communications about the planning process and for distributing additional materials.

- Invite all interested members of the organization to participate in a "treasure

Treasure hunt at the capitol or city hall

Directions: Plan a business-hours visit to your state capitol, county office, or city hall for members of your planning committee plus any stakeholders you want to involve in your organization's lobbying effort. Allow three hours for this adventure. Plan to visit with your own elected representative, if possible, to get acquainted. Have fun on your "treasure hunt" as you do the following:

❑ Find the building. (Provide a map; one new lobbyist's first visit to her state capitol left her perplexed. There were no other cars in the parking lot. How could this be? She was at the nearby cathedral, which looks a lot like the capitol building but isn't!)

❑ Find the information office. Look for the house information office and the senate information office (except in Nebraska, which has a unicameral legislature).

❑ Learn where on the governmental website you can find the following:

  ❑ Information about how the legislative process works

  ❑ Information about the executive branch and administrative agencies

  ❑ How to find out who represents your area

  ❑ How to teach your constituencies to learn who represents them

  ❑ Information about committees: their issue areas, members, and staff

  ❑ Meeting minutes

  ❑ Information on audio and/or video coverage of meetings and press conferences

❑ Find out how your nonprofit can reserve a space for meeting at the capitol when you have a Day on the Hill

❑ Sign up to get publications and meeting notices by mail or e-mail.

❑ Visit the index office. Ask how you get copies of bills, current calendars, agendas for legislative sessions, and official records of votes. Is there a system for tracking bills on the Internet? Ask for a demonstration of how to track a bill.

❑ Visit the legislative reference library. Is there one? What resources and services does it provide?

❑ Visit the legislative chambers. Where does the house, senate, county board, or city council meet? Ask how you get messages to elected representatives when they are on the floor debating issues.

❑ Visit committee meeting rooms. Where do the elected officials sit? Where do witnesses sit or stand when presenting testimony?

❑ Visit the press-conference room. Is there a space for media events? How can you reserve it if you want to use it?

❑ Visit the press corps offices. Where are they? Stop and introduce yourselves.

❑ Where can people park? What are the public-transportation routes for your constituents?

❑ Is the governmental complex fully accessible? Are there interpreter and translator services?

❑ Is there a cafeteria or other food service?

In addition to your public policy-oriented tour, suggest that planning committee members take the architectural-historical tour of your capitol, often offered by the state historical society or capitol staff. These tours give historical context and provide some intriguing stories.

hunt" in your chosen arena for change. (See the sidebar Treasure hunt at the capitol or city hall opposite.)

- Sponsor a training session. Ask your planning team members and someone experienced in nonprofit lobbying to do a three-hour session on how the process works, who has power, and how to reach them effectively.

Summary of Planning Step 4

At this point in your planning process, you have set your issues agenda and learned a lot about the arenas where you want your issues to be addressed and acted upon. Before your next meeting, members will need time to complete their research assignments, perhaps meet for a "treasure hunt" at the arena of influence, and pull together all the information gathered. Once this has been completed and information has been compiled and distributed, the team can meet to focus on lobbying strategies and tactics—getting the work done well!

Planning Step 5: Choose Strategies and Tactics for Effective Advocacy

Planning Step 5 is where you decide on the basic approaches you'll use to carry out your lobbying work. You will choose from a checklist of typical strategies and add some of your own. After you know your broad strategies, you will turn to Planning Step 6: Design Organizational Infrastructure. The agenda for your fourth meeting, which should take from three to four hours, follows. (See the summary of the agenda for the fourth meeting in the box to the right.)

Agenda—Meeting 4

Preparation: Assign one planning team member to read about direct lobbying and grassroots mobilizing in Chapter 3 in preparation for Item 2 below.

Planning Step 5: Choose Strategies and Tactics

1. Conduct a *brief* review of what has been decided about your agenda of priority issues and the arenas of influence where those issues will be decided.
2. Discuss direct lobbying and grassroots lobbying.
3. Decide on the key components of each type of lobbying that your organization wants to implement in your legislative work.

BREAK (15 minutes)

Planning Step 6: Design Organizational Infrastructure

4. Discuss decision-making structures. Determine the role of the board, key staff, a public policy advisory committee, and a rapid-response team.
5. Identify the role of staff. Develop the job description for the lobbying coordinator. Determine who will carry out key responsibilities for tracking legislation, direct lobbying, and mobilizing support for your positions.
6. Identify costs in staff time and financial resources that the organization will need to commit to lobbying.

Review Completed Work

Your public policy planning team has covered a lot of ground. Before choosing lobbying strategies, take a few minutes to review the decisions made about priority issues and desired outcomes. Review Worksheet 5: Issues, Objectives, and Positions; Worksheet 6: Identify Arenas of Influence; Worksheet 7: The Legislative Arena; and Worksheet 8: The People of the Process. In addition, team members may have gathered more information based on the assignments made at the previous meeting. Be sure that all members of the planning team have received and reviewed information added to the worksheets by team members.

Discuss Direct Lobbying and Grassroots Organizing

Whether your arena of influence is the state legislature, the county board, or the city council, your nonprofit will be most effective if you use a two-pronged approach: direct lobbying and grassroots organizing. Direct lobbying is the action that your organization takes to persuade elected and appointed officials to adopt your position and vote the way your organization wants them to on your bills. Grassroots organizing involves educating and activating the public to persuade elected and appointed officials to vote to support your positions.

Nonprofits have two primary sources of power: valuable information and the voices of people who care about your legislative priorities. Direct lobbying and grassroots organizing enable your nonprofit to use those two sources of power effectively.

Your nonprofit has unique and valuable expertise and experience about your issues. Without this information, elected officials may make uninformed decisions. In direct lobbying, you provide information—data and anecdotes—that shapes the debate.

When you tap your members, friends, and allies and reach out to the public, you mobilize people who care about the issue. Therefore, they are willing to share their concerns (and your nonprofit's positions) with decision makers, especially their own elected officials. Your supporters can use their influence as constituents. This is a great advantage to your nonprofit. Constituents elect government officials and can hold them accountable on election day. In a representative democracy, constituents' voices are sure to be heard, and your supporters can be persuasive with those whom they elect.

Chapter 2 will guide your nonprofit through the "how-to" steps of both direct lobbying and grassroots mobilizing. Prior to the fourth meeting, assign one planning team member to read through Chapter 2 to help guide the discussion around grassroots organizing and direct lobbying.

Choose Lobbying Strategies

At this point in your planning process, your planning team should consider lobbying strategies and tactics and determine which you want to have in your repertoire.

Knowing the general types of lobbying activity that you will want to employ over time will help you to develop a lobbying plan and anticipate the resources needed to carry it out. Worksheet 9: Lobbying Strategies on page 231 outlines basic lobbying strategies and includes a checklist of tactics you might take. As mentioned above, the most basic division of strategies is between lobbying and organizing. Tactics within these strategies include:

Direct lobbying

- Build positive relationships and trust with elected officials.

- Monitor the legislative process and identify activities that affect your issues.

- Provide expertise to elected officials.

- Persuade legislators to support your position.

As you can see, direct lobbying strategies focus on providing valuable information to legislators and working with them in positive and respectful ways to influence their decisions. Over the long term, your information and unique expertise can make you a resource that elected officials and their staff will turn to as they shape their own priorities and positions.

Grassroots organizing

- Build your base of supporters.

- Mobilize your supporters.

Grassroots strategies can multiply your overall effectiveness. Grassroots lobbying involves first developing a base of supporters (including your most direct stakeholders but reaching out to many others as well), keeping them informed and updated, and then mobilizing those who care about the issue and who are willing to have their voices heard. Read more about grassroots organizing in Chapter 2, pages 101-107.

As a group, read and discuss the options in Worksheet 9: Lobbying Strategies. Select those that, at least for the present, fit your goals. This checklist is an overview of choices about direct and grassroots lobbying approaches. Consider your team's responses as a preliminary catalog of the types of activities that you will undertake. But remember that your unique circumstances—your existing relationships with elected officials, the readiness of your supporters and allies, the work already under way on the issues that concern you—will create specific needs and opportunities for your lobbying effort. The checklist allows you to make some tentative decisions about basic activities that can be used or held in reserve as circumstances require. (Because Worksheet 9 is self-explanatory, no sample is provided.)

Planning Step 6: Design the Organizational Infrastructure You Need

You have made key decisions at this point in the planning process. Your planning team has examined

- How public policy advocacy and lobbying will enable you to fulfill your mission.
- Public policy goals.
- Priority issues, positions, and desired outcomes.
- Information about arenas for change where your issues will be decided.
- Lobbying strategies that you might employ.

To lobby, your organization needs to have enough internal capacity to do this work well and sustain the effort. Whether you intend to lead a major lobbying effort or dedicate a few hours a month to communicating with elected officials, plan for the infrastructure that will meet your organization's expectations. In Step 6, you will examine internal decision-making structures, roles and responsibilities, and resource commitments needed to meet your lobbying objectives.

Planning Step 6 can often be accomplished in the second part of the fourth meeting (see Meeting 4 Agenda repeated at right). It's natural to follow up choices about likely activities with the development of a structure that will support those actions.

Discuss Roles, Responsibilities, and Decision Making

Public policy decisions require both long-term strategies and short-term responses to unanticipated crises or opportunities. To ensure that policy decisions are made with adequate information and by those in the organization with authority to set the organization's policies, your nonprofit needs to establish decision-making roles in your public policy work.

Typical roles for board, staff, and advisory committee are described below.

- The Board of Directors. The board has final authority over your policy agenda and the resources allocated to public policy work, consistent with the governance role of nonprofit boards. The board must ensure that policy efforts are helping the organization meet its mission.
- Staff. Usually, your organization's executive director and any staff designated to carry out lobbying activity will need to work with the board in setting the issue agenda and identifying resources. In addition, the director and staff will shape the work plan for implementing the lobbying effort and ensure that staff members have clear direction about roles and responsibilities.

- Public Policy Advisory Committee. In addition to board and staff involvement, many nonprofits find great value in forming a public policy advisory committee. It can be a committee of the board or a committee composed of a mix of stakeholders interested in the public policy dimension of your work. These people may be your link to other organizations working on related issues. They may be community members who care about your issues, stay informed, and are eager to be active in policy efforts. When the public policy advisory committee is not a committee of the board, it should include one or two board members who can serve as liaisons to the board.

Board, staff, and public policy advisory committee roles need to be clearly defined so that this strategic work can proceed in a timely and focused way. Legislative activities often require on-the-spot decisions and adjustments in plans to meet changing circumstances. In advance of actual lobbying, your organization needs to decide who will make decisions about your organization's policies and activities.

Many nonprofits designate a rapid-response team made up of a few board and staff leaders. This team is empowered to deal with fast-moving action in a legislative arena and to make decisions when there is little time to consult widely or convene a board meeting.

Consider the wide array of public policy job descriptions that you might want to adopt or adapt to your organization's particular structure and culture. The sidebar Public Policy Job Descriptions on pages 56 and 57 provides a menu of possibilities. Consider both the decision-making hierarchies in your organization and the ways in which you want to assign responsibility for lobbying activity. As a group, read through all the options. Use Worksheet 12: Roles and Responsibilities (page 243) and Worksheet 13: Decision Making (page 247) to designate staff for the positions you'll need and to note who has authority for decisions. Sample worksheets are on pages 75 and 80.

Identify Staff and Financial Costs

Public policy work requires thoughtfulness, energy, creativity, and time. It doesn't always require much cash.

Your organization needs to determine what your lobbying costs will be and build that need into your development and resource-allocation plans.

Develop a public policy guide for your organization

Your organization will need its own public policy guide, complete with internal policies and procedures and information about the policy arenas you work within. Begin now by saving relevant worksheets and adding notes and documents provided by guest speakers or uncovered in your own research.

Public policy job descriptions

Board Chair

The board chair leads the board in ensuring that the organization has been intentional in adopting public policy as a component of its work. The board chair works with the board to affirm the organization's positions on public policy measures and to determine the priority of public policy in the overall mix of the organization's work. The board chair guides the board as it shapes plans and allocates resources for lobbying. In some organizations the board chair may be a community leader in a strong position to be a public spokesperson for your issue.

Board Members

Board members make the key decisions to move the organization into public policy initiatives that are consistent with the organization's mission and goals. Board members may serve on the planning team that determines what role public policy will play in the organization's program, and they may also serve on the public policy advisory committee if one is created. Board members' responsibilities for the management of organizational resources and for organizational accountability are important in their governance of policy work. Often board members have relationships and status in the community that position them to be good spokespersons and lobbyists. Their role should include advocating on behalf of your organization's public policy positions in coordination with the board chair.

Executive Director

The executive director has oversight responsibility for public policy and works with the board chair to ensure that the board shapes the organization's direction on policy. The executive director may also serve as spokesperson for the organization and is likely to be one of its official lobbyists (registered, if required by state law). His or her responsibilities for hiring, program design, program accountability, and resource management all apply to the public policy component of the nonprofit's work.

Public Policy Coordinator

This staff person or volunteer tracks and manages all information relevant to your nonprofit's public policy work. He or she is the steward of the plans and systems essential to your policy initiatives. This person also coordinates communications and activity. The coordinator's responsibilities may range from knowing how to access all statements ever made by the organization on a given policy issue to being sure that there is enough postage to get out a call to action on schedule! This person knows where every policy spokesperson is and needs to be. The coordinator ensures that all spokespersons are promoting the same key messages, that the lobbyist's report from the capitol gets to the organization's directors and members, and that the rapid response team is convened to deal with a crisis or course correction.

Lobbyist

The lobbyist works to persuade decision makers to adopt your organization's position on an issue. Some nonprofits have a full-time lobbyist because of the priority placed on lobbying and the intensity of the issue. For many nonprofits, an executive director or program staff person serves in this role. If you plan on long-term involvement in policy work or are addressing a complex major issue, your organization may want to have at least one lobbyist who is often (preferably always) present at the legislative body where you are working to create change. He or she should know the legislative process and players. Your lobbyist's credibility, timeliness, savvy, and ability to present clear and compelling arguments will be a keystone to your success.

Some nonprofits may hire a contract lobbyist who is familiar with nonprofit lobbying. Contract lobbyists have developed experience and access to the legislative arena that can serve you well, especially when you expect to have only short-term involvement in a lobbying effort. Because smaller nonprofits can rarely afford their own lobbyist if they are seeking someone with significant experience, hiring a contract lobbyist can be cost-effective. The contract lobbyist will need to have clear responsibilities, and the lobbyist's work will have to be coordinated well with the efforts of the organization's staff and board. The policy coordinator should work closely with the contract lobbyist in such cases.

Public Policy Advisory Committee
This committee can be either a committee of the board or an advisory committee that includes both board members and other interested stakeholders. This committee can add a focus and perspectives that you might not otherwise have. Its role can include shaping your organization's long-term policy agenda and assisting in building grassroots support for positions. A key role for this committee is to work with your organization in building strategic relationships with public officials, nonprofit colleagues, and other sectors.

Rapid Response Team
The team should include the executive director, a board member, the lobbyist, and up to two other people who are authorized by the board to mobilize quickly and make crucial decisions during the fast-changing legislative process. Compromises, media opportunities, and proposed alliances will have to be addressed between board meetings, and this is the team to do it.

Organizer
This staff person or volunteer organizer informs and mobilizes your supporters by building support in key legislative districts; holding briefings or press events that garner understanding and attention; and managing an action alert network that can muster calls or letters to decision makers on short notice.

Media Specialist
This person builds rapport with the members of the media who cover your organization's issues. This communications specialist knows how to reach the media, how to handle the tough

questions, and how to become a resource—the person the reporters call when they need a community connection on a story about your issue.

Just a note: **DON'T LET THIS LIST BE DAUNTING**. In most nonprofits, the lobbyist, the organizer, the policy coordinator, and the media specialist are the same person. For small nonprofits, even those with only a few staff and volunteers, some minor shifts in work priorities make it possible to do the advocacy work that furthers your mission strategically. Advocacy requires good planning and strategic thinking. It does not always command a lot of time if you focus on a very specific agenda and especially if you collaborate with other organizations.

Many organizations support lobbying work with unrestricted funds such as dues, fees from events or publications, and fees for services. While some governmental and foundation grants prohibit lobbying with grant funds, many will fund educational efforts and outreach related to your public policy issue priorities.

Once you have selected your issues and some key lobbying strategies, you will be able to identify budget needs. Use Worksheet 14: Identify Resources on page 249 to build a preliminary cost projection for your lobbying effort. Base your personnel costs on the anticipated percentage of staff time spent on public policy. For example, an executive earning $70,000 a year who is anticipated to spend 5 percent of her time on public policy would cost $3,500, plus benefits. A sample is on page 81.

Summary of Planning Steps 5 and 6

At the end of your fourth meeting, you have gone as far as you can to determine the infrastructure you will need for public policy work. You have looked at possible ways to define roles and assign responsibilities to carry out your public policy work. You have determined how decisions will be made and by whom as you engage in a process that can present crises and opportunities without much warning, and you have done some initial calculations of the costs that you will incur as you lobby.

Planning Step 7: Create Your Plan

Your nonprofit's public policy planning team has carried out a wide range of tasks and made some key decisions throughout the planning process. Now it is time to put it all together in a work plan to propose to the organization's leaders for approval. Your work plan will combine all the decisions you've made and indicate the activities that you will carry out. If you are following the meeting schedule on page 33, this will be your fifth meeting. (See the summary of the agenda for the fifth meeting in the box on the opposite page.)

Review and Include Key Documents

You have already gathered much of the information you'll need to create a public policy work plan. Review and compile the information you've gathered on your mission, vision, and goals, your issues and strategies, and your infrastructure.

Mission, vision, and goals

Begin your public policy work plan with your overall thesis that public policy advocacy is a strategy for meeting your organization's mission. Include in your work plan the statements about your public policy vision and goals developed in Worksheet 2: Mission, Vision, and Goals. Review these statements and change them if needed. Your core positions are not likely to change, but you may have more details to add as you complete your planning process.

Issues and strategies

Next, review your issue priorities and the advocacy strategies you will use to meet your policy objectives. In Worksheet 5, you identified your issues, positions, and objectives; in Worksheet 9, you identified some advocacy strategies that match your needs and organizational strengths. Now you develop a preliminary plan of action that shows which strategies you will put into place to meet your policy objectives and achieve the desired outcomes. This is a preliminary but important plan that identifies some concrete options for how you will eventually advocate. It will be shaped and reshaped by your staff, board, and public policy advisory committee once it is adopted.

Infrastructure

Compile the work completed in planning for the infrastructure required to carry out your public policy initiatives. Here you will integrate into your plan the thoughts developed in Worksheets 12, 13, and 14, which were completed during your last meeting.

Worksheet 15: Public Policy Work Plan on page 251 will give your organization a sense of your planned efforts. Assign one person to compile the worksheets as reviewed and amended by the group during this fifth meeting. As necessary, have the full team review and respond to the draft plan before forwarding it to the board for approval. A sample of Worksheet 15 is on page 82.

Prepare a Proposal Letter to Your Organization

After you've drafted the plan, assign one member of the team to write a cover letter to the organization that makes the case for accepting the plan. Be persuasive. Ask for authority to implement the public policy plan.

Agenda—Meeting 5

Planning Step 7: Create Your Work Plan

1. Review and include key documents developed in the planning process relating to your public policy vision, goals, and objectives.
2. Present your issue priorities and determine which lobbying strategies you will employ to meet your objectives.
3. Review and include key documents developed relating to organizational infrastructure.
4. Assign one member of the team to write a cover page requesting the organization's approval of the work plan.
5. Return to Worksheet 1: Public Policy Readiness Inventory and see how far your planning team has progressed.

Summary of Planning Step 7

Your planning team has completed a thorough process and developed a proposed work plan for your organization to adopt and implement. Now it is time to present the work plan to the decision makers within your organization who can review it, revise it (if needed), and set it into motion. Set a meeting date and time. Be certain that key leaders who need to be involved in discussions and decisions can attend, and provide participants with your cover letter and work plan in advance of the meeting.

This is a good time to retake the Public Policy Readiness Inventory presented in Worksheet 1. By following this planning process, you have made great strides in increasing your organization's readiness to advocate. Your progress will be clear when you go back to your baseline inventory and compare it with the present.

Planning shortcut

For nonprofits that are using a shortcut version of the planning process, this is a good time to reconvene your planning committee for its final meeting. Staff should present proposals based on Planning Steps 4, 5, and 6. Staff may also present a draft work plan to stimulate and focus discussion as the full planning team completes its planning.

Planning Step 8: Present the Plan and Secure Organizational Commitment

This is the final stage of the planning process. In presenting your work plan to your nonprofit's organizational leadership, make your case interesting and compelling. You might invite a leader from another nonprofit to explain how advocacy helped his or her organization make a difference. Or ask an elected official to speak briefly about the critical role nonprofits play in advising policy decisions. Focus on mission and on the specific steps you've outlined for an intentional, systematic, and strategic way to select issues and lobby for changes that affect the lives of the people and communities that you serve. Since the presentation is done at a full board meeting, the agenda is not under your control. The box on the opposite page, however, suggests an agenda for the sixth meeting that might be incorporated into the board agenda.

Summary: You're *Set!*

You have done the critical work of establishing a plan, a foundation for your advocacy and lobbying systems and activities:

- You have articulated your vision, goals, and policy objectives.
- You have taken the first steps in identifying the arenas of influence where your issues will be decided.
- You know who has power and influence within those arenas.

- You have chosen some of your strategies for advocacy and lobbying.

- You have planned the infrastructure that ensures your advocacy and lobbying is an effective and sustainable strategy for fulfilling your mission.

Be sure to thank the members of the public policy planning team for their time and talent. Their work is the bedrock of the policy changes that your organization will influence in the years ahead.

Celebrate! The planning team has completed its assignment. Your nonprofit's staff and board are ready to begin the work outlined in Chapter 2: *Go!:* Implement Your Advocacy and Lobbying Plan. Let's GO!

Agenda—Meeting 6

Preparation: Distribute the proposal prior to the meeting. Review it with your organization's decision makers and then formally present it to the board at a board meeting.

Planning Step 8: Present the Work Plan

1. Report on the planning-process steps.
2. Discuss the planning team's proposal for your public policy work.
3. Participate in the board's discussion and track changes made to the proposal.
4. The board formally adopts the proposal.

WORKSHEET 1   Public Policy Readiness Inventory

*There are two parts to this assessment. **Part A** looks at the substance of your organization's public policy objectives. **Part B** looks at your organization's current capacity to do the work.*

Use this assessment to create a public policy readiness profile. This profile will help you to see how prepared you are to do this work effectively and examine your capacity to do the work. Refer to it as you complete planning and assess your first months of policy work. Mark your progress along the way. Remember that your response marks a starting point. Consider this a tool to inspire a sense of direction.

Part A: Public Policy Objectives

1. What are your issues?

In the context of our mission, goals, and existing work, we have identified issues and objectives that can be furthered by engaging in debates about public policy and specific legislation.

YES   NO    IN PROGRESS

Our public policy issues are

- State support for job training and education—good programs, adequate funds
- Inclusion of all potential and incumbent workers in state training and education programs
- Coordinating state and federal workforce development programs
- Livable wages
- Work supports: child care, housing, transportation

2. What are you already doing to address these issues?

We have organizational involvement and expertise in the public policy areas we most want to influence.

 YES   NO   DEVELOPING

Expertise and experience are demonstrated in

Programs:

Job training: GREAT! has three programs that provide training and education to workers. These programs have been in existence for

(continued)

4 years, and GREAT! has been recognized as innovative and experienced based on their accomplishments. These three programs are

- *Starting Up.* A Program for New Workers. It covers work-readiness skills, including language classes where needed.

- *Moving Up.* A Program for Incumbent Workers. This provides skill training, often in cooperation with potential or committed employers, for individuals who need additional skills to move up the career ladder.

- *Entrepreneurial You.* A Program for New-Business Builders. This supports individuals and partners seeking to form new businesses with everything from business-plan development to examination of business-finance options.

Services:

GREAT! provides

- Language training

- Work-skills training

- Personal employment counseling

- Child-care and housing referrals

- Job placement

- Post-employment support

Research:

GREAT! does limited research, mostly tracking our clients—job placements, wages, job retention, types of requests for follow-up support. On an as-time-allows basis, we also track programs that support our clients in multiple ways: child care, etc. When possible, we conduct research into good model programs throughout the country. We also research new sources of state and federal funding.

Education, awareness, community outreach:

GREAT! has done only limited outreach, mostly to program officers at the state economic-development agency and with employers who are partners in shaping specific job-training and placement efforts.

(continued)

Advocacy:

None

Lobbying:

Limited. We testified each year over the past three years at state legislative committee meetings to explain how we use state funding to improve people's self-sufficiency potential.

3. Where are your issues decided and debated?

- ☑ Congress
- ☑ State Legislature
- ☑ County Board
- ☐ City Council
- ☑ State Administrative Agency
- ☑ City or County Agency
- ☐ Court
- ☐ Don't know
- ☐ Other:

Arenas for influence where we have an interest in shaping policy decisions are

Mostly state. But we need to figure out how county policies affect our budget and clients. Need to get a better handle on federal action. Are feds doing more since the workforce shortage is a national issue? Need to check this out.

4. What policy changes do you want?

We know the actions or changes that are needed in legislation to address the problems and opportunities that we have identified in our priority issue areas.

      YES   NO   (SOME)

Desired changes in laws, ordinances, or budget and tax policy are

- **Need more money for workforce training.**
- **Also need to be sure people get enough training (especially welfare recipients, new immigrants, youth, and other first-time workers) to really be self-supporting.**
- **Need better coordination of state programs and state and federal programs.**

(continued)

Worksheet 1– continued

- Include simpler single-form grant and contract applications, single reporting form.

- Need better coordination with employers and "next-millennium" industries so we prepare people for the jobs of the present and the future.

5. Will you be reactive or proactive?

We will be proposing policy changes and need to prepare a campaign to introduce and lobby for a new idea.

 YES   NO

The ideas above are proactive. We hope to work with other groups on them.

We will be responding to an existing legislative proposal or another group's efforts by supporting it.

 YES   NO

Other groups are talking about forming a coalition to work on a proposal for coordinating state programs and providing more extensive training and education. GREAT! could work with them on this.

We will be lobbying to stop a measure that we think will have negative impact on our community or the people we serve.

 YES   NO

If the rumors are true and the legislature plans to cut funding for community-based workforce-development programs, we'll fight that effort. Lots of organizations would be likely to join together to oppose that proposal!

6. Will you be lobbying onetime only or are you in it for the long haul?

ONETIME ONLY    ONGOING COMPONENT

(continued)

Check the approaches compatible with your organization's strengths and objectives:

- ☑ Background research and information gathering to "make the case"
- ☑ Public education and awareness
- ☑ Responding to issue alerts by organizations taking the lead on issues
- ☑ Direct lobbying of elected officials
- ☑ Mobilizing grassroots support (at least clients, employer-partners)
- ☑ Working with other organizations in a coalition or an informal alliance
- ☑ Media advocacy
- ❑ Other: _____

Part B: Organizational Capacity for Public Policy Work

1. Who is the organizational champion of public policy work, and how deep is the organization's commitment?

The person(s) serving as key conveners of the discussions about policy work and the stewards of organizational readiness for policy work are

Name: **Jane S.**   Title: **Executive Director**

Name: **Mai M.**   Title: **Board Chair**

Name: **Larry L.**   Title: **Board member (former legislator, too!)**

We have begun the organizational discussion about why and how to do policy work.

  YES   NO   (IN THE SEEDING PHASE)

The board of directors has made a commitment to policy work.

  YES   NO   (IN DISCUSSION) (They're almost ready to vote.)

Our organization's staff share a commitment to policy work.

  (YES)   NO   A FEW SKEPTICS

Members, clients, stakeholders, and other supporters are ready to go.

  YES   NO   (NEED TO TALK TO THEM)

(continued)

Worksheet 1– continued

2. Do you have a public policy plan?

Our organization is engaging in a planning process to decide how to incorporate public policy work into our organizational strategy and work plan.

 YES   NO   PLAN TO

3. Who's doing what and when?

We have designated a person to coordinate our policy planning and work.

 YES   NO   RECRUITING

The role of the board is clear.

 YES   NO   WORKING ON IT

Staff roles are clear.

 YES   NO   WORKING ON IT

We have a "rapid-response" team ready to make decisions and set the course for action when we are in the midst of fast-moving policy action.

YES   NO   WORKING ON IT

We have decided to form an ongoing public policy advisory committee, and its role has been defined.

YES   NO

4. Where is the voice of the community?

We have systems in place to educate, inform, and mobilize our members and our constituencies in support of our issues.

 YES   NO   WORKING ON IT

5. Do you understand legislative processes and structures?

We know how our state (or local) government moves an idea through the legislative process to become law.

YES   NO   LEARNING

(continued)

We know the key structures (house, assembly, commission, committee, political caucuses) and the players (leadership, members, staff) whom we will need to influence.

YES   NO   (LEARNING)

6. What are you prepared to do now?

We are ready to

- ☑ Compile and present the information that makes the case for our position
- ☑ Identify legislative proposals that affect our issues
- ☐ Identify decision makers and our supporters who are their constituents
- ☐ Monitor the introduction and progress of bills
- ☐ Record all of our action on our issues
- ☐ Inform all interested people as the debate progresses
- ☐ Issue calls to action to people ready to act
- ☐ Record all press coverage of our issue
- ☐ Maintain a record of our activity

7. The best things are not always free. What resources will you commit to policy work?

We have budgeted for staff time, materials development, and information dissemination.

YES   NO   (PLANNING FOR NEXT YEAR)

8. Media matters. Are you camera-ready?

We have included a media advocacy component to our lobbying plan.

YES   (NO)   WORKING ON IT

9. Nonprofits can and should lobby, but do you know the rules?

We understand the IRS rules governing 501(c)(3) lobbying and reporting.

YES   (NO)   WORKING ON IT

We understand the registration and reporting requirements our state has in place.

YES   (NO)   WORKING ON IT

WORKSHEET 2   Mission, Vision, and Goals

Record your mission statement. Then brainstorm a public policy vision and related goals for the organization. What will change in three to five years as a result of your public policy efforts? What broad goals will get you there?

Your mission statement:

Gloriously Responsive Employment Advancement Training! (GREAT!) was formed to address poverty issues through workforce development. Our formal mission statement is: To support people with barriers to employment in moving out of poverty and into jobs that provide a career path and livable wages.

Your vision statement for public policy work:

If we fulfill our dreams for our public policy work, we will be able to assess our status and accomplishments in 3 years and say:

- GREAT! is more effective at supporting people with barriers to employment to get jobs and the assistance they need to maintain the highest level of self-sufficiency possible.

- We have a good plan in place and have worked it well.

- We have lobbied successfully for state and county policies that address the training, education, and work-support needs (child care, health care, housing, transportation) of our clients.

- We have the skills, financial resources, and organizational systems in place to be effective lobbyists on our key issues.

- We have a strong communications strategy that helps us to get our key messages to decision makers, the media, and our supporters.

- We have increased support for our issues in the nonprofit sector and the community at large.

- Other organizations involved in workforce development and self-sufficiency, including employers, have a better understanding of the needs of those with employment barriers and understand the strategies for overcoming those barriers. They see GREAT! as an important organization on these issues.

(continued)

Your broad public policy goals:

GREAT! Goals:

1. State support for job training and education—good programs, adequate funds

2. Inclusion of all potential and incumbent workers in state training and education programs, especially low-income workers, welfare recipients, new immigrants

3. Coordinated state and federal workforce-development programs

4. Livable wages

5. Work supports: child care, housing, transportation

WORKSHEET 3   Criteria for Selecting Issues

Issues and priorities will change as the policy landscape changes from year to year, sometimes from day to day. Identify the criteria that your organization will use to decide whether or not to advocate on an issue. Be sure that your criteria keep you close to the core of your mission and goals.

Based on our mission and goals, we will select public policy issues and action strategies that address the following principles:

1. The issue is a priority in our work and is essential to GREAT!'s mission.

2. The proposed legislation presents a threat to our organization, our mission, our services, and the people and communities that we serve.

3. The legislation involves an issue area where we have unique and valuable information to contribute to the policy debate.

4. The legislative issue presents an opportunity for us to involve people who will be affected by decisions in the public dialogue, thereby increasing their participation in the decisions that affect their lives.

5. The issue presents an opportunity for our organization to establish a leadership position that enhances our role in the community.

WORKSHEET 4   Identify Issues

On the table below, list those issues currently in discussion, those anticipated over the next year, and those you wish to initiate. Then place a check (✓) if the issue fits with your mission, goals, and criteria.

	Serves mission	Fits goals	Consistent with criteria	Ranking priorities
Issues already in discussion				
Make training comprehensive to include all workers	✓	✓	✓	3
Increased child-care funding	✓	✓	✓	6
Issues to anticipate				
Possible proposal to cut workforce-development program budgets	✓	✓	✓	2
Possible proposal to increase minimum wage	✓	✓	✓	5
Issues to initiate				
Adequate state support for workforce development; requires increased funding	✓	✓	✓	1
Increase coordination of state and federal workforce-development programs	✓	✓	✓	4

WORKSHEET 5   Issues, Objectives, and Positions

List in priority order your selected issues, policy objectives, and positions.

Issues	Policy objectives	Positions
1.& 2. Adequate state support for workforce training	a. Increased funding	a. Initiate new proposal to fund demo programs ($2 million) and fund current programs ($13 million increase over current budget)
	b. Defeat efforts to cut funding	b. Monitor proposals
3. Comprehensive workforce training is needed in state programs	a. Include new workers	a. Initiate mandate to provide increased training to welfare recipients before requiring workforce entry
	b. Include immigrants	b. Support bill for ESL, translators at work sites, cultural-awareness programs for employers
	c. Include hard-to-serve	c. Initiate bill to design and fund programs meeting needs of potential workers with mental or physical disabilities, displaced homemakers, others
	d. Support dislocated workers	d. Support proposal for increase in funding for dislocated-worker programs and improve systems for identifying needs. Support continued employer tax for dislocated-worker program

(continued)

Worksheet 5-continued

Issues	Policy objectives	Positions
4. Federal and state programs need to be co-ordinated and consistent	a. Design coordinated system	a. Oppose department's plan and offer alternative that includes a new work-force coordination office that has multiagency and intergovernmental authority
	b. Develop common application and reporting forms	b. Work with agency staff to accomplish this administratively
5. Wages	a. Increase minimum wage	a. Support union proposal
	b. Incentives to employers	b. Support Chamber tax incentive proposal
6. Work supports for housing, child care, transportation	a. Comprehensive system of work supports, well-coordinated	a. Support welfare-coalition proposal

WORKSHEET 6   Identify Arenas of Influence

For each issue identified in Worksheet 5, note the arenas of influence where your lobbying efforts will occur. Also note any actions you've taken so far.

Issue	Arena of current debate (or likely arena for new initiatives)	Action to date
State support	Legislature, Economic Development Committee	None
Inclusive training	Legislature, Economic Development, and Human Services committees	None
Coordinated state and federal program goals, delivery systems, and application and reporting requirements	Legislature, Administration	Four agencies requested by Legislature to propose a coordinated system. GREAT! has asked to be included in discussion.
Wages	Legislature	Union has proposed bill to increase minimum wage; GREAT! has signed on to support.

WORKSHEET 12   Roles and Responsibilities

Record below the positions you will create, the individuals who will fill those positions, and their responsibilities. Remember, in most organizations, the positions are incorporated into existing jobs.

Position	Person/title	Job description/Role in public policy
Board Chair	Mai M. (board chair)	Serves as part of rapid-response team. Is a public spokesperson for the organization to the press and elected officials as needed. Ensures that the board has complete and timely knowledge of public policy activity and fulfills its responsibilities in shaping GREAT!'s legislative agenda.
Board	All 22 board members	At least one board member serves on the public policy planning team. Once the board approves the public policy plan and a public policy advisory committee is created, two board members serve on that public policy advisory committee. They are the key liaisons between the public policy advisory committee and the board of directors. They ensure that the work of the public policy advisory committee is consistent with the mission of the organization and organizational policies. They facilitate the annual discussion of policy agenda proposals presented by the public policy advisory committee to the board. While the board members who serve on the public policy advisory committee have a specific role as liaisons, all board members participate in the lobbying efforts and other aspects of public policy work.
Executive Director	Jane S. (executive director)	Has responsibility for oversight of the public policy component of GREAT!'s work. Hires and supervises the public policy coordinator. Works with the board chair to ensure that the board is involved in setting the agenda and supporting it. Serves as part

(continued)

Position	Person/title	Job description/Role in public policy
Executive Director (Continued)		of the rapid-response team and collaborates with the public policy coordinator as needed on the shaping and implementation of the public policy work plan. Serves as a public spokesperson for GREAT! with the media and elected officials. Educates external and internal audiences about GREAT!'s agenda.
Public Policy Advisory Committee	25 representatives, executive directors, and lobbyists from other nonprofits involved in workforce development and economic justice issues	The public policy advisory committee serves as a network that informs and advises GREAT!'s public policy agenda and lobbying strategies. Committee members may propose initiatives that should be incorporated into GREAT!'s public policy agenda. The committee provides information, intelligence, and analysis of legislative issues and proposals. Committee members may be involved in lobbying efforts. The committee facilitates the coordination of GREAT!'s public policy work with the initiatives of other organizations and coalitions to ensure that shared interests are served well by GREAT!'s work and by involvement in collaborative efforts. The committee will meet four times a year—more often during legislative sessions, as issues need attention.
Public Policy Coordinator	Jason W. (public policy coordinator— new hire)	The public policy coordinator (PPC) is responsible for all aspects of GREAT!'s public policy work. The PPC convenes and sets the agenda for the public policy advisory committee. The PPC is key in the development of the policy agenda and work plan. For now, the PPC also serves as the organization's lobbyist and organizer. The PPC, with the executive director and key board members, establishes and maintains relationships with

(continued)

Position	Person/title	Job description/Role in public policy
Public Policy Coordinator (Continued)		supporters, elected officials, and the media. The PPC represents the organization on a day-to-day basis with elected officials and with other organizations and coalitions. The PPC also maintains internal systems for monitoring policy debates and legislative activity, informing supporters of organizational and legislative action on GREAT!'s issues, and alerts supporters to act as needed. The PPC works with GREAT!'s management-information system (MIS) director to set up and maintain databases of supporters, elected officials, and the media as well as files of all legislative activity. The PPC keeps records of all legislative activity in which GREAT! engages for purposes of reporting to the state and the IRS. The PPC coordinates all training and events relating to public policy, including GREAT!'s "Action Day at the Capitol."
Lobbyist	Jason W. (also public policy coordinator)	For now, the PPC will also act as lobbyist. The PPC may supervise interns and volunteers who work on public policy issues and some lobbying activity for GREAT! As resources allow, GREAT! may contract with a lobbying firm for lobbying services on major issues. The contract lobbyist would be selected by the executive director according to GREAT!'s usual contracting protocol, which involves multiple bids, reference checks, and interviews in which the PPC and board chair participate. The contract lobbyist would serve as GREAT!'s "eyes and ears" at the capitol, provide a constant presence for the organization, and

(continued)

Position	Person/title	Job description/Role in public policy
Lobbyist (Continued)		work with the PPC and the executive director to determine when others need to be present and engaged in the process. The contract lobbyist would also help to facilitate GREAT!'s access to elected officials and the press.
Organizer	See PPC	The PPC will conduct outreach to supporters and clients and on public policy activity as much as possible.
Media Specialist	See PPC and executive director	The PPC and executive director will share responsibility for developing a media strategy to support lobbying activity. They will hire a media consultant to carry out this activity.
Rapid Response Team	Mai, Jane, Jason, and one member of the board who also serves on the public policy advisory committee	The rapid-response team (RRT) assists the PPC with decisions and strategy plans that need to be addressed quickly. The RRT is authorized by the board to make decisions about media responses, changes to legislative initiatives, and other activities that surface during the lobbying process and need to be resolved in a short timeframe. The decisions of the RRT will be reported to the board.
Spokesperson(s) for the organization on public policy issues	Mai (board chair), Jane (executive director), and Jason (public policy coordinator)	The board chair, executive director, and PPC serve as spokespersons and decide who should address each targeted audience. Other members of the board and public policy advisory committee may be called on to speak as needed, given the issues, their expertise, and standing in the community.

(continued)

Position	Person/title	Job description/Role in public policy
Other staff (researcher, support staff, program staff with lead responsibility in key issue areas)	Appointed as needed	Program staff will provide information and supportive testimony as needed when the public policy agenda focuses on their areas of experience and expertise. They will assist the PPC in compiling information needed to build GREAT!'s case for an issue, and staff will recruit clients and colleagues who can serve as speakers and "story tellers" in meetings with elected officials, the media, and others. All staff will dedicate time to educating those they serve about GREAT!'s public policy agenda and encouraging their participation in responding to action alerts. The role of the MIS director has been addressed above. One clerical support staffer will be dedicated to half-time work with PPC on public policy efforts.

WORKSHEET 13   Decision Making

Record below the individuals who have key responsibilities for decisions in your organization. This information will become essential in the fast-changing legislative environment. Keep it as part of your public policy guide.

Decisions to be made	Key decision makers
Adopt the organization's policy goals and strategies	Board of directors
Shape the organization's policy agenda	Executive director, public policy coordinator
Set the organization's formal policy priorities	Board sets final priorities. (Staff and ongoing policy advisory committee <u>propose</u> agenda items; the planning team <u>recommends</u> priorities.)
Assign responsibilities to board	Board chair requests board members' support and involvement.
Assign responsibilities to staff	Executive director assigns staff responsibilities.
Allocate financial resources	Board sets budget; executive director manages public policy budget; public policy coordinator tracks expenditures and time on lobbying activity.
Manage organizational activity in carrying out public policy activities	Public policy coordinator
Approve public statements about the organization's position	Executive director (in consultation with the rapid-response team if issue is controversial)
Approve positions in negotiations with elected officials when issues are in hurried stages of debate	Executive director and lobbyist (in consultation with rapid-response team when possible)
Other: **Track changes in federal laws and implications for GREAT!'S issues**	Public policy coordinator

WORKSHEET 14   Identify Resources

Create a preliminary budget for your policy work. Determine the amount of time that each staff person will dedicate to public policy work and budget the required amount of salary and benefits. Plan for all related program activities, such as printing, postage, travel, and meetings. Don't forget administrative costs.

Item	Cost
Personnel: Salaries	
Executive director **(.2 FTE x $60,000)**	$12,000
Public policy coordinator **(1 FTE x $51,300)**	$51,300
Lobbyist **(same as public policy coordinator)**	$0
Support staff **(.2 FTE x $24,000)**	$4,800
Other as determined by roles identified in your nonprofit	$0
Personnel: Benefits **(24% of salary)**	$16,344
Total Personnel Costs	**$84,444**
Public Policy Program Activities	
Technology: hardware and software, as determined by plans to reach elected officials and mobilize supporters	$0
Website	$0
Broadcast fax	$0
E-mail	$0
Telephone	$1,250
Printing, as determined by plans for educational materials and alerts	$3,500
Postage	$3,000
Travel	
Board and public policy advisory committee travel to meetings	$3,000
Staff travel	$1,500
Public policy advisory committee meetings (space, food)	$1,000
Events (Day on the Hill, policy training, briefings)	$1,000
Administrative (% of organizational administrative budget as determined by % of overall work that is public policy)	$1,250
Other	$0
Total Program Costs	**$15,500**
TOTAL	**$99,444**

WORKSHEET 15   Public Policy Work Plan

Gather together Worksheets 1 through 14. Compile and edit them into the format in this work-sheet. Route the draft to the rest of the planning team, rewrite as necessary, then seek the team's approval to send the plan to the board for approval. Save this as part of your public policy guide.

I. Organizational mission

GREAT!'s mission is to support people with barriers to employment in moving out of poverty and into jobs that provide a career and livable wages.

II.   Public policy vision and goals

A. Vision

In three years, as a result of our public policy efforts:

- GREAT! is more effective at supporting people with barriers to get jobs and the assistance they need to maintain the highest level of self-sufficiency possible.

- We have a good plan in place and have worked it well.

- We have lobbied successfully for state and county policies that address the training, education, and work-support needs (child care, health care, housing, transportation) of our clients.

- We have the skills, financial resources, and organizational systems in place to be effective lobbyists on our key issues.

- We have a strong communications strategy that helps us to get our key messages to decision makers, the media, and our supporters.

- We have increased support for our issues in the nonprofit sector and the community at large.

- Other organizations involved in workforce development and self-sufficiency, including employers, have a better under-standing of the needs of those with employment barriers and understand the strategies for overcoming those barriers.

(continued)

B. Goals

GREAT! has the following public policy goals:

- **State support for job training and education: good programs and adequate funds**

- **Inclusion of all potential and incumbent workers in state training and education programs, especially low-income workers, welfare recipients, and new immigrants**

- **Coordinated state and federal workforce-development programs**

- **Livable wages**

- **Work supports: child care, housing, and transportation**

III. Issues

For each issue, state the objective, the arena of influence where that issue can be addressed, and how the organization will lobby. Identify the roles and responsibilities of staff, board, and volunteers in carrying out those lobbying activities.

Many organizations choose a single issue for their primary focus. Often, this is the best approach, especially for an organization just beginning its policy efforts. In your plan, focus on just the one issue that will dominate your work in the next year. If you plan to address multiple issues, indicate which ones will get the emphasis in your work and which you might simply monitor.

Issue 1

Our top priority is <u>increased funding</u>. We will lead by getting a legislative proposal introduced, debated, and supported.

Objective:

A $2 million increase in state spending for workforce-development programs targeted to serve new workers (including new immigrants, welfare recipients, and people with disabilities) and low-income workers. (This number could change pending the research for the initiative.) Workforce-development programs intended to serve these specific populations should be funded by the state and delivered by community-based service providers. (NOTE: GREAT! would be eligible to compete for these funds. But

(continued)

the objective is to expand the pool of resources available for workforce-development strategies that serve those who most need training and support to move out of poverty and into maximizing their ability to support themselves and their families.)

Arenas of influence:

1. *State legislature.* Key decisions will be made in the House and Senate Committees on Jobs and Economic Development. The legislature is the primary arena of influence, the place where the final decision about the appropriation will be made.

2. *State Department of Jobs and Economic Development and the State Finance Agency.* The commissioners of those two agencies propose programs and budgets for legislators to consider as they shape the state appropriations proposal for the next biennium.

3. *Governor.* She has the ability to line-item-veto legislation. We need her support for this increase in workforce-development spending.

Tasks/Activities	Who	By when
Prepare the case: research/write report identifying all state spending on workforce development	Jason (Public Policy Coordinator)	June 1
Write one-page legislative proposal: statement of need, funding request, rationale	Jason	June 1
Public Policy Advisory Committee reviews/amends proposal	Public Policy Advisory Committee	June 15
Board reviews, amends or approves proposal	Ex. Dir., Board, Jason	July 30

(continued)

Issue 1 work schedule *(continued)*:

Tasks/Activities	Who	By when
Prepare supportive educational materials and final proposal. Promote to stakeholders in summer newsletter.	Jason	Aug. 15
Present proposal to Commissioner of Jobs and Economic Development and State Finance Commissioner. Ask for support, inclusion in Econ. Dev. agency budget proposal.	Board Chair, Ex. Dir.	Aug. 15
Involve Welfare Reform Coalition (and others) in supporting the effort. Attend their meetings, begin reciprocal support arrangements for their issues that relate to ours.	Jason	Begins Aug.; ongoing thereafter
Identify chief authors for House and Senate versions of bill. Request support from Economic Development Committee chair or senior member of committee. Serve as resource for chief author.	Jason, Ex. Dir., Board, or Policy Advisory Committee member from author's district	Sept., Oct.
Secure additional authors; meet with all Economic Development Committee members to seek their support.	Jason, others who are constituents of authors (as needed)	Oct.– Dec.
Briefing and training sessions for grass-roots and coalition supporters; letter, fax, e-mail, personal-contact campaign	Jason	Nov.
Ask authors to introduce bill	Jason	Jan.

(continued)

Issue 1 work schedule *(continued)*:

Tasks/Activities	Who	By when
Find witnesses/prep testimony	Jason, Public Policy Advisory Committee	Jan.
Meet with Economic Development Committee members to explain proposal and seek support. Follow up their questions.	Jason, Ex. Dir., constituents	Jan.
Media contacts begun	Jason, Ex. Dir., Board	Immediately prior to introducing bill
Monitor legislative activity; alert all supporters to first and subsequent hearings/urge direct contact. Send weekly alerts. Participate in negotiations as requested. Keep governor's office focused on issue.	Jason, Rapid-Response Team	As dates set, Jan.-May

(Note: **GREAT!** will focus on only one issue for the first year of effort.)

IV. Organizational infrastructure

A. Roles and responsibilities

Insert and edit your completed Worksheet 12: Roles and Responsibilities.

(Editor's note: sample Worksheet 12 not included in this sample plan)

(continued)

B. Decision-making authority

Insert and edit your completed Worksheet 13: Decision Making. (An organizational chart for your public policy work could be included here to illustrate the roles and responsibilities of the people involved and the lines of decision-making authority.)

(Editor's note: sample Worksheet 13 not included in this sample plan)

C. Resources needed

Insert and edit your completed Worksheet 14: Identify Resources.

(Editor's note: sample Worksheet 14 not included in this sample plan)

V. Conclusion

The organization should discuss, amend if needed, and adopt the work plan when it is presented to the board by the planning team. Once the plan has been accepted, the executive director should assign staff responsibilities and develop task and timeline plans with each staff member involved. This may involve significant revisions to job descriptions or creation of new positions. The hiring process for such positions should be launched as soon as possible.

The executive director should provide oversight to the process and convene involved staff on a regular basis, at least weekly, to ensure that tasks are coordinated and proceeding. Throughout, the work plan should serve as a guide.

Go!
Implement Your Advocacy and Lobbying Plan

You are ready to act!

Your planning team has developed a work plan. Your organization discussed and adopted that plan. You have a clear statement of your public policy goals, your issue priorities, the arenas of influence where those issues will be decided, and basic commitments of organizational resources.

To begin your lobbying effort, you will need to take two more steps:

1. First, you must *put the plan in place.* This means instituting the infrastructure that you planned, from assigning specific positions to specific people, to setting up good internal systems, to securing the funds to lobby effectively. The first section of this chapter walks you through the establishment of your infrastructure.

2. With the infrastructure in place, it's time to *initiate advocacy and lobbying activity.* This means conducting any one of (or, more likely, a combination of) six activities: proposing a new law; supporting an existing legislative proposal; defeating proposed legislation; lobbying the executive branch; building and mobilizing grassroots support; and advocating through the media. In many cases, you'll be working on three or four of these fronts at once. The second section of this chapter explains how to conduct each one of these activities.

Implement Your Advocacy and Lobbying Plan Step 1: Putting the Plan in Place—Building Capacity

It's always a bit rough to move from the *design* of a plan to its actual implementation—assigning the tasks, rewriting job descriptions, hiring people as needed, getting the funds in place, and so forth. Expect it to be a bit messy. The important thing is to simply get things going.

Putting your plan in place involves five steps:

1. Assign the roles, responsibilities, and decision-making structures outlined in your work plan

2. Provide training to motivate (and activate) your organization, especially board, staff, and volunteers

3. Create and implement the internal information systems and outreach systems you'll need to mobilize support and track activities

4. Secure the finances necessary to make the plan go

5. Activate the public policy advisory committee

Worksheet 16: Components of Organizational Infrastructure on page 261 is a checklist of the activities you'll need to accomplish. Use it to keep track of your progress.

"Lobbying is just another word for freedom of speech . . . Call it government relations, public policy advocacy, or whatever—lobbying is one of the central mechanisms of democracy, and speaking up for what you believe is about as American as you can get. The framers of the Constitution explicitly assumed that citizens would get together to press their case, and both the letter and spirit of the law have grown to accommodate that process. . . . If we don't lobby, that just means 'the other guy,'—often an opponent—is the only voice that gets heard."

—John D. Sparks, *Best Defense: A Guide for Orchestra Advocates*

Assign Organizational Roles and Responsibilities

Once your organization's board has adopted the work plan and said "Go!" you must *name* the board members who will be key decision makers on public policy questions, including those who will serve on the rapid-response team when decisions have to be made between regularly scheduled board meetings. For guidance, refer to the decisions reflected in your work plan and in Worksheet 12: Roles and Responsibilities and Worksheet 13: Decision Making.

If your nonprofit will be hiring new staff or consultants, decide the level of board involvement in the hiring and name board members to the task. And, if your plan calls for the creation of a public policy advisory committee, name the board member or other organizational leader who will chair that committee. Name board members who will serve on the committee and recruit additional advisory committee members.

A simultaneous step is for the executive director to name a public policy coordinator and other members of the staff who will be responsible for your organization's advocacy and lobbying efforts. Some organizations may need to develop a new position and hire additional staff. Other nonprofits may choose to revise job descriptions to include new responsibilities and balance workloads. In either case, you need to design and distribute to board and staff an organizational chart that clearly shows the lines of responsibility and authority for your staff—paid, volunteer, or consultants, such as contract lobbyists. And each of these people needs a job description.

Develop a Public Policy Advocacy Committee
Susie Brown, Minnesota Council of Nonprofits

A policy committee can be one of an organization's most strategic tools for lobbying and advocacy. Policy committees are often composed of board members, staff, and other stakeholders and typically carry out roles such as **planning, implementing** and **supporting** the organization's advocacy efforts. The composition and role of your organization's policy committee will depend on the history and role of advocacy in your organization and the array of stakeholders that have something to offer.

A policy committee typically serves the function of developing, discussing, and approving the issues of focus for a nonprofit organization. Additionally, the committee and its members may be those who actually do the advocacy work or connect the organizations with key relationships. Prior to establishing a policy committee, consider the following questions, which will shape the composition and role of the group.

1. What role will advisors play in how your nonprofit chooses the advocacy issues it will pursue?

2. Which key stakeholders should be considered in developing your advocacy agenda?

3. Do you have dedicated staff for advocacy, or will you rely on volunteers? How much involvement will you request from advisors as part of the advocacy team?

4. Which relationships in government and policy making will you need, and how will you build them?

5. Whose voices are needed in your advocacy efforts?

6. To what extent does your board desire an active role in advocacy?

An important consideration is whether your policy committee is a part of the organization's formal governance structure or is advisory in nature. For many organizations the planning function, including approving the annual policy agenda, is a governance function, appropriate for a board-level conversation and formal board approval. The steps that precede a board vote could be carried out by a formal policy committee of the board (set out according to the board's other standing committees) or could be informed by an advisory committee whose role is less formal. Whether the committee is part of the board's governance is up to each organization, but it is critical to be clear with all involved which model is being used. Advisory committees might be larger and more inclusive of a broad range of participants, with the goal of maximizing participation and attracting diverse voices, skills, and relationships. A governance committee might be composed solely of interested members of the board and staff, with the intent of doing pre-work before board meetings or providing leadership for board-member engagement. In either case, the planning, implementing, and support functions may be similar, but the composition and relationship to formal board governance will differ. Careful consideration of this question by staff and board prior to launching a policy committee will provide clarity as the committee is assembled and undertakes its work.

Committee Composition

Considering these questions will help define the group of people who will be most strategically aligned to carry out the advocacy goals of the organization. Starting with the organization's key staff (executive director, designated policy staff) and interested board members, there are no limits to the possibilities of who could be included: constituents of the organization, representatives of like-minded organizations, state or local policy makers (or retired policy makers), funders aligned with your policy goals, or others of the organization's key stakeholders. Composition of the group should be focused on building a team that meets the organization's needs while ensuring inclusion of those without whom your efforts will be limited.

Committee Structure and Role

Assembling the right group will ensure that they are able to play the role that your organization needs and how it will operate. A key decision (see sidebar, page 91) will be whether the committee is a part of the formal governance structure of the organization or more advisory in nature. If it is included in your organization's governance, building its structure and work around your board's typical cycles and processes will ensure that it is consistent with organizational norms. Another critical decision is whether the committee is standing or ad hoc. A standing committee assumes there is on-going work to do and perhaps a perpetual agenda. This is useful for organizations that have consistent cycles and predictable needs. It is also useful for an organization whose committee is counted on for significant input and carrying out the work. An organization with a well-developed policy staff, clear positions on most issues, and a history of work in this area might establish an ad hoc committee. In this case, the committee has a clear charge that is assumed to be as-needed, rather than ongoing. In these cases, the committee chair, working with staff, determine when the organization's advocacy efforts will benefit from the input or support of the committee.

Committee Function:

Your organization may need a policy committee to carry out all three functions—planning, implementing or supporting—or just one. Or, very likely, needs will change as your advocacy efforts evolve. Clear understanding of need will help your organization develop the right structure and group. Core functions—planning, implementing and supporting—can be developed as follows.

Planning—The planning function of a policy committee is a critical role used to ensure that the organization's policy efforts are aligned with mission and focused on the issues and strategies most likely to make a difference. Planning needs can be in the early stages of an organization's advocacy efforts, such as laying the foundation for determining the way issues are chosen, identifying resources that will be needed and which outcomes are desired, or can be an on-going need, such as considering and approving the organization's annual policy agenda. Whether one-time or ongoing, making use of a policy committee can be a strategic way to engage key organizational stakeholders in planning for advocacy success. Examples:

> A food shelf that doesn't currently do advocacy is interested in following the process outlined in Chapter 1. They assemble a group of board, staff, and partner organizations to discuss their goals and the path toward successful outcomes. They plan a process for choosing issues, conduct an analysis of the needs and opportunities in these issue areas, determine staffing needs, and consider the resources required. They meet for six months, concluding their work when they have developed the plans and supporting documents to launch the organization's advocacy effort.

> A mental health council that was founded to provide state-level advocacy and education for families has perpetual planning needs as new policy ideas are developed amid a changing political and economic environment. In order to keep their strategies and positions up to date and aligned with the interests of their constituency, they create a policy committee to engage in ongoing planning. Meeting quarterly, this group includes staff, board, and members of the organization's two core constituencies: people with mental illness and members of their family. This group shares information about current issues, developments in other states, possibilities at the legislature, and challenges to advancing their agenda. They often invite elected officials, lobbyists, members of the administration, health providers, and allied advocates to speak to their committee, which recommends policy priorities and positions to the organization's staff and board. The committee is ongoing, with staff and board serving as consistent members and representatives of the organization's constituents rotating through two-year, staggered terms.

Implementing—Some organizations utilize policy committees to implement their advocacy strategies. Particularly when the organization lacks dedicated advocacy staff, a carefully assembled policy committee can bring the energy, skills, and commitment to advance the advocacy plan. An implementing committee is assembled of active, knowledgeable, and dedicated volunteers who, in partnership with staff and board, carry out the lobbying, grassroots organizing, education, or other activities that are designed to advance their advocacy goals. Participants commit to periodic committee meetings and frequent work, carried out either independently or directly with other committee members. This committee counts its success as the direct efforts and outcomes related to the organization's policy goals. Example:

> A river-cleanup organization operates on a largely volunteer model. With an executive director and two part-time staff, they rely on volunteers for both their program

activities that enhance the current quality of life and the advocacy efforts that provide long-term river protection. Their policy committee is composed of their executive director, two board members, a contract lobbyist providing pro bono assistance, a former state senator who was on the environmental committee, and the mayors of two towns along the waterfront. They lobby state government for river protection and resources for environmental cleanup, each focusing on their particular relationships with policy makers and knowledge of the policy-making process. Throughout the legislative session, they are in constant e-mail contact and meet in person each Friday for strategy meetings and policy updates. This committee provides an all-volunteer policy team that is effective and highly credible, successfully implementing the organization's advocacy priorities.

Supporting—In a variety of circumstances, an organization will benefit from the support of a policy committee, available to be deployed in a variety of ways depending on needs. Sometimes, an organization needs expert testimony, and a policy-committee member has the right knowledge and credentials. Occasionally, advocacy staff find themselves in a highly complex or unexpected situation, and a rapid response from strategic policy thinkers supports staff as they find a path forward. Other times, organizations need connections to key decision makers, and policy-committee members can help open those doors. A policy committee designed to support the organization's leadership and staff as they advance advocacy effort can put the best people in place for strategic assistance, drawing from a group that is intentionally assembled, frequently kept up to date, and put to use in ways that maximize their unique contributions. Example:

An affordable-housing organization that both provides housing and engages in advocacy has a strong policy staff, a history of advocacy success, and many allies in the legislature. But they know that they operate in a highly complex policy and funding environment, and there are multiple and sometimes competing views on housing priorities. Recognizing that policy making inevitably includes many twists and turns of financing and regulatory proposals, the staff has assembled a strategy team to support them when the policy process gets complex. Late in the legislative session, they encounter complicated choices and trade-offs as the final version of the housing-appropriations bill is being developed. Having a team ready to go and including a housing researcher, a community-development lender, two board members, the head of the local homeless shelter, and a Realtor philanthropist, the staff can assemble this group on phone meetings for consult as needed, to help them navigate the nuances and implications of various proposals. Staff members know that the Realtor likes to do media interviews, and the community-development lender has a close relationship with the speaker of the house. Deploying the policy committee in these ways is intended to support the work of staff, and ultimately add value to the advocacy efforts of the organization.

Regardless of whether your organization's advocacy efforts are new or mature or if you need substantial ongoing support or just periodic discussions with your policy committee, establishing a committee structure will add value to your efforts. Nonprofit organizations enjoy a vast array of community support, often knowledgeable about and interested in the policy issues that intersect with the organization's mission and services. Determining what your advocacy effort needs and who has something to offer will help set your organization on course for making the most of the planning, implementing, and support functions your policy committee can offer.

Provide Public Policy Training for Your Organization

Public policy eventually involves the *entire* organization, its clients, allies, and other stakeholders. While some are only passive recipients of the benefits of policy work, many can become active participants. Get the ball rolling by starting a series of training events.

The first training you conduct should be a briefing to board, staff, and key volunteers so that everyone understands the work plan, roles, and timelines. Build enthusiasm for the work. Let them share in the excitement of this new effort to meet your nonprofit's mission. Explain new staff and board assignments. Invite everyone's support for the work. Answer questions. Be sure no one is mystified about this component of your work and how it will affect the operations and effectiveness of the organization. In most organizations, all board and staff will be aware of the planning process that has been carried out, since you have consulted them along the way. But as you implement the work plan, be sure that it has been shared and that everyone is "in the loop."

Provide training opportunities for those who will be lobbying or making decisions about your lobbying efforts. A variety of sources can train your supporters, including state associations of nonprofits and national organizations such as Charity Lobbying in the Public Interest. (See Appendix B: Resources for Nonprofit Lobbying.) Civic organizations such as the League of Women Voters offer training for citizen activists.

Organizations in specific nonprofit subsectors (arts, housing, welfare reform, environment, human services, human rights, child care, health) may provide training that covers lobbying skills and specific issue strategies. If no formal training is available in your area, try these steps:

- Invite an experienced lobbyist to consult with your organization.
- Invite your supportive elected officials to share their insights about what works and what doesn't.
- Invite legislative staff—those who work for individual legislators or committees and those who serve as information officers for legislative bodies—to share their expertise about how you can be effective in your lobbying efforts.

The training you provide will advance your work if it includes the basic information that inspires confidence and core knowledge of the issues and skills required.

Build Internal Systems for Information and Communications

To meet your advocacy goals, you will need to establish systems for gathering information, managing the information, ensuring that your internal team is doing fully coordinated work, and reaching your target audiences effectively and consistently. Worksheet 16 Components of Organizational Infrastructure provides useful guidance. Systems to sustain your work include:

Systems for outreach and building your organizing and advocacy efforts

- Love your lists. Maintain a database that includes all of your contacts for your advocacy work and that includes enough detail to allow you to identify supporters and audiences with micro-targeting, i.e., identifying them based on specific characteristics for the purpose of contacting them at times and with messages that are meaningful to them. At a minimum, you should be able to identify the legislative districts of all supporters and the types of activities that they have said interest them. As you design the fields in your system, think about the things that you want to do: expand the reach of messages, tap the supporters in districts of key decision makers, match supporters to the tasks that are a good fit. At a minimum, you want to be able to reach people at accurate addresses for e-mail, postal service, and social-media outlets.

- For good organizing strategies, you want good information about the mapping of districts at the state level as well as local governmental districts, wards, and precincts. These are readily available from state and local governments. If you know where you have concentrations of supporters, you know where you have concentrations of power. Your goals in organizing are to engage people in the life of their communities through civic engagement and advocacy, and, if you know where they are located, you can connect with them based on their ideas, communities of interest, and importance as constituents of decision makers.

- Build and maintain lists of target audiences in addition to your supporters: the media (from TV reporters to bloggers), decision makers and their staff, allied organizations, and community leaders all matter to the success of your issue campaigns and long-term movement-building work. Because relationships are so important in advocacy work, lists that are current and detailed allow you to provide updates, maintain an ongoing conversation, and reach your audiences in timely ways with multiple media.

- Put into place the communications tools that you will use in your advocacy work. These may range from regular newsletters and eNews to websites, blogs, videos, direct mail, and more. Internet-based communication is critical, and people depend on e-mail for timely information. You will need systems that allow you to use these tools with outreach to specific audiences.

  - Meet the need for internal communication modes that keep your staff connected. For example, your advocacy team will meet regularly and share the same information that you post publicly. But you will also need to communicate often and nimbly. Plan for this. For example, e-mail and texts have helped members of an advocacy team make real-time connections when working at a state capitol and ensure that people have information and know where they are needed when issues are in debate.

  - You are likely to use other modes of communication for external audiences. How will you reach all of your supporters on a given issue? Your donors?

  - Learn about the tools that have the most appeal to decision makers and the media. Often this requires asking individuals about their preferences. When you meet with elected officials, for instance, it is a useful part of relationship building to ask what forms of communication work best for them. Do they accept phone calls and when? Which e-mail addresses do they really use and want you to use? Are there staff members to whom you should copy all communications in order to ensure that everything from scheduling requests to urgent persuasive messages get attention?

- Decide on the way in which you will brand your public policy communications. What are the images and words that will trigger instant and positive responses from your audiences when you are breaking through the flood of information that each person faces every day?

- Determine the ways in which you want to receive input from those who communicate with you on all aspects of your policy work. Be sure that you promote the mediums and the addresses at which your organization and your advocacy-team members may be reached. For the media and elected officials, it is important to give them contact information that allows them to reach you at times outside of regular office hours if policy work is in progress. When you are serving as a resource to a legislative champion or a reporter, you want that person to be able to contact you—even at midnight when your issue is being discussed or written about for the morning enewspaper.

- Assign responsibility for the design and maintenance of communications systems and lists of target audiences. These are essential tools for effective advocacy. Communication systems are worth an upfront investment and staffing to keep them current.

Systems for tracking information

- It is important to have timely and accurate information about your issues and activity in the policy-making process. To ensure that you are receiving the research, analysis, schedules, and activity reports that you need, set up files for systematically collecting and disseminating information from your most valuable sources.

- Subscribe to informational resources so that you have an ongoing stream of information that adds to your knowledge base as you develop and promote your issue.

  - Most governmental bodies—executive offices, legislative entities, administrative offices—have websites at which you can sign up for everything from schedules of hearings and events to press releases from the governor or mayor.

  - Research centers will provide alerts to data and analysis so that you are always ahead of breaking information that has implications for your work on issues. Subscribe to the vehicles that they offer for regular updates.

  - Organizations working on your issue, whether they share your position or not, help to keep you informed about how your issues is developing, what data and stories they are using to be persuasive, what their latest information is, and more. Get on their lists so that you don't miss anything about the context and activity in your issue area.

Systems for tracking your legislative activity

- Keep a file for maintaining records of lobbying activity for reporting to the IRS and regulatory agencies.

- Set up a system for recording and sharing information about elected officials and contacts with them. This should include a method for filing notes from meetings so that people in your organization can benefit from what is learned and can use those notes as background for future contacts. Begin by keeping a set of files for each of your organization's lobbying issues, and expand them as you contact legislators, attend legislative sessions, and add more issues to your plan. For example, GREAT!, the fictional nonprofit introduced in Chapter 1, organized a set of files on building state support for workforce development. Within this set are files for each bill drafted as well as proposed amendments, each marked to show the date the legislature debated the bill or amendment and the action taken. Other files hold dated notes from all committee hearings and floor debates. Still others hold handouts and media clips. There is a separate file for each legislator with whom GREAT! has contacts, and these include notes on the meetings, dates meetings occurred, and ideas for next contacts or followup. GREAT!'s lobbyist refers to these files before the next contact with a legislator.

Secure the Resources for Policy Advocacy

When you wrote your work plan, you created a budget appropriate to the scale and scope of your advocacy effort. (See Worksheet 14: Identify Resources.) Most organizations can do a minor amount of advocacy without significant additional financial resources. For a major initiative and ongoing public policy capacity, most organizations will need additional resources. If you have determined that additional resources are needed, begin working to secure funds as early as possible. Options to consider include

- Reallocation of existing unrestricted funds and staff time.

- Requests for grants from philanthropic sources for the information and education components of your advocacy efforts.

- A *public policy* fundraising campaign to members and supporters. For example, send a letter requesting donations to cover the costs of literature and mailings for a lobbying campaign on a particular issue. Members, clients, supporters, and community leaders are often willing to help meet the costs of a lobbying campaign on an issue that matters to them.[3]

Coordinate any fundraising that you do to support your public policy work with your nonprofit's other development plans. Many foundations are increasingly supportive of public policy work, and foundations that support your programs may be willing to provide additional support for the advocacy component of your mission-related work. All types of foundations may support education and outreach efforts. Community foundations may also support lobbying. Chapter 4 provides some basic information about foundations and the laws on lobbying, but nonprofits should recognize that general operating support and project-specific funding may be available. Increasingly, national, regional, and local foundations recognize that nonprofits play an important role in adding data, stories, experience, and expertise to an informed policy dialogue. Some have identified policy as a key strategy for meeting their own philanthropic organization's goals for making a difference in our communities. Work with any foundations that support your ongoing programs and services to explore their willingness to fund advocacy, and research foundations that have created policy support programs. State associations of nonprofits, state and regional associations of grantmakers, The Foundation Center, and such publications as the Chronicle on Philanthropy provide up-to-date information about where the best prospects for policy support are in your field of interest. You may be able to expand your organization's funding sources by seeking support for enhancing the public dialogue on the issues that affect your organization's constituencies.

---

[3] Like any charitable contribution, these donations from individuals to a 501(c)(3) organization qualify for charitable-giving tax deductions or credits. Foundation funding for lobbying activity is more restricted. For detailed explanations of how (and how much) foundations can support public policy work, see the Alliance for Justice publications at www.bolderadvocacy.org.

Activate Your Public Policy Advocacy Committee

Finally, convene the initial meeting of the public policy advisory committee to review the "charge to the committee" and the public policy work plan. The first meeting should also provide committee members with a clear understanding of your organization's mission and how that mission is to be served by your public policy work.

Set a schedule of committee meetings for the year. Each meeting should include the following regular agenda items:

- A briefing on the substantive issues that are your lobbying priorities. This will ensure that all members of the committee have a solid grounding in the issues. For example, GREAT! might include a briefing on the role of child-care supports in work-transition programs. The next meeting might feature a briefing on the role of employers in workforce development.

- Updates and discussions on current activities. Don't just describe what you're up to; ask for the advisory committee's advice! Let your advisors know what information or recommendations you want from them, give them ample time to provide their ideas, and listen carefully. Create feedback loops so that advisors will know how their ideas have shaped your lobbying activity.

- Thoughtful discussion and creative ideas. Make committee meetings a place where people come for the ideas, the debate, and the opportunity to network. Make the meetings fun—serve food, invite guest speakers, and celebrate successes. Invite legislators who can explain their agenda and forecast highlights of upcoming legislative sessions, agency staff who can provide background on issues, experienced lobbyists who will tell their stories of successful strategies and grisly mistakes, proponents and opponents to debate an issue, and media representatives with expertise in your issues.

Identify additional ways in which members of the committee want to be involved in your lobbying efforts. They may be willing to use their media contacts to help you get coverage of your issues. They may serve as spokespersons for the organization. They should be expected to answer "calls to action" and call, write, or meet with elected officials as needed. Learn about their interests, talents, and connections—and tap them.

Getting your organizational infrastructure in place for your public policy work is a crucial step in implementing your public policy work plan. Once the essential components are in place, especially the authority for decision making and the assignment of responsibilities for coordinating public policy activities and lobbying, you are ready to act.

Implement Your Advocacy and Lobbying Plan
Step 2: Initiate Advocacy and Lobbying Activity

Advocating for Change

As you launch your policy work, keep in mind the basic structure for building an advocacy campaign. As the policy triangle reflects, you begin by having your policy goal and the key messages that support your position. Then there are three strategies to put in place: lobbying (and the education that leads up to lobbying), organizing a base of supporters, individuals, and organizations that will be a strong community voice for your cause, and media advocacy.

"Lobbying is presenting facts, opinions, concerns, expectations, theories and ideas. . . . It is persuasion of your point of view. Politics is essentially the attempt by humans to agree on a course of action. Real power rests less in coercing people to do what you want and more in persuading them to do what you want. Real power is getting other people to share your goals—and lobbying is one avenue for doing just that."

—John D. Sparks, *Best Defense: A Guide for Orchestra Advocates*

Four key questions drive your issue work:

1   What is the problem or opportunity?

2   What, exactly, do you want to have happen?

3   Who decides? (City, county, state? Executive, legislative, or judicial branch?)

4   What are the effective strategies for persuading decision makers to adopt your position?

How to Organize and Mobilize Community Support

Over the long term, your organization will need a base of supporters who will be citizen activists, committed to your issues and the public policy changes that are your goals. Organizing involves bringing people together for a shared purpose and building power at the community level to make a difference in the policies and priorities for the public good. Collective action has long been used by nonprofits working for social change. Indeed, organizing fulfills an important role for nonprofits: serving as

"One of the resources nonprofits can turn to as they develop advocacy plans is their own board of directors. What often makes the difference in building support is access and attention. Often, board members have personal contacts with elected officials and in the corporate community and can tap these relationships to build support for nonprofits' issues. We've found that board members are willing and excited to be advocates for their nonprofit organization or the whole sector, but they need to be asked."

—Kristin R. Lindsey, Vice President, External Relations, Donors Forum of Chicago

a vehicle through which people have a voice in the decisions that have an impact on their lives. Some organizing is referred to as grassroots organizing: organizing that engages and gives a strong voice to the community residents, the people. Grasstops organizing is often a term applied to building support from community leaders who have influence because of their status in the community. Both are important.

Consider organizing as the foundation of your advocacy work. Your organization establishes its leadership by serving as the convener of people with shared purpose. Your movement has power in numbers if a group of people stand together with clear intent, well developed information, compelling messages, and skills for communicating with the people who are, in fact, accountable to the public. As we discuss in later chapters, organizing is also key to nonprofit, nonpartisan election activity. If the base of supporters who share in your advocacy work are also voters, your collective power increases significantly. Remember that elected officials review the voter rolls and know who votes (not HOW they vote). If your area has high turnout, you get the attention and consideration that you want for your issues.

Organizing also refers to your nonprofit's ability to join with other organizations in some form of collaboration to build deep and broad support for your cause. For small nonprofits or those only beginning to do advocacy, working in collaboration (from ad hoc task forces to more-formal alliances and coalitions) provides the option of being part of something bigger and needing to add their unique value without being responsible for a full issue campaign. In most states, coalitions that address homelessness, mental health services, environmental causes, or human rights or that form to support or oppose a specific bill or initiative exemplify the power of bringing together organizations and individuals with shared concerns to be a force for change.

Good organizing involves:

- identifying people who do or might have a stake in your policy work
- recruiting them to work with you in support of shared goals
- informing them about the issues and policy process
- preparing them to take action
- mobilizing their support
- engaging with them in evaluating the effort
- involving them in shaping the work ahead from the ground up

Organizing supports your current work. Perhaps more important, sustained organizing builds leaders for your cause and creates ever increasing power and effectiveness for your work.

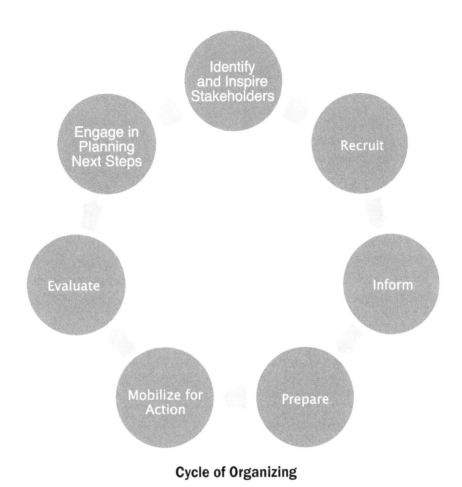

Cycle of Organizing

1. Build a base for support

Numbers count in politics. Constituents count in politics. Leadership voices—organizations, individuals, media—count in politics. Public will, the voices of constituents (especially if they vote!), and strong community partners are essential components of effective advocacy. As you move your public policy plan into implementation phase, organizing is an important initial step. Your organizing should build and expand on the support that you already have as early as possible. Build your grassroots base and continue to build and engage that base year after year.

Conduct a stakeholder analysis

Stakeholders are all the people who have an interest in your organization's success at achieving its mission. In public policy work, stakeholders include the people who care about your effectiveness in passing or stopping legislative proposals. In a stakeholder analysis, you identify the specific segments of the general public who care about your organization's work and public policy agenda. For each of your public policy goals, you may have different stakeholders.

Begin your analysis by stating your organization's mission and one public policy goal that you will advance to meet your mission. Then brainstorm all the people or groups who might be affected by or care about that goal. These stakeholders will include the following.

People and groups that will *benefit from the proposed law.* These may include your customers or clients, other people who struggle with the problem you are attempting to solve, groups and individuals who support the intended beneficiaries of the proposed law, and people in other states or countries who will base their efforts to change laws on the precedents that you set. You need to get these stakeholders involved in your effort so they can tell their own stories, persuade decision makers that the problem you have named is real, and emphasize that the proposed solution will help.

People and groups that will *benefit from your organization's success.* These stakeholders include board, staff, donors, and funders who support your work; allied organizations that rely on your services; and similar organizations that want to follow your model. This group of stakeholders is likely to rally behind you because they are loyal. You will need them to use their power as constituents, experts, and informed citizens to help make your case to decision makers.

People and groups that *influence opinion and make decisions.* These stakeholders include the people whose support you need in order to convince elected officials to adopt your position: community leaders, political leaders, and members of the media; the elected officials who will vote on your proposal; and the executive branch leaders who will support, oppose, or veto your proposal. These influences and decision makers are the ultimate targets of your efforts, because they shape the policy dialogue and make policy decisions.

For each group of stakeholders, determine

1. Which issue they care about
2. Why they care
3. What they can do
4. What you want them to do
5. How to present your key messages so that you persuade them to join your cause
6. How you will reach them, educate them, and keep them up to date on your issues and arguments
7. How you will mobilize them to act strategically at critical times

After you have determined your stakeholders and the kinds of activities necessary to educate and motivate them, you need to set priorities; rarely will you have enough resources or time to reach *all* your stakeholders. Placing your stakeholders on an x-y grid such as the one below can help you decide which ones you had best concentrate your energies on. Rank them by influence (on the vertical axis) and ease of accessibility (on the horizontal axis). Concentrate your actions toward the upper left of the grid—but don't forget that many voices with "low influence" can become *very* influential when combined.

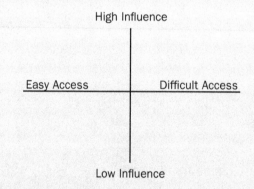

Decide which stakeholder groups are priorities, based on how much they can influence the people who will be making decisions about your legislative proposals. Focus your time, energy, and resources on these stakeholders. Build your efforts to educate and mobilize supporters around the insights gained from this stakeholder analysis.

Your base of supporters should be broad, and it should include people who have diverse points of impact on decision makers. For example, the people you serve can persuade legislators to support your cause because they will enjoy improvements in their lives or communities. Their strength is their personal stories and their power as constituents of elected officials. Legislators who care about your cause and your organization can be mobilized to use their influence with their colleagues, and they are among your best potential lobbyists. Board members are often key leaders in the community and can command the attention and respect of decision makers. Members of the press always capture the attention of people in policy and politics; it helps to have them covering your issues the way you want them covered.

Your objective is to know who your stakeholders are, determine how they can help you win support for your legislative position, and educate and mobilize them strategically. The sidebar Conduct a stakeholder analysis on the opposite page will help.

- Do a stakeholder analysis. Create a chart that allows you to see who cares about what issue, why they care, what they can do, and how to persuade them to join the cause and act. It is important to have 1:1 discussions with individuals whom you are trying to recruit. Explore in a structured conversation what they think about the issues that you address. You will want to know if they agree with you intellectually. That is a good start. You will want to know if they see their self interest connected to your issues and positions. Even better. You will want to know if they share the core values that drive your policy work. This is best. Your strongest and most enduring supporters will be those with whom you connect on all three levels.

- Prioritize your stakeholders. If helpful, use the influence-access grid described in the sidebar.

- Set up a system for identifying and reaching specific individuals. This will require you to have and continuously build good lists of people you want to keep informed and call to action. Lists are part of your well maintained database. They should include as much information as possible: names, addresses, phone numbers (office, cell, phone), e-mail addresses, job title and organization, relationship to your organization (volunteer, program participant, donor, neighbor), congressional district, legislative district, local government districts, types of activities in which the person expressed interest (testimony, phone calls, data entry, graphic design, events, etc.). It is helpful to be able to organize them into specific groups, i.e., constituents in a specific district, supporters with specific expertise, and so forth.

- Build supporters' interest and understanding of your policy issues over time. Include materials and ongoing updates about your policy positions and efforts in communications with all of your audiences.

- Teach supporters how to communicate effectively with elected

What is a 1:1 conversation?

Serious organizing depends on getting to know an individual and identifying the degree to which that person is interested in your cause, able to contribute something of value to the effort, and willing to take action. As with all advocacy, relationships and conversations are ongoing priorities. A 1:1 is a structured conversation in which your nonprofit meets with a person (sometimes a group) for some give-and-take about the issue, the level of connection, and determine if there is benefit and will to work together. See *Tools for Radical Democracy*, cited in the resources on page 175, for examples of structured conversations.

officials. Provide information on how to write letters, leave persuasive phone messages, use e-mail and social media effectively, and build ongoing contact with their own elected officials. Consider holding lobbying-training sessions for supporters who want to build their skills and confidence in lobbying.

- Once supporters know your policy positions and have decided to lobby, tell them where the decisions will be made, when, and which key elected officials need to be lobbied. Provide e-mail and mailing addresses, phone numbers, social media sites with postings by the elected official, and some biographical information about the official.

2. Use the best strategies for grassroots support

Grassroots supporters will want to know how they can use their time and energy to really make a difference. Legislators agree that they are persuaded most by

- **Meetings.** Legislators value personal meetings and discussions with constituents and with advocates who have valuable information on an issue. Schedule meetings rather than "dropping in" and keep them positive, respectful, interesting, and full of useful information. Provide your grassroots supporters with a single-page handout and collateral resource packets that they can give to the official and that the official can use in framing a debate or proposing legislation.

Nonprofit organizations that hold a "Day at the Capitol" or "City Hall Days" often include meetings with elected representatives as part of the program. On such occasions, when many representatives of your nonprofit are meeting with elected officials, wear buttons and hand out brochures that give your issue visibility. Ask public officials to show support by wearing your button.

Strange bedfellows

In doing a stakeholder analysis, be creative. Building unexpected partnerships can be an effective strategy. For instance, the American Medical Association and other health organizations joined anti-violence organizations in support of gun-control legislation. The issue became part of the public health advocacy agenda. Creative partnerships bring increased people power to your legislative effort. And new partners may have access and influence in arenas new to your nonprofit organization.

- **Letters.** While meetings are the best way to contact legislators, personal letters, especially from constituents, are also highly effective. You can provide key points to help supporters focus their letters, but those letters should have a personal touch. They can be handwritten or prepared electronically, as long as they are readable. Constituents should identify themselves as residents in the legislator's district. Their letters should state the key points about the issue, and they should tell why the issue makes a difference to them in some specific way. The important element is personal concern.

- **E-mail.** While some people may still consider e-mail impersonal, it is increasingly the way that many elected officials communicate with others. Indeed, some legislators use e-mail and social media to have ongoing conversations with individuals and the public about issues. Introductory e-mails should have the same structure and formality as a written letter. Further communications may be less formal depending on the relationship with the decision maker and how that person responds to the initial letter. Some hints: include important clues in the subject line of an e-mail.

How do you activate supporters? Let us count the ways

1. Provide briefings, stories, and informational materials. Win people's support.

2. Offer training on the legislative process and communicating with legislators.

3. Identify what you want them to do and suggest specific steps to take. Make it easy.

4. Develop effective communication tools. Alert people to take action when they have a solid background on the issue and are committed to supporting your position. Give them talking points to guide their communications and reinforce your key messages.

5. Ask supporters to write to their legislators. Identify their representatives or the key legislators you want to reach. Provide addresses, fax numbers, and key points to include in a personalized letter.

6. Bring people together to see the process at work and get comfortable meeting with their elected representatives. Hold rallies and "Days at the Capitol" that engage people in the public dialogue. Make it fun!

7. Share victories and be generous with thanks.

Elected officials are inundated with e-mail, so a subject line that identifies you as a constituent, as a group making a scheduling request, or as an important piece of information related to issues that they work on can help you to get their attention and a response. Also note that, at the congressional level, e-mail messages are favored over regular mail because of delays in processing regular mail. Also keep in mind that most governmental entities caution against the use of e-mail attachments based on security concerns.

- **Social media.** Most elected officials now have social-media profiles that they use for communications. It is perfectly acceptable to engage with elected officials via these channels. However, maintain your professional voice. Your communications may not be private. Use discretion about what you post.

- **Phone calls.** Constituents get priority attention from their legislators, especially those who have made an effort to get to know the public official prior to the home stretch of the decision-making process. Callers should identify themselves by name and address and leave a clear message that will fit on a message slip.

- **Press attention.** Letters to the editor have enormous impact. No matter how busy they are, public officials always want to know what is in the hometown newspaper (or online) that relates to their district and their work. Supporters should send letters to their local weekly or daily newspaper.

The sidebar How Do You Activate Supporters? on this page has more ideas for mobilizing grassroots support.

Appendix D: Samples includes Tips for Contacting Your Representative, adapted from materials developed by the Minnesota Citizens for the Arts.

Initiate Lobbying Activity

Your organization will need to combine six tools to accomplish its public policy goals. You will need to know

1. How to propose new legislation
2. How to support legislation that has already been proposed
3. How to defeat proposed legislation
4. How to lobby the executive branch
5. How to build and mobilize grassroots support
6. How to advocate through the media

You'll be using these basic tools for as long as you have public policy goals. Learn to use them, and you will serve your mission well.

How to Propose New Legislation

The following section presents basic steps in developing an idea and working proactively with elected officials and supporters to have it adopted as law. As you refer to your work plan, choose the steps presented here that will enable you to meet your policy priorities as articulated in Worksheet 5: Issues, Objectives, and Positions.

There are four steps in proposing new legislation. They are

1. Research and write your proposal for a bill
2. Gain the support of your bill's chief author in the legislature
3. Lobby for passage
4. Celebrate success, learn from failure

1. Research and write your proposal for a bill

Each legislative initiative has a research phase. Your planning team identified priority issues for your organization in Worksheet 5. When the issue you've chosen falls under the often harsh light of political scrutiny, you need to know your facts. Conduct whatever information-gathering steps are needed to ensure you can make your case.

Know current law

The first step is to be sure that you know current law. This information is available in a variety of ways: government websites often allow you to access state statutes and local government ordinances. You might ask your own elected officials to have staff help you review the existing law in the area of interest. Sometimes experienced advocates will be a good resource if they have worked in this area of policy. Know the law and what you need to add or change to achieve your objective.

Identify the problem and explain how your proposal will address it

To make your case, be prepared to explain why the existing law doesn't achieve the desired ends and how your proposal will make the needed changes. As you prepare the evidence, rely on your own organization's information as a starting point and build from there.

Prepare a statement that describes the problem and that introduces your proposed solution. Follow this with the justification for your position. Build your case with facts and anecdotes. If your proposed law promotes a program, service, or tax policy that you have experience with and that has demonstrable results, be sure to include that information as part of your case for your proposal.

Learn about the people who will be important to your lobbying efforts

Once you have solidified your case, you need to know the people and organizations that will be players in the dialogue about your proposal. This includes getting to know decision makers, allies, and opponents. Refer to Worksheet 8: The People of the Process. Confer with the public policy advisory committee and build on its ideas about which people you need to influence to move your legislation forward. Get to know the people who will make or influence decisions on your issues. (See the sidebar Quick tips for building relationships with public officials on page 112.)

Invite public officials and their staff to visit your organization's site. The time they spend with the people you serve will help these officials understand community needs as well as your organization and its accomplishments. For public officials, such visits often build deeper understanding and a personal connection to the way in which your work benefits their community.

Read everything available about the decision makers. Observe them in action at legislative meetings, in the community, on local television access stations or radio, wherever they are in your community.

Learn everything that you can about other organizations, academicians, journalists, business leaders, politicians, and celebrities who might be your allies or opponents. Reach out to supporters and people who benefit from your work to strengthen their willingness to act on the issues. Build positive relationships and make friends!

Before you begin, review what you know about the arena of influence where you will be lobbying for a new initiative. See Worksheet 7: The Legislative Arena.

Relationships matter. Nonprofits committed to working on public policy make the time to build trusting working relationships with allied organizations, decision makers, and the media. Good relationships ensure that your nonprofit will have timely access to those who can help to move your issue agenda forward. Those same relationships allow you to fulfill your role as a leadership organization, counted on as a resource for shaping sound policy.

Shape key messages as you write your proposal

Your organization needs to shape its key messages in the very early stages of preparing your legislative work. *Key messages* are clear and consistent statements about the issues, ideas, and actions that you are promoting. They are a critical part of the way you build understanding and motivate people to respond. Your organization will need to identify the key messages that you want to convey, the audiences that you are targeting, and the vehicles that will help you to get your key messages to your target audiences. In lobbying, key messages usually include the following:

Case statement: This is a clear articulation of the problem that you have identified, the solution and position that you are advocating, and the rationale that supports your position.

Results: You need to state the expected outcomes of your proposed solution to a problem and identify the ways in which those outcomes will be measured and experienced. Be as clear as possible in describing how people's lives and communities will be different if the measure you support passes or the measure you oppose is allowed to progress. For example, advocates of clean- and safe-water policies need to address the specific consequences of allowing fertilizers and manure to run into streams, rivers, lakes, and aquifers as part of a campaign to stop feedlots from expanding.

Slogans: Your lobbying campaign will want to include repetition of key phrases that capture the essence of the issue. For example, advocates for violence prevention have repeated one brief slogan as part of every written statement or public notice, whether it's about stopping domestic abuse or ending gang warfare: "You're the one who can make a difference. You can make the peace."

Persuasive statements: There are the oft-repeated statements that capture your ideas and touch the particular audience that you have targeted. These statements appeal to a specific audience's interest in the issue. Advocates for the right to bear arms have approached mothers with the statement "You not only have a right to protect your children; you have a responsibility." They might reach another targeted audience, hunters, by noting that "the right to bear arms is part of the American way of life. Don't let anyone limit your right to hunt." To yet another target audience, lawmakers, they might use persuasive statements relying on legal issues and election strategies: "The Constitution guarantees the right to bear arms. Voters in your district—lots of hunters—want to be able to hunt and protect their property."

The annotated samples in Appendix D provide a good example of effective key messages.

Write your proposal

Keep your written proposal brief. Make it compelling. Your aim is to compress all the work that you have done into a brief but persuasive case. You want to inspire a legislator to have a bill drafted, to make it his or her priority, and to work for its passage. In a short, one- to three-page proposal

- Identify the need or problem. Be clear about who is affected by the problem and what it means in their lives and to the community.

- State the solution that you offer.

- Identify expected outcomes if the legislation passes. Identify the consequences of failing to make the policy change that you recommend.

- Be clear about points of controversy that your proposal may provoke.

- Describe other places where this solution has been tried and has succeeded (if this information is available).

- Demonstrate support for your proposal. Who else will "sign on"?

- Address costs of the proposal.

Give your proposal a short and catchy name that captures the essence of your idea. This will become its informal name as it moves through a legislative process. Efforts to legislate a refund for recycling glass containers have been known as "bottle bills." Use the title to suggest how the public interest is well served by the idea. States have passed tax deductions for charitable giving for nonitemizers, calling these "charitable-giving tax-relief acts."

A sample legislative proposal can be found in the annotated samples (Exhibit 2) in Appendix D on page 194. The sidebar Shape Key Messages As You Write Your Proposal on page 110 contains more information on effective proposals.

2. Gain the support of your bill's chief authors in the legislature

Here is some good news: *you don't have to draft the technical language for the bill!* In almost every state, a legislator—at the state, county, or city level—who wants to author a bill asks legislative staff to draft the actual bill language. In the state legislature, there are usually two *chief authors*—one in the house and one in the senate. Your chief authors will want to use your proposal as the starting point for having a bill drafted by legislative staff. Drafting a bill is often done at the state level by the "revisor's office," which is a nonpartisan office serving all members. Revisor's office staff members put ideas into bill form and identify where the proposed law will fit in the state's statutes.

Nonprofit lobbyists should work closely with the bill's chief authors to ensure that the bill, as drafted, captures the proposal as intended. Ask to see the bill when it comes back from the revisor's office and discuss any changes that you recommend with the chief authors. Changes can be made before the bill circulates to additional authors and is introduced.

Find legislative authors for your proposal

In addition to chief authors, other legislators may sign on as coauthors (usually referred to simply as *authors*). Each legislature and local governmental body has its own rules for how many legislators can be named on a bill as authors and where a bill will first be discussed when it is introduced. (Note: Some states use the term *sponsors*, while others use *authors*.) Be strategic about selecting your chief authors. You want a chief author in each body of your legislature who has "the four *Ps*": passion, position, power, and persuasiveness. These people will have the primary responsibility within the legislature for moving the bill toward passage.

Passion. Your bill's chief authors must care deeply about the problem that you are addressing and must be convinced of the value of your proposal. It's best if the chief

Quick tips for building relationships with public officials

You will have a much easier time getting support for your positions if you have worked, ahead of time, to build relationships with legislators and administrators involved in your issues. Here are a few pointers to remember:

- *Be of value to public officials.* Know what issues they care about and become a reliable source of accurate information.

- *Be a good host.* During times when the legislature is not in session, invite legislators to visit your organization and see what you do.

- *Be a good listener.* Meet early with key legislators, be respectful, and listen.

- *Ask for help early.* Public officials are much more likely to be invested in your bill if they've been involved in it from the start.

- *Understand the environment.* It's politics. Show that you have strong constituent support for your position.

- *Reward support.* Whether you fail or succeed, thank those officials who supported you. When you do succeed, thank them in public and invite reporters.

- *Stay in touch.* Show public officials the positive outcome of their acts.

- *Never burn bridges.* Today's enemy may be tomorrow's ally.

authors adopt it as their own top priority. Best case: your chief authors will have worked on legislation to address similar needs in the past and will know the problems, people, and communities affected; the advocacy groups likely to be involved in the issue; and the legislative path that the bill will need to follow to pass.

Position. Chief authors can be most influential in getting a bill heard—and taken seriously—if they are members of the key committee that will decide on the bill's merits. In most legislatures, there are policy and finance committees in every major policy area: education, health, human services, economic development, governmental operations, agriculture, crime. Choose chief authors who are members of the committees that will hear the bill. This is crucial because these committees could (1) recommend passage to the full house or senate, (2) kill the bill by either denying it hearings or referring it to other committees that will hold it up, or (3) vote it down in committee and thus stop its progress. (There are ways to bring a bill to life after it dies in committee, but it is better to start with chief authors who have a good chance of shepherding it through committees with positive votes.)

Power. Look for chief authors with political power. The committee chair, the majority leader of the house or senate, or a long-standing and well-respected member of the committee has more power to influence the committee's agenda and action than a rookie. It is almost always best to have the chief authors of a bill be from the dominant political party, and it helps if the legislators have a powerful position within their political caucuses. If you can choose chief authors who provide a display of bipartisan support, so much the better.

Don't forget about the governor's office!

It will be helpful to scope out the feelings of the executive branch on your proposal as state agency staff are often solicited in committee to provide testimony as to the impacts of a bill. You don't want to be surprised with executive opposition. On the contrary, strong support from the ultimate "implementers" of your proposal (following passage) will only add to the reasonableness of your idea. If you don't have a personal connection to the governor's staff, ask to speak with a policy aide, or government-relations staff who is assigned to your issue area. It is common for executive staff to specialize in various categories (e.g. budget, taxes, health or human services, environment, etc.).

Persuasiveness. Sometimes a legislator has power as the recognized expert in an issue area such as housing, insurance regulation, or technology development. Your chief authors will have to be your bill's best lobbyists! They must care enough about the issue to move it through all the steps by which a bill becomes a law. This will require a clear understanding of the bill and the process and the ability to influence a wide variety of decision makers along the way.

Some other considerations in selecting chief authors and coauthors:

- Work with someone who knows and trusts your organization. You'll want the chief authors to call on you when decisions have to be made and compromises considered.

- To the extent possible, invite a mix of coauthors whose "signing on" reflects support from all political parties and all geographic areas of the state.

- Look for gender balance and full representation of the community in the list of authors.

- Seek leaders as coauthors. It can be very helpful to have a speaker of the house or a senate majority leader as a coauthor. They may be too busy to be chief authors, but their names on the bill signals to others that they are on board.

3. Lobby for passage

As you prepare to lobby for passage of your bill, convert your research and writing on the issue to attractive forms for supporters, the media, the public, and public officials. Be creative, interesting, persuasive, and do it all with materials that are brief and compelling. Several samples of such materials can be found in the annotated samples in Appendix D.

With materials in hand, your primary goal is to shepherd the bill through the legislative process, working tirelessly to see it pass. In this all-important process, the lobbyist's duties include working to

- Introduce the bill
- Move the bill through committee
- Influence decision makers *after* your bill passes in committee
- Be there on the day of the vote

Introduce the bill

The bill is usually formally introduced (often called "given a first reading") before the full legislative body, assigned a number, and referred to a committee for consideration. Your lobbyist should work with your chief authors as the bill is ready to be introduced. Some tips:

- Urge the legislator who is the chief author in the house and the legislator who is the chief author in the senate to have the bill introduced and assigned to a committee in each body early enough in the session to give it time to be heard and to meet any committee deadlines.

- Allow time for supporters to be alerted to the bill's introduction and the names of committee members who will be hearing it, and to contact key legislators to voice their support. Identify and mobilize supporters and stakeholders from key legislators' districts. They will understand and make convincing arguments to legislators about the impact of your proposed public policy on their district.

- Build in time for unexpected delays or legislative maneuvers. Many bills that are introduced independently are rolled into more comprehensive bills, sometimes called "omnibus bills" or "committee bills." This occurence may require an extra committee hearing or that the bill be heard independently before it can be considered for inclusion in an omnibus bill.

- Remember that, in many states, if the house and senate pass bills that are not identical, a joint committee (sometimes called a "conference committee") will be convened to reconcile differences.

Move the bill through committee

Prior to any committee hearing, learn about the members. This information is available from the legislative information services and should be on file in your office. Refer to Worksheet 8: The People of the Process to review your earlier detective work on committee membership.

Meet with each member of the committee prior to committee hearings. You should be sure that each committee member knows what the proposed legislation is intended to accomplish. Your role is to describe the problem that needs to be addressed, what solution the bill offers, and why you think this legislation will provide an effective solution to a problem.

How to testify at a committee hearing

Committee testimony is one form of formal, strategic communication. Your lobbyist and the bill's sponsors can help get you into a position to testify. You have already prepared your key messages as you developed your lobbying materials. Draw your testimony from your key messages. (See the sidebar Shape key messages as you write your proposal, page 110.) Make your testimony clear, brief, and compelling. Use real-life stories to make complex issues meaningful and personal. Here are some tips for testifying.

- *Prepare a formal statement of your position.* Explain that position in clearly enumerated points. This can range from a one-page handout that is the most direct statement of your position to letters of support, press clippings, pictures, and artifacts.

- *Learn everything possible about the committee members.* It is important to know the audience. And legislators are always pleased to be addressed by name.

- *Choose a person to provide your primary testimony.* Choose someone who is articulate and convincing and has status within your organization or coalition. Your board chair, executive director, or the staff person with the highest level of expertise may be more appropriate for this role than your lobbyist, who serves as "stage manager." The organization needs its own best and most influential voice.

- *Provide an additional person or two to testify.* Choose people who can state why they support your position and how they expect it to impact their lives or communities. If time is limited, include their stories in written form.

- *Respect committee protocols.* Address the committee correctly (Madam or Mister Chair and Members of the Committee). Respect time constraints.

- *Anticipate questions and opposition.* Research who opposes your position, why, and what they are saying about the issue. Assume that opponents, too, will have lobbied committee members and their staff. Assume that you will get requests to explain your facts. Also be prepared for questions driven by a different position or perspective on the issue. You and your legislative supporters should identify these potential questions and how you will address them. Write out the questions and answers to the best of your ability.

- *Rehearse. Critique. Revise.*

- *Relax.* Remember that you know more about your issue than almost anyone else in the process and you are prepared to make a case for something that matters. Square your shoulders, take a deep breath, and do your best.

- *Ask the committee members to vote in support of your position.*

In meetings with individual committee members, ask them how much time they have. Respect their time constraints. Get to the point early in the discussion, and leave written information with the committee member and his or her staff person. Limit the meeting to two or three individuals from your organization and include a representative from the committee member's legislative district if possible.

Before you conclude a meeting with a committee member, *ask for his or her vote for your position.* Remember that not everyone will agree with your position. If you know that a legislator opposes your proposal, find out why. The more information you have about how strongly a legislator opposes or supports you, the better you will be able to work to gain or strengthen support for your issue. Keep careful notes of a legislator's commitments to support you and questions or concerns.

If the elected official needs additional information or has concerns about the bill, offer to get the information (if you believe this can be done and will make a difference). Always follow up on promises to provide additional information, whether those are facts, lists of supporters, examples of the problem, or models of similar bills and their impact in other locations.

Be prepared to address questions that committee members are likely to raise about your bill during committee hearings. Know as much as possible about how they are likely to vote. Your bill's sponsor will appreciate knowing ahead of time how much support and opposition to expect when the bill is heard by the committee.

Work with your chief authors and those legislators who support your bill to pass it in each committee and return it to the full legislative body for passage. Here are some tips:

- Ask the chief author to request that the committee chair hear the bill (rather than let it languish on the roster and die for lack of action).

- If you wish to present expert witnesses and constituents who have personal stories, find out how the committee sets the agenda of speakers and get on the list. The bill's author will be expected to introduce and explain the bill to the committee. He or she can tell the committee chair and staff that you are there to testify about the bill and its intended impact. (See the sidebar How to testify at a committee hearing on page 115.)

- Be sure that your lobbyist has observed the committee and knows the committee protocol. Your presenters will need to know how to formally address the committee members (usually "Mister or Madam Chair and Members of the Committee") and how long their testimony should be to conform with committee rules and attention spans.

- If you are not initiating a bill but want to respond to an existing proposal—for or against the measure—the same approach applies. Work with your strongest ally in the legislature to ensure that you will testify. Involve your lobbyist and citizen activists in persuading committee members of the merits and importance of your position.

Influence decision makers *after* your bill passes in committee

During and especially after the committee process, your focus must embrace all members of the legislative body who will have a final say in the passage or failure of the measure you hope to enact. Your lobbyist and your grassroots supporters need to reach every legislator with your message. In the best case, your lobbying will deliver key messages and materials to every elected official or his or her key staff, and every legislator will hear from supporters in his or her legislative district.

Resources for such full coverage may be limited, so your strategy should include priorities. Focus your efforts on

- Strong supporters who need to be encouraged to provide leadership for your cause

- Undecided officials whose vote can make the critical difference

- Elected officials from areas where you have strong and well activated grassroots support

- Key leaders in political caucuses who can encourage their colleagues to support your position

- Opinion shapers who are respected as experts and policy leaders in your issue area

Be there on the day of the vote

When your legislative proposal has proceeded through the committee process and is scheduled for a hearing in the full house and senate, you should make a timely effort to reach all members of the legislature with a final reminder. This is where your preparation of key messages, the materials you have developed, and your education and mobilization of supporters can make a difference in the final vote. Some steps that you can take on the day of the vote:

- Get a final reminder to each elected official about your position. This reminder may take many forms, including electronic messages. Supporters not present at the capitol can send e-mails or texts or utilize social media. You could leave a final "fact sheet" at the legislator's desk before the floor debate begins, the day before or early in the morning of the vote. You could urge supporters to make final phone calls or to "catch legislators in the halls on the way to session" to get in a final word. When resources are limited, target these final reminders to the undecided legislators who can make the key difference in whether your measure passes or fails.

- If you can get a supportive editorial from a newspaper or other media outlet, try to time it for the days prior to the vote. Deliver it to legislators before the floor session in which they will debate the issue begins.

- Have supporters present in the house and senate galleries as the issue is debated and the vote taken. Wear identifiable buttons so that elected officials know that people care and are watching the debate and final action on the bill.

- Many government hearings and full sessions at all jurisdictional levels (city, county, state) are available to the public through live streaming or cable television broadcasts. These broadcasts enable supporters across the area to observe proceedings in real time from their offices or homes or at the capitol and outside the legislative chambers. Your organization can then communicate quickly with elected officials while the debate is in progress and votes on amendments or final passage of a bill are pending. This is when the use of electronic media can be effective for showing support for an issue and also for communicating information to champions. If an author of your bill, or a key leader supporting your position, suddenly faces an unanticipated question or unexpected amendment, your organization can share information and recommendations instantly using electronic communications. An e-mail exchange during a floor debate has saved more than one important policy from amendments that could weaken or defy the original intent. Let your legislators know how they may reach your experts and that you will be available to support them.

- In some legislatures, it is possible to send messages to members of the house or senate when they are in floor sessions debating bills. Constituents who are present in the capitol building will have a good chance of getting their representatives to meet with them for even a minute or two so that they can get a final lobbying statement in on behalf of your organization's cause.

Greet legislators when the vote is over and the session has recessed. Thank them for their support. Avoid any recriminations if they have failed to support you. For opponents, a genuine statement that you hope that you can work together on these and other issues in the future will do more good than an expression of anger or frustration.

4. Celebrate success, learn from failure

At the end of any legislative campaign, brief or extended, simple or complex, take some time for lessons learned. Here are some steps to take:

Debrief. Within a few days of final legislative action on your proposal, convene those most heavily involved in the legislative effort for a debriefing. First reactions may be victory shouts or groans of defeat. Give people a chance to express their reactions. Then guide them into an evaluation of the work. Pose some key questions for the group to address collectively:

1. What were the strengths of our campaign?

2. What were our weaknesses?

3. What were the three most important factors leading to our victory? How can we build on these so that our strengths grow in future efforts?

4. What three factors had the most influence in defeating us? How can we redesign our approach to overcome these weaknesses?

5. What surprised us? How can we be better prepared next time?

6. Was any damage done that will require immediate remedial action on our part?

7. Whom do we need to thank? How do we build on the support they provided here for future efforts?

Be critical. Be forward-thinking about how to build for a next effort. But DON'T be too tough on yourselves; many factors in legislative debate and action are simply outside of your control. Learn to identify these. Then work where you can make a difference. This is always a steep learning curve.

Report. Write a summary of the effort along with your findings (What happened? What went well? What went poorly? Why? What are the next steps in growth?). This report can be written by one person, often the public policy coordinator, based on the group discussion.

Discuss lessons learned and next steps. Present the summary to the full public policy advisory committee for discussion and recommendations. This will serve many purposes: advisory-committee members will be included in your analysis of how the organization can build on strengths to improve its lobbying capacity; advisory-committee members may add ideas and insights that those involved in the day-to-day campaign didn't consider; and advisory-committee members will use what they learn from this experience in their next efforts to inform the organization's public policy work.

Win or lose, **celebrate your good work**. Even if your bill didn't pass this time, celebrate your accomplishments: you made a good case; you educated elected officials about your organization and issues; you built a base of supporters that you can develop for the future; and you learned some lessons that will improve your next efforts. Thank everyone who contributed—warmly and often. Have a party for supporters. Take time to be proud of what you did accomplish!

How to Support Legislation That Has Been Introduced

Often your role is not one of a bill's creator but of a key supporter. When this occurs, you will use many of the same techniques as when you have been the primary mover of a bill. You will need to take extra care to be sure your efforts complement those of the bill's creators and existing supporters.

Sometimes, you will be working alone or alongside others to support some proposed legislation. Other times, you may choose to work as part of a coalition. When groups want to see the same outcomes in a public policy debate, they can increase their chances for success by working in coalitions. Coalitions can share both direct and grassroots lobbying efforts. This strengthens the information base and increases the numbers of constituents that elected officials hear. It is a powerful organizing strategy, provided the coalition serves as a means to a shared goal and doesn't consume time and energy that drains your ability to lobby effectively.

There are essentially four steps in supporting legislation proposed by someone else:

1. Do adequate research to affirm that you agree with the proposal.

2. Identify what added value you bring to the effort to support the existing proposal. Can you help to make a difference in support of the cause?

3. Determine whether you will work in coalition with others or alone.

4. If you intend to work with a collaborative effort, initiate the discussion about your specific role and responsibilities.

1. Determine whether to work alone or in coalition with others

When you choose to support an existing legislative proposal, find out which individuals and groups inspired the legislation and are working to support it. An easy way to get this information is to talk to the chief sponsor of the bill in the legislature. He or she will want your support and will be willing to discuss the genesis of the bill and the groups that support and oppose it.

If a coalition of supporters exists, contact key leaders to discuss their objectives and strategy and to determine whether or not your participation will help you meet shared goals. If no coalition exists, your nonprofit can take the leadership position of inviting supportive groups to meet to discuss the merits of coordinated work. In building a coalition, consider new allies. Often organizations that might seem to be unlikely partners have a common agenda on a specific legislative issue. Working together, you and a new partner may broaden the base of support for your work and signal to decision makers that your issue touches diverse constituencies.

Some criteria can help you to assess if a coalition effort is an effective way to reach your goal. The following questions will help as you weigh the merits of joining or forming a coalition.

Do you share a common objective?

Do you agree that the proposed legislation is the best way to solve a problem that all potential coalition members have identified as a priority? Sometime organizations agree on a definition of a problem but have different and contradictory solutions to offer. If a shared legislative solution can be crafted that all agree will address the problem, your nonprofit can avoid competing with multiple proposals about the same issue. Elected officials will appreciate this sorting out of options and a unified focus on a solution that all agree is best.

Do you agree on key messages and arguments to support your shared position?

Working in coalition, organizations that have a common message can present a powerful and unified voice. Compare the arguments and key messages you would use with those of your potential allies.

Do you agree on the lobbying strategy for supporting the proposed bill?

Even when the end goal is the same, some groups use tactics that may be in direct

Coalition partners build power to influence policy choices

Contributor: Patti Whitney-Wise, Executive Director, Partners for a Hunger-Free Oregon

The work of Partners for a Hunger-Free Oregon (PHFO) exemplifies multiple dimensions of the value of work in coalition. This nonprofit grew out of a 1989 legislative initiative, the Oregon Hunger Task Force (OHTF). The mission of OHTF was to study the problem of hunger in Oregon, make recommendations for policies and programs to alleviate hunger, and help local communities implement changes. OHTF includes community-based organizations, nonprofits, and faith-based organizations, as well as legislators and state agency representatives.

In 2006, the Task Force helped to launch a private, non-profit organization to advance the implementation of the key policy agenda created in the "Act to End Hunger". Progress was made on 30 of the 40 action items. This creation story reflects that governmental and nonprofit partners, working with a shared goal, can collaborate in ways that build broad momentum, support, and action on an issue. Partners and the Task Force created a new five-year action plan in 2010, "Ending Hunger before it Begins," and is focused on implementing that new plan.

Partners and the Task Force, working in alliance, bring together the perspectives, knowledge, skills, networks, and clout of many partners and is a force for change. Key components of their collaborative strategy include:

- **Organizations working across sectors and interests can be powerful when united in common cause.** Partners for a Hunger-Free Oregon now supports and participates in several issue coalitions that include legislators, nonprofits, lobbyists, and business representatives. OHTF/PHFO helps lead the Temporary Assistance to Needy Families (TANF) Alliance and the Earned Income Tax Credit coalition and participates in the Housing Alliance. Partners reports regularly to the Human Services Coalition of Oregon and draws other issue organizations into its work during legislative session. It is obvious that the depth of knowledge, the reach, and the combined power of these many entities make change possible.

- **Planning matters.** Both the five-year plan, "Ending Hunger Before it Begins: Oregon's Call to Action," and advance legislative agendas from OHTF/PHFO help shape the policy dialogue in focusing on shared commitment and direct specific responsibilities for meeting the plan's objectives.

- **Message matters.** All involved have adopted a clear and simple statement as their signature statement: "Hunger is an Income Issue." They have developed talking points with coalition partners to use with the media and legislators. This straightforward statement reflects the bias of the strategy developed to end hunger and invites a broad range of organizations and individuals concerned about income disparities and the impact of poverty to support the five-year plan and actions. The message reflects a strategic frame.

- **Positioning matters. Work with partners who are decision makers and have strengthened their leadership and improved policy outcomes.** In this instance, it has worked well for OHTF/PHFO, born of a legislative initiative, to continue strong bonds with the legislative, executive, and administrative components of government. With four state agencies as partners, and the legislators who are part of the ongoing Oregon Hunger Task Force on board, PHFO/OHTF has well informed and deeply committed champions in policy arenas. The reach included Governor Ted Kulongoski who took on a highly visible role because of his dedication to ending hunger from 2003 to 2011. Currently, First Lady Cylvia Hayes has continued and broadened that legacy to include a new Prosperity Initiative and Governor John Kitzhaber (2011-) is supporting both hunger- and poverty-prevention initiatives. Information must be timely and accurate. OHTF/PHFO is able to ensure that it is always working with good policy and analysis and is succinct. Tapping into academic partners and fiscal-policy analysts as well as coalition partners, OHTF/PHFO produces one-page fact sheets that clearly lay out the issues at hand and are widely used by legislators and partners alike.

(continued)

- **Outreach is essential.** OHTF/PHFO works with leadership organizations from all sectors. Therefore, it has the reach needed to engage the media, opinion shapers, and the people of Oregon to make hunger, as an income issue, a high priority.

- **Opportunities for citizen engagement matter.** A coalition with a broad range of partners presents multiple and diverse channels for citizen activism. Individuals and groups can join this collective effort through any entry point: an organization with which they are already affiliated, the coalition itself, or the leaders who invite them to the work.

- **Coalitions build mutual accountability.** A formal coalition, working from a shared plan, requires each partner to fulfill its commitments. Too many respected partners will know if some group isn't meeting its promises to advance the plan.

- **Collective action can lead to success.** The first five-year plan to end hunger in Oregon made significant progress on 30 of its 40 objectives. The second plan has brought new partners to the table and helped to spur the Oregon First Lady's Prosperity Initiative, which is focusing on poverty reduction as the long-term solution to hunger and includes many of the hunger plan's objectives.

- **Coalitions seed long-term change.** The combined strengths of OHTF/PHFO and its many allies make it bigger than a single bill, a single plan, a single moment in time. This coalition is the core of a social-change movement.

Each collaborative effort has its unique purpose, structure, and value for nonprofits advocating for change. This example presents a high-profile issue, an engaged group of elected officials, and nonprofits with much experience and expertise. Some other collaboratives may need to be structured as basic ad hoc working groups meeting a short-term need, informal alliances for ongoing work mostly on parallel paths, or issue-campaign-specific formal coalitions. In all of these cases, partnerships create increased knowledge, outreach, and power in working for change.

conflict with your organization's values. A coalition of such groups—when they do not agree to abide by the same strategies—can be damaging to both parties.

Will your combined efforts provide needed strengths that no group can bring alone?

Assess whether or not working in coalition will strengthen your effort enough to justify the effort that goes into the work. It takes time, money, and resources to agree on lobbying tactics and activities. Weigh the potential costs against the likelihood of success with either approach.

Do the groups trust one another?

Without trust, it is impossible to coordinate efforts for very long. Member groups may not share essential information or work from the agreed-to lobbying strategy.

Are there leadership and capacity to coordinate coalition efforts?

Someone needs to be designated as the convener of the coalition. In addition, the organizations in the coalition need to create a common system for sharing information, making decisions, and sending out calls to action. Be sure that a coalition that you join or form has the capacity and resources matching its goals.

2. Identify your unique contribution

Whether you work in a coalition or lobby independently, identify and use the unique contribution that you make to the cause. Following are some specific strengths that you might have that would enhance the debate. (See also the sidebar Coalition members build power to influence policy choices on page 121.)

Exclusive information

This could be data about the clients that you serve or the programs and services that you provide. What unique information could you bring to the effort?

Access to people who will be directly affected by the bill

Organizations and people who are the intended beneficiaries of proposed legislation have an important role to play in providing feedback about whether or not proposed legislation will meet their needs. Access to them may be your strength.

Credibility on the issue

If your organization has in the past provided essential information that shaped related legislation, elected officials will be expecting you to make your position known on allied bills being proposed. Once you establish that you have expertise in an issue area, your support will carry weight.

Access to legislators

Your board, staff, volunteers, and clients may be able to reach elected officials in a unique way. You will have great influence with legislators from your own district. And you may have friends in the legislature who know and trust you and will give credence to your messages of support. You can tap members of your board who are key leaders in the community to use their influence with elected officials.

Never assume that groups already in the debate can represent the interests of your organization's stakeholders. Always assume that your expertise, insights, and credibility in the community allow you to make a difference in whether a proposal passes or fails.

3. Support the bill

The actions that you take in supporting a proposed bill will be similar to the legislative efforts described in the section How to Propose New Legislation, pages 108-119.

Learn what has been done on the issue. The organization or coalition that is initiating the proposal will have conducted research and prepared a case statement. The group is likely to have arranged to have chief authors and to have a bill drafted. You will need

Even if your issues are not "popular" with political leaders in a particular time or at a specific level of government, maximize the value of your nonprofit's nonpartisanship. As a 501(c)(3) organization, you are not engaged and should never be identified with a political party or candidate. You work with all "people of the process" to advance your issues, build support across the aisles, and serve the people of the community in your mission-driven work. There is extraordinary opportunity in being a facilitator of nonpartisan cooperation on issues that matter to your community. Be the bridge builder. It isn't always easy, but it is almost always important!

to review the organization's work, determine if you have any differences of opinion with the proposal, and assess where you can contribute additional information to the effort. Work with the originators of the proposal to use your unique contributions strategically. Sometimes, you may wish to weave your organization's specific research, stories, and ideas into the overall case statement. At other times, you can provide more support by being a separate voice, supporting the bill but providing your own rationale, stories, and perspective. The crucial step is to cooperate with those who have taken a lead on this issue so that your efforts are complementary and coordinated.

Build relationships. As you would with any advocacy campaign, learn about the people who will be important to your lobbying efforts. In addition to the originators of the proposal, you will need to develop relationships and good communications of your own with people important to this process: legislators who are authors and coauthors, committee members, other groups supporting the proposal, your own supporters, and the media. If your voice is going to add strength to the effort already under way, these relationships will be essential to your ability to be an effective voice.

Lobby for passage. Here you will *coordinate* with the primary supporters of the bill, but you will nevertheless carry out a full range of activities. You will meet with legislators to make your case; prepare fact sheets and materials to persuade elected officials and the media to support your position; educate and mobilize supporters who will add their voices to the groups already weighing in on the issue by meeting with legislators, writing letters, making phone calls, and activating others; and provide testimony at committee hearings.

4. Celebrate success, learn from failure

This, of course, goes without saying—but never forget to pat yourself on the back and learn from experience.

How to Defeat Legislation That Has Been Proposed

Nonprofits are often drawn into public policy lobbying to fight proposals that will damage their organizations, hurt the people and communities they serve, or create new problems in their areas of interest. Approaches to *defeating* legislation parallel the steps described in this text for passing and supporting legislation, with a few additional considerations:

- Before launching a full campaign in opposition to a proposal, make overtures to proponents of the measure if possible. You may be able to persuade them to withdraw or amend the proposed law. At a minimum, they will be forewarned that you will be opposing their bill.

Mistakes to avoid

Whether you are proposing new legislation, joining others in supporting an existing bill, or trying to defeat a bad idea, there are some common mistakes to avoid:

- *Lone Ranger expectations.* Don't expect one person in an organization to do it all! It takes many voices to make a difference in policy arenas.

- *Petitions and postcard campaigns.* These lack the personal voice that persuades officials that constituents really care about the issue.

- *Crying wolf!* Don't sound so many alarms that your supporters can't sort out the real need for action from the stack of alerts in their e-mail.

- *Showing up at a hearing without following the protocol for signing up to testify.* Witnesses are expected to call ahead. Learn the local customs and rules on testifying.

- *Missing the boat.* Don't wait until late in the decision-making process to voice your support or concerns.

- *Surprises.* Public officials expect honesty and full disclosure. Don't leave your supporters in the legislature, county board, or city council in the lurch by failing to tell them all the facts about an issue. It is part of the lobbyist's job to tell elected officials who opposes a position, as well as who supports it, and why.

- *Angry, hysterical, or threatening communication.*

- Remember to work with the executive branch. In most states, the governor can exercise veto authority over legislative proposals that he or she deems to be detrimental to the state.

The next section guides you as you proceed to lobby the governor and other members of the executive branch.

How to Lobby the Executive Branch and Administrative Agencies

The executive, or administrative, branch of government plays a key role in shaping public policy. Governors, commissioners, and mayors can develop policy and funding proposals that shape priorities in all segments of community life. Therefore, you should have ongoing contact with executive branch officials, agency directors, and those staff within agencies who work in your program areas. These connections will allow you to seed discussions with information and issues that need to be addressed.

As you prepare to lobby the executive branch, review your identification of key leaders in the executive branch in Worksheet 8: The People of the Process. Following are some steps you can take to maintain good relations with the people in the executive branch who have an impact on your mission. By following these steps, you will be better prepared to ask for their support on your key issues.

1. Work from the bottom up

Continually work to have good relationships with the staff of the executive branch of government. You can have an impact on the policies they shape and their funding decisions, and you can persuade them to support your position in working with the legislative branch. Work to gain executive branch support and endorsement for your position and to insulate your issue against a veto. More than one nonprofit issue has been saved from the veto pen by a governmental agency director who advised a governor to follow a legislative recommendation and keep a nonprofit's priority in place.

Know which agencies have policy and funding authority in your issue areas

Learn about the organizational structure in those agencies that have policy and funding authority over your issues. Build ongoing strategic relationships with these agencies' leaders and staff. Focus on developing regular communications with the agency program staff who have oversight responsibility for any funding and regulations that affect your issues and organization. These people make recommendations to people in power about your program. They can also alert you to anticipated opportunities or crises.

Build relationships with the people who control your funds

If you get government grants or contracts, be certain that contract officers who administer your funding and monitor your work understand what you do and what needs you meet in your community. Get to know them and gain their trust in your knowledge of the issues and ways to address those issues. If you don't have an existing relationship with staff in government agencies who administer the programs and policies that you care about, ask to meet with these key people. Introduce your organization and explain your case.

Become a trusted resource to administrative offices

Make it your goal to be a resource to administrative departments and executive offices as they develop new policies and set priorities. If agency staff accept your ideas for how to solve problems, they are in a position to make recommendations to agency directors. When this happens, your ideas may turn into a governmental agency's recommendation to a mayor or governor. *Thus, you get a voice in the developmental phase of policy shaping and budget planning.* This is a plus for your lobbying campaign.

2. Work from the top down

Create a good relationship with the chief executive. You will have a better chance of the chief executive's support if you make sure he or she has had a chance to understand your cause and looks to your organization for reliable information.

Know the chief executive's priorities and positions

Know the chief executive's priorities and positions on the issues that you care about. This information can be gathered from campaign statements, public statements while in office, and documents presented to the legislative branch and the public, including budget proposals and "State of the State," "State of the County," and "State of the City" addresses. If you meet with the chief executive or have him or her as a guest speaker at an event that you host, keep a record of his or her comments about your nonprofit and your issues. Most units of government have a website that includes a section maintained by the chief executive's office. It may include biographical information as well as the official's vision and policy positions.

Know the chief executive's responsibilities and deadlines

Know the responsibilities of the chief executive and the timeline for carrying these out. Know when he or she presents budget proposals and annual reports to the legislature or other body, and what the rules are that govern veto authority and veto timelines. You may also want to explore the extent of executive authority a governor or executive official has. "Executive orders," may be an attractive alternative to legislation.

Know the chief executive's staff

Learn the organization of the chief executive's staff and the people in key roles that affect your nonprofit's work. Positions that are usually most important are chief of staff, government relations director, and communications director (also called press secretary). Once you know the structure of the chief executive's office, learn about and meet with the key staff. Acquaint them with your organization and your public policy agenda.

Get to know the governmental-relations staff person responsible for your issue area. He or she needs to know how you can be a resource in your areas of expertise. This is also the person who, along with the administrative agency director, will provide information to the chief executive to shape the executive branch agenda and make decisions about policy and funding that you propose. Provide executive office staff with written information about your organization, including your issue priorities, lists of types of information you have available, names of contact people with expertise, and information about your supporters. Invite the government relations staff to meet with you at your organization's location if possible. Time your request for a meeting so that you have established this relationship before policy debates have begun and as the executive branch is shaping its proposals to the legislature.

Get to know the communications director. The communications director can be an ally in arranging press coverage when the chief executive and your nonprofit share the same position on a legislative issue. For example, if you are working for affordable housing funding, the mayor of your community may be eager to hold a press conference at your shelter facility to underscore the importance of the city council's agreeing to fund affordable housing units for those who are working but cannot find stable housing.

Understand the organizational chart of cabinet-level positions and agency staff

Generally, the higher the position (e.g., commissioner or state-agency director), the more political the position. Cabinet-level staff are generally appointed by the executive and serve at the pleasure of the executive for the duration of the elected official's term. What may be of more value to you in your advocacy is the cadre of program-manager staff, who are often content experts who serve numerous administrations over a long period of time.

3. Maintain systematic communications

Have a systematic way of maintaining communications with the executive offices in your issue area. Send regular updates on your issue. Call with new information or progress reports on your legislative initiatives. Alert executive staff to anticipated attacks on positions that you share with the executive branch. Include staff in regular mailings about your organization, such as your newsletter and annual report.

Provide honest feedback when you disagree with an executive decision. Emphasize points about which you agree. Note that you respectfully disagree on other points and explain why. Express hope that you will be able to work together in the future to reach a mutually acceptable position. Invite a discussion about next steps at which you will provide new information or stories to strengthen your case. Never threaten and never limit the possibility of future collaboration.

Above all, thank the executive for any support. Awards, letters of appreciation, invitations to address your supporters at meetings or events, and letters to the editor applauding good work on your behalf strengthen your relationships.

Nonprofit Lobbying on Ballot Measures
Susie Brown, contributor

In some states, ballot questions are common; in others, they have recently gained a foothold as a policy-making strategy. Whether as a proactive strategy or something requiring an unexpected defense, nonprofit organizations may encounter ballot questions as an advocacy approach that is new and unfamiliar. This section provides information and guidance intended to help your organization be ready to be active and effective participants in this kind of policy making, which is both the same as other advocacy in many respects and has several important differences to be considered.

What are ballot questions?

Unlike legislative policy making, ballot questions take the policy making to the voters.

Establish trusting relationships in the executive branch

Keep in mind that agency program staff often prepare preliminary policy proposals and budgets for consideration by the agency leadership: the commissioner, director, or deputies. The agency leaders, in turn, propose policies and budgets to the governor's staff and the governor. The cabinet members have access to the chief executive on a regular basis and are essential in shaping proposals, informing the policy process in concert with the experts in the agency, and negotiating final decisions about policies and appropriations.

It is important for the many nonprofits that receive government support and/or work in programmatic partnerships with government to build strong and ongoing relationships within the agencies that address your issues. You are an important resource to the staff and political appointees who are charged with building policies and allocating resources to address needs. Be sure that they know and trust you and that they have access to you and your organization's expertise, data, stories, and spokespersons when needed. Work with agencies is ongoing, year-round work in the cycle of advocacy.

You can learn a lot about the way in which state or local governments structure their agencies and the people who hold program positions within the agency at the agency website. Reach out to the people who have lead roles in your issue areas. Meet them before you are promoting a specific policy to acquaint them with your mission, program, and accomplishments. Ask whether there are specific "government-relationships" staff in the agency whose responsibility it is to work with legislators, and get to know those people, too. Cabinet members often speak at public meetings or nonprofit gatherings. Learn about their priorities by showing up, understanding their perspective, and making an effort to meet them (catch them!) for a brief introduction. As more and more nonprofit leaders also work in government, you may find that you have people whom you know in agencies who can help you to navigate the bureaucracy and target the staff and leaders who will want your information and respond to your requests.

Even if your issues are not popular with political leaders in a particular time or specific level of government, maximize the value of nonprofit nonpartisanship. As a 501(c)(3) organization, you are not engaged and should never be identified with a political party or candidate. You work with all "people of the process" to advance your issues, build support across the aisles, and serve the people of the community in your mission-driven work. There is extraordinary opportunity in being a facilitator of nonpartisan cooperation on issues that matter to your community. It isn't always easy, but it is almost always important!

The specific mechanism for this to occur differs from state to state. Some states, such as Oregon and California, are initiative and referendum states. In these cases, citizen petitions bring an issue to the voters, and, if they pass, the issues become statutory changes similar to those made by the legislature. In other states, ballot questions are originated by the legislature before going to the voters. This is the case in Minnesota, for example, where questions before voters result in changes to the state constitution. Each state has its own mechanism for questions coming to the voters and the

A word about terminology

Language varies from state to state and even within states, describing policy questions on the ballot. Some of the language describes the process (such as initiative and referendum), and others describe the outcome (constitutional amendment). Still others indicate what the actual question on the ballot is called: for example, ballot measure, ballot question, or ballot initiative. Uniformity in language is less important than understanding what the language you or others are using refers to. It would be incorrect, for example, to use Initiative and referendum terminology in a state whose process is legislative, rather than citizen-driven. This book uses the general and universal term *ballot question*, although the terminology used in your state is likely to be different.

place where the policy change occurs (statute or constitution). You can learn about the process in your own state by contacting your secretary of state's office.

How can this be the same as other advocacy work when it feels so different?

As nonprofit organizations plan their advocacy strategies, ballot questions should be considered both similar to and different from the legislative advocacy strategies we are more commonly familiar with. The main similarities include: for the purposes of the IRS, this work is considered lobbying, allowable under the federal laws that govern our sector; these are often issues that are of significant importance to the communities we serve; and our organizations may have critical information and views to inform the debate. Meanwhile, the ways that ballot questions differ include: while we may educate the public about other choices on the ballot (candidates), we may not take a position—but, in this case, we may; it is likely there are state-level regulatory and reporting requirements governing this activity; and it is likely that timelines, activities, and strategies differ substantially from the advocacy we are accustomed to.

Can we take a position on ballot questions?

Yes, nonprofits may lobby on ballot questions. In this case, the voters are the decision makers. For more information on the law governing advocacy and lobbying, including lobbying on ballot initiatives, see page 155 of this Handbook.

Whom are you trying to influence? Different strategies required

While many nonprofit organizations may be comfortable and familiar with lobbying elected officials, they will likely find that lobbying the public on a ballot question demands a very different approach. In the state of Maine, for example, the job of influencing the legislature—a group of 186 people whose names and contact information are readily available and whose job is to listen to information presented on issues and formulate a position—is substantially different from influencing the nearly 1 million registered voters in the state who are widely dispersed and potentially disinterested in the questions that are before them. Time-tested strategies such as testimony, personal stories, research papers and citizen engagement may not be the strategies needed to reach the public. Rather, nonprofits must learn from strategies honed by political campaigners, a group accustomed to activities such as message testing, polling, targeting, direct mail, and paid media. The nonprofit concern about issues coupled with the need for different strategies suggests that new partnerships or new staffing models will be needed for effective advocacy. Formulating your plan with the assistance of an experienced campaign strategist will lay a good foundation, and seeking unusual allies and staff with political campaign experience may be necessary.

Short-term campaign, long-term strategies

In addition to requiring new skills and different partners, ballot-question advocacy is orchestrated as a campaign, much like campaigns for elected office. By nature, campaigns are short term with a single, identifiable goal and end date. Win or lose, those seeking elected office are on to another thing the following day, either preparing to take office or returning to private life, their campaign staff often on to another job. But for nonprofit organizations building ballot questions into their year-round, long-term advocacy work, the immediate focus will shift on the day after the election, but the long-range work and the core advocacy function of your nonprofit is as present as ever. You might experience a feeling that the momentum stops and your partners disperse, but the next critical role in your cycle of advocacy is just around the corner. Take a short rest, learn from what happened, reconfigure your policy agenda based on the outcome, maintain the new relationships that were built, and pursue your strategies with the vision and long-range approach that will best serve your community. Most important, while you are engaged in ballot-initiative advocacy, tend to the core needs and long-range goals of your organization. Can you use this opportunity to build your list? Have you attracted the attention of potential new funding sources? Did the campaign produce information such as polling, research, or messages that can be used in your long-term work? As with all advocacy efforts, ballot-initiative campaigns should be carried out strategically in ways that support your long-term goals—the community you serve is counting on it!

Media Advocacy and Social Media Advocacy

Strategic media advocacy is an important extension of the strategic communication that you do when you advocate and lobby. Media coverage expands your ability to reach key audiences, including the general public, people who are affected by your issue, and elected officials and their staff.

Strategic use of media is a specialty unto itself, and there is a wealth of publications on the topic. However, you can accomplish your advocacy goals by following a few principles:

1. Be media ready
2. Clarify your position, goals, and audiences
3. Use media that will accomplish your goals

1. Be media ready

Nonprofit organizations advocating their cause via news media need to build the organizational infrastructure to do this work well. Key components of building capacity for media work are, first, to put someone in charge of media relations and, second, to have him or her build relationships with key media people.

Put someone in charge of media relations

Aim for clear designation of board and staff responsibility for media work. Identify one person in the organization as the media specialist. Your media person can facilitate communications with the media and maintain internal systems for media advocacy. Official spokespersons may be chosen based on issues and expertise, but, for every lobbying issue, it is important to determine who will speak for the organization in various situations.

Build relationships with key media people

The person in your nonprofit who is responsible for advocacy and media needs to know the diverse media that are available to you for moving your messages. For traditional media, including newspapers, radio, and television, it is important to know what the outlet covers, who does the key reporting in your issue area, and how to gain access to that person. Keep in mind that, in the newspaper industry and news radio—in print, on the air, and online—there is a firewall between the reporters who cover news and those who take and publish opinions: the editorial board. It is time well spent to read, listen, watch, and know about the people on the news, feature, and editorial components of the medium. Do they care about your issue in general? Do they reach an audience that matters to you? Are there long-standing journalists and editors with whom you can build a professional relationship?

Build a list of the media that matter for the purposes of your work. Most outlets have information online about how to contact them. Where possible, get to know the people of the press and encourage them to trust you as a source by giving them good information about the issues and access to interesting spokespersons, including those who have personal experiences and stories to tell. This approach is important with traditional media, with bloggers, with partner nonprofits that have a reach to your audiences, and with nontraditional sources.

Research and get to know the specialty press, which serves specific constituencies: student newspapers, online forums, and radio stations may be influential in your area. The weekly paper in your region is likely to be read carefully by residents in the area. Targeted press aimed at women, people with disabilities, communities of color, religious groups, immigrants, and language groups have loyal and important audiences. Work with them over time. Effective work with members of the media depend on a few basics:

- Provide good information. Be accurate, clear, and reliable.

- Be interesting. Provide solid data and interesting stories to make your point.

- Maintain the highest levels of integrity and trust. Don't invent facts, don't gossip, and don't overstate your case.

- Be respectful of deadlines and other constraints of a particular medium. Ask reporters how you can best communicate with them.

- Be responsive to the media. It is always okay to ask for time to formulate a response or track down information. But follow through on commitments to get back to reporters.

- Don't be naïve about media work. Always assume when talking to a reporter that you are "on the record," and don't say anything you wouldn't want to see in print or hear on the air. Building relationships with the media will enable you to know how an individual journalist works and what to expect.

Produce your own media

Nonprofit organizations are not dependent on traditional media to move their message for them. With access to everything from regular newsletters, letters to the editor, and free public-service announcements to websites and ever-growing forms of social media, your organization can promote your ideas and positions yourself. When you develop the communications component of your public policy plan, place an emphasis on what you will do, using all the tools available to you, to tell your story the way you want it to be told. This increased control over the content and targeting of messages has made earned media (i.e., not paid advertising) a powerful resource for advocates.

2. Clarify your position, goals, and audiences

Effective media advocacy requires that you are very clear about your position, what you want to accomplish through the media, and the audiences you want to influence. Elected officials have a keen interest in what their local newspapers, radio stations, TV stations, bloggers, Facebook friends, and websites of groups in their districts are saying about issues.

Know your position, goals, and key messages

- What do you know about the community need and the proposed solution? This is important background information necessary for those covering your issue. Even though the reporters may not print the background, it will help them formulate their stories.

- What is the point you want to make (your position)? This is the statement of your fundamental stance about the issue.

- What do you want to happen as a result of your media advocacy? These are your goals. Make them specific, as in "Ten letters to the editor supporting our issue will appear over the next two weeks. We will reproduce these in large size and hand-deliver them to the heads of the appropriate senate and house committees."

- How do you want your position and knowledge of the need and solution to be presented? These are your key messages.

Much of this work has already been done at various stages. Assemble the information developed when you prepared to make your case to the legislative or executive branches, and adapt it as appropriate for the reporter.

Know your audiences

- Whom are you trying to reach? Legislators? Executive branch officials? Grassroots supporters who can influence these policy makers? List each group you are trying to influence.

- How much does each audience already know about your issue and the context in which your issue is being debated? Is it a highly visible issue with lots of public debate and media coverage of pros and cons, or is it a hidden issue with little general appeal? Tailor the key messages and kinds and amount of background information to fit the audiences you'll use and the media who will reach them.

- How much complexity is your audience willing to deal with based on its interest in the issue? Often your job will be to help the media explain a complex issue in simple and straightforward ways so that people understand why they should care about it.

3. Use media that will accomplish your goals

If your organization has a person responsible for community relations or media, that person should brief you about the media and the media outlets that you can target with your message. This information can also be obtained by monitoring the media, asking experienced lobbyists, requesting (or buying) a few hours of consultation time from a media-relations firm, and contacting your state's associations of newspapers and broadcasters. Also check the resources recommended in Appendix B. You will want to know the following information:

- Who reaches your target audiences and how? While we're all familiar with the larger papers, radio stations, and television stations, there are a host of more tightly targeted media that reach specific audiences. Find out the daily, weekly, and specialty newspapers that reach each of your audiences. Legislators and executive branch leaders almost always read the clippings from their hometown or neighborhood newspapers. It is a high priority for them to know how an issue is playing in their *own* district and what their constituents are saying about it. An editorial or letter to the editor in a local newspaper or coverage of a local event has a very good chance of getting an elected official's attention.

- Which radio programs have news and feature coverage or run public-service announcements? Who are the producers and hosts? Listen to the kinds of coverage and questions they favor.

- What television coverage is possible in your area? Whom do individual stations, including public television and local-access cable stations, reach? What feature segments of the news or public-affairs programs do they have that might be interested in covering your issues? Who are the producers and key reporters?

- If you are working on an issue at a state legislature or city council, who are the beat reporters in all media assigned to the capitol press corps or city hall? They will be ever present in the arenas where you are working for change, and you will want to establish good working relationships with them.

- When you choose media to reach specific audiences, remember to package your message in the way that is most useful to the particular medium. Television is very visual; so, if you choose TV, illustrate your story visually. Radio is very friendly to interviews with "real people" that illustrate the issue you are dealing with. Newspapers can go into great depth. Newsletters can reach and motivate smaller but perfectly defined audiences. Bigger is not necessarily better. If the key people you need to influence can all be reached via a trade newsletter, go with the newsletter, and don't waste energy on other outlets.

- Get to know the local policy websites and blogs. Bloggers often are connected with a smaller audience than mass media, but their specific audience may be more likely to take action to support your issue.

For more information on media advocacy, refer to Worksheet 11: Media Advocacy Checklist and Messaging Strategy.

A word about paid media:

Large organizations or coalitions that are working on a high-profile issue may need to use paid media advertising to promote issue education or call on people to take action. This is especially true with ballot measures, when the voters, not elected officials, are the decision makers. For most nonprofits, doing paid media will require guidance and support from public-relations professionals, who have the experience of designing the message, targeting the media that will reach the desired audience most efficiently, buying media time, and keeping the process moving in a timely way. Many nonprofits have access to public-relations firms that may provide discounted or pro bono work. If you know that you are likely to need this type of high-profile media tactic, begin early. Work with potential consultants to understand the cost, timelines, and oppor-

Working with the press

Nonprofits need to develop strategic relationships with the press. The goal is not only to get coverage of the issues and ideas that you are promoting but also to become a resource to the press. You are positioned well when members of the media come to you for information and seek your reaction to proposals and points of debate.

tunities that exist so that you can incorporate this component into your planning and budget setting in the initial phases of that work.

Use Worksheet 11, page 235, to make sure that the media component of your work is getting the attention and development it deserves as an important part of your lobbying effort. The checklist is self-explanatory, so no sample is provided.

Social-media advocacy
Contributed by Josh Wise

Effective nonprofits work with multiple communication strategies. While some earned-media work may focus on traditional media outlets—newspapers, radio and commercial TV—social media has become a major component of media advocacy. Additionally, as access to the Internet and even smart phones become the norm, your supporters will prefer electronic forms of communication, and you'll be able to save time and money by making the switch from print. Indeed, social-media sites are where people of all ages and demographics are choosing to communicate. Social media presents three unique opportunities to advance your cause. First, it allows your organization to communicate with a large audience on a regular basis with little effort. Second, it provides for two-way communication in real time to evaluate the effectiveness of your message. Finally, it serves as a rapid-response system to make your position known whenever there is a development in your efforts, be it positive or negative.

What is social media?
Social media is any form of communication that allows the people you're communicating with to communicate back. In reality, this means any thing from an oral conversation to correspondence, but in common practice means a set of online tools and sites that allow for instant two-way communication between you and your audience, be it the media, your members, or the public. The most common types of social media are blogs and articles with a comments section, micro-blogging sites such as Twitter, and online communities such as Facebook, Google+, Pinterest, and many others. These sites also can link to your website and to each other and can be integrated with a level of sophistication limited only by your social-

media savvy. For example, if you have a blog on your website, every time you have a new blog post, you can use your social media to provide a direct link to your site. Once you get hooked on social media, you'll find endless ways to make it work for you.

Getting started – know your audience
As with other communications, the most important things to consider in your social-media strategy are what the intent of your message is and who the audience is that you intend to reach. It is important to remember that a strong social-media presence is not a substitute for other modes of communication, especially personal conversations. Social-media posts for your advocacy campaign will generally fall into one of these categories:

* Educating your supporters about an issue
* Mobilizing your supporters to take action (call your legislator, etc.)
* Promoting and driving turnout to an event related to your campaign
* Rapid response to current events

Understanding whom you are targeting is important for each of these situations. If you want people to call their legislators, it makes sense to post during a time when people are likely to be free to make a call. There are free programs available that allow you to schedule when a post occurs. Another example is engaging reporters. If you know a story is developing and you want a quote included, it makes sense to tweet them directly, with plenty of time before a deadline. Worksheet 11 will help you map out what types of messages you want to deliver, the modes of communication for delivering the message, and which target audience will be moved most by each mode of delivery. Also, for each of the above categories, there are specific tools within social-media sites to help you out. You want to make sure to spend plenty of time exploring all of the tools you get with a social-media account.

Who does what

The next step of your social-media campaign is to set clear boundaries about what will be posted and who will have access to the social-media accounts. Having multiple people administering your account will enable you to post more content and engage more people, but it's important to make sure that everyone is on the same page with your message and how it gets disseminated. For example, while live updates from a legislative committee hearing may be interesting on their own merit, they can clutter your profile, and the message that you most want to get across may get buried. Second on this point is that there also needs to be a clear distinction between one's personal accounts and the account of the organization. Obviously, it is helpful to have staff sharing and promoting your organization to their own networks. However, when posted under the profile of the organization, posts should be directly relevant to the objectives of the advocacy plan and not simply a recounting of events that happened during the workdays of a given staff member.

Engaging audiences:

The third step of your campaign is building a network of supporters. The best way to do this is to "lead by following." Look for people and organizations with similar goals and interests and engage with what they are already posting. Share and re-post things from their profiles, and invite them to follow your posting. Eventually, as you begin to get noticed, your network of supporters will expand. For example, if you are starting out on Twitter, the first thing you want to do is search for the people and organizations you are affiliated with in the "real world" and follow them. By retweeting their material and mentioning them in your own tweets, not only will you get them to follow you back, but their existing followers, who likely also share your values, will see what you are posting and will begin to engage with your organization.

It's also important to remember that your job doesn't stop at posting. Especially for organizations, it's important to stay tuned to who is engaging with your posts. Foremost, you don't want people making comments that are offensive or irrelevant, so monitoring for that needs to be done. In addition to bad comments, you want to make sure to acknowledge good comments and use the two-way communication to inform future posts. It may sound obvious, but social media ism by its nature, social—and that means you must take time to interact, and, if you don't, your social-media campaign will suffer. Posting without taking the time to engage in the rest of what's happening in an online community means your network will be less engaged and your communications less effective. By keeping disciplined and engaged, you will be able to build a solid network of online supporters for your campaign.

After you've built your network, you want to make sure you're still evaluating your reach. Most sites offer some sort of free analytic system to see if you're reaching whom you want to reach. For example, both Google and Facebook will tell you how many people your posts are reaching and let you see activity over time in graph form. You should use these tools to evaluate your social-media program.

Words to the wise

It's important to remember, however, that the rapid pace of social media requires a high level of caution and discretion in order to avoid straying off message or inadvertently misspeaking or posting inappropriate content. Indeed, just like talking to the press, whatever you post is "on the record." As the prevalence of sites such as Facebook and Twitter have gained in popularity, so have the scandals due to off-the-cuff tweets and posts that were either misunderstood or poorly thought out, and a lot of damage control has had to be done. Finally, you need to understand that the landscape of social media is constantly changing. The best practices for each site change as the user bases become more savvy and the sites are developed to provide a better experience. As with advocacy, success in social media comes from active participation. The more you engage, the more savvy you'll become, and the more effective you'll be!

Summary: Now *Go!*

In the first half of Chapter 2, your planning team developed a work plan for your lobbying work. In the second half, the focus has been on the tactics that you employ to implement your plan. You have learned how to

1. Build the organizational infrastructure that enables you to manage, implement, and monitor your lobbying efforts systematically

2. Build strategic relationships with legislators and lobby the legislature to

   - Propose a law

   - Support an existing proposal for a law

   - Defeat a law

3. Build strategic relationships with the executive branch, and lobby for its support for your issues

4. Build and mobilize grassroots support for your legislative initiatives

5. Carry out a media advocacy strategy that supports your lobbying effort

From all that you have learned thus far, it is clear that your nonprofit can have a significant impact on your issues. But you're not quite there yet. Reporting requirements and regulations govern nonprofit organizations, and you must learn how to lobby within the legal guidelines. Nonprofit lobbying and the law that governs this activity will be discussed in the next chapter.

CHAPTER THREE

Sustaining the Cycle of Advocacy: Expanding Impact through Civic Engagement

CONTRIBUTOR, JEFF NARABROOK

You have created your advocacy campaign and are ready to go. Congratulations! We hope you are ready to win and that you are in it for the long haul. While specific policy initiatives may be focused on a single legislative session or local-government budget cycle, major social change takes years if not decades to realize. That is why your ongoing advocacy work will be strongest if you adopt a cyclical (rather than linear) model of change. This not only helps insulate your efforts from the vagaries of political fortunes but, done well, even allows you to create favorable conditions to advance your issues.

This Handbook has emphasized attention to sustained work on the Cycle of Advocacy, above. Civic engagement in elections follows a complementary path, the Cycle of

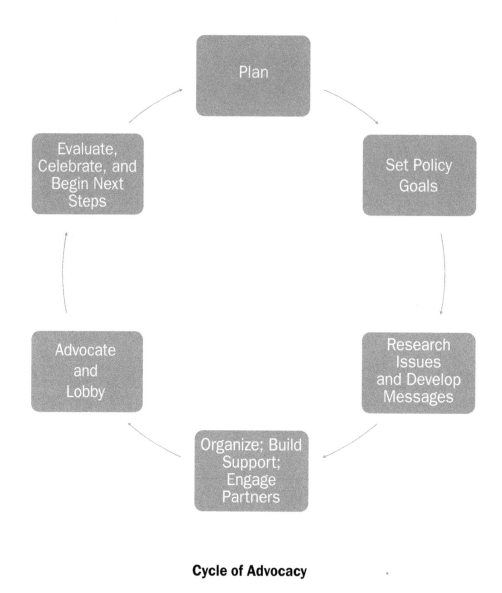

Cycle of Advocacy

Elections. The cycle of civic engagement reflects the ongoing process of engaging voters as part of the approach to improving policies. In our democracy, we elect representatives and hold them accountable for their policy choices in an ongoing sequence of elections. Nonprofits have an impact on policy choices through advocacy and, in elections, through promoting voter participation. Civic engagement may already be a part of your campaign, such as mobilizing community-based support for your position or hosting public discussions on issues. Nonpartisan voter engagement is a particularly powerful form of civic engagement that can advance your cause for the long term.

Advocacy campaigns benefit immensely from an informed voting public that shapes candidates, elects them, and holds them accountable once in office. Your organization

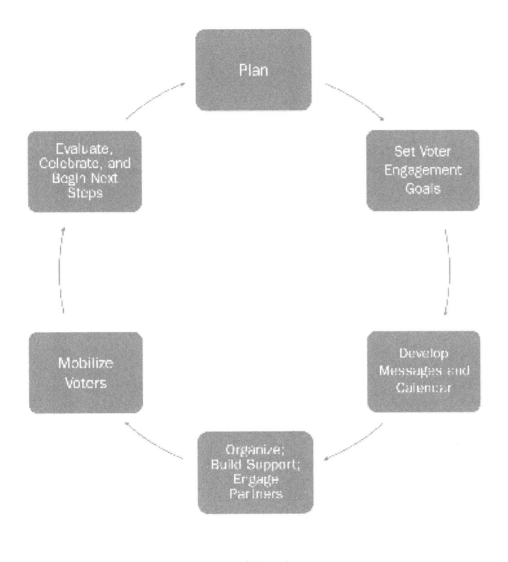

Cycle of Elections

can and should play a part in that process. While a 501(c)(3) nonprofit organization may not support or oppose, explicitly or implicitly, a candidate or party for public office, there are dozens of legal and effective ways to educate and mobilize voters. When you do this, you not only keep the spotlight on your issues but also build a base of voters to tap later for grassroots activism.

Many organizations advocate for and with people who are disproportionately on the margins of the political process, are less likely to know how to participate and vote at lower rates. Young people, those who are in poverty, and people with only a high school education or less vote at much lower rates. Such disparities can weaken your advocacy campaign. When the lack of voter participation severs the connection between communities and elected officials, fewer of their issues will be heard, and legislators will be less responsive to community needs. Elected officials feel accountable to those who show up at the polls.

The good news is that nonprofits already have the skills and assets needed to be successful at voter engagement. Your organization already interacts with potential voters who are clients, constituents, staff, volunteers, or board members. When trusted organizations engage voters, they tend to be more willing and interested in participating. Moreover, as nonpartisan entities, you can promote issues that matter to voters without wading into partisan electoral politics. All these conditions position your organization for success in voter registration, voter education, and voter mobilization.

Voter registration is required to vote in nearly every state and is an important first step. When planning voter-engagement activities, consider the kind of contact you already have with your constituents, members, and volunteers. How can you maximize these interactions as an opportunity for voter registration? Registration drives should educate the public about the importance of voting, and activities cannot show bias for or against any candidate or party. Nonprofits can target areas in nonpartisan ways. For instance, you may target low-turnout areas, low-income populations, minority populations, students, and the areas or people you serve.

Once your nonprofit registers a voter, there are many opportunities to educate him or her about issues and the voting process and to make sure they get to the polls on Election Day. You may choose to host or co-sponsor a candidate forum to help your community familiarize itself with candidates and where they stand on the issues. Likewise, you can create and distribute nonpartisan candidate questionnaires or voter guides. These activities must be open to all candidates, be conducted in a balanced way, and include a broad range of nonpartisan questions for the candidates.

Many organizations also create fact sheets and information on the key issues that affect their organization or the people they serve. During an election year, these may be included as a part of your voter-education efforts. Organizations can demystify the voting process by explaining where, when, and how to vote. You can also provide information about who is on the ballot and any ballot-measure questions in play by providing sample ballots.

Voter-mobilization activities help motivate and assist potential voters to get to their polling places and cast their ballot. In the days and months leading up the election, having conversations with voters can be very effective. Remind them to vote and ask if they know where and when to vote. You can do this through face-to-face conversations at your office, organized community door-knocks, or phone banks to supporters and participants of your organization. You may also decide to host an Election Day celebration in the community to tap into the social nature of civic participation. Some organizations distribute door-hangers, send direct-mail pieces, and pass out leaflets and other handouts with basic information about polling-place hours and where to call for assistance in locating their polling place. Nonprofits can also provide transportation for voters to the polls.

In addition to connecting candidates to voters, you can make presentations on your organization's issue to political-party platform committees, campaign staff, candidates, media, and the public. Just as elected officials rely on community knowledge and expertise to inform their policy work, so too do candidates rely on organizations to brief them on important issues in their community. Consider sending an informational packet to the slate of candidates running for a particular office. After the election, you can loop back to the winners and continue building their knowledge and your relationship with them.

Nonprofits can ask voters to support or oppose ballot-measure questions, which the IRS classifies as direct lobbying and not electioneering (IRS guidelines regulating your total amount of lobbying still pertain). You can adopt an organizational position for or against a question; educate staff, board, donors, volunteers, and program participants about what it means; or connect to a ballot-measure campaign to provide resources, such as space, staff time, e-mail lists, or funding.

Your voter-engagement work connects back to your legislative advocacy in a powerful way. To maximize your impact, find ways to gather contact information for those you engage (if you do not have it already) so that, after the election, you can match those lists to the public voting roles. When your issues are up for action in the legislature, call upon this unique set of voters who have a stake in the issue and bring with them the power of their constituency.

The following checklist comes from Nonprofit VOTE, a national nonprofit that assists nonprofits in helping the people they serve to vote. Find more factsheets, toolkits, and state-specific rules at www.nonprofitvote.org.

Getting started with voter engagement: A CHECKLIST
Contributed by Jeff Narabrook

Get started

Before you begin, think about why this work is important. Make a list of the benefits to your organization, your community, and the individuals you serve. This might include advancing your issues, building clout, or empowering your clients by promoting engaged and active citizenship.

Capacity

Get buy-in from your Executive Director or other leadership

Choose a staff lead who can involve and motivate other staff and volunteers

Consider ways to engage the people you serve in your election activities

Identify assistance and resources from a community partner, your local or state elections office

Knowledge

Understand the guidelines for 501(c)(3)s on how to stay nonpartisan

Learn about voting in your state—deadlines, how to register, and early voting options

Find out what's on the ballot in your locality and state for the upcoming election

Plans

Choose your target audience—clients, constituents, staff, your local community, or others

Select appropriate opportunities for engagement: as part of daily services, in classes, at trainings or events, as a project for a youth group, or incorporated into community outreach

Create a specific timeline for your plan

Voter registration

Decide on your approach. Some nonprofits actively register voters, while others focus on promoting registration by announcing deadlines, making forms available, or helping voters register online. If you plan to conduct voter registration make sure to:

Familiarize yourself with your state's voter registration procedures at www.canivote.org.

Set concrete and attainable goals and tie them to deadlines

Target pre-existing opportunities—as part of services, tabling in your lobby, at events, or in the community at citizenship ceremonies, graduations, or other events

Enlist volunteers and staff to enhance your efforts

Engaging candidates

Plan at least one activity that engages local candidates on your issues.

Identify a race that's important to your community—city council, mayor, state representative, congressional representative, or others

Choose from five main candidate engagement options: Candidate Forums, Candidate Appearances, Sharing Research, Candidate Questionnaires, or Asking Questions at events

Be familiar with nonpartisan guidelines for candidate work, which requires equal treatment of all candidates in the same race

Ballot measures

The majority of states ask voters to weigh in on laws, referendums, constitutional amendments, local bond issues for public programs, and other issues.

Find out if any ballot measures, amendments, or other questions are on the ballot

Learn what 501(c)(3) nonprofits can do to influence passage and educate the public

Decide your approach: Will you take a position for or against the issue? Or will you stay neutral and share nonpartisan information highlighting both sides of the issue?

Voter education

There are two kinds of voter education. The first covers the when, where, and how of voting, while the second identifies what's on the ballot.

Identify voter-education opportunities at your events, classes, and in your communications

Develop an internal and external communications plan for the election

Get out the vote and Election Day

Don't forget that some of the most important work happens near and on Election Day when you encourage, help, and mobilize your community to vote. The final push

takes preparation and a clear understanding of the payoff: research shows that the most effective messages come from trusted messengers—people of similar interests and backgrounds—made in-person or through peer-to-peer social media. You can activate voters simply by:

Promoting early voting by mail or in person

Providing personal reminders

Giving out information to help your community vote—help lines or polling hours and locations

Linking the election to the future of your issue or nonprofit services

Making Election Day special by treating it as a holiday for democracy!

See the sample materials on the following page for Voter Registration Drives. For additional materials and ongoing updates, go to www.nonprofitvote.org.

NOV 6, 2012
I PLEDGE TO VOTE
BECAUSE MY COMMUNITY, MY FAMILY, AND MY FUTURE ARE WORTH IT.

FIRST NAME   MIDDLE INITIAL   LAST NAME

CELL PHONE

ADDRESS

CITY   STATE   ZIP

EMAIL

By filling out this postcard, you are granting permission to be contacted by our organization. Your information will not be sold.

TAKE THE PLEDGE & VOTE.

VOTE BECAUSE YOUR FAMILY IS WORTH IT.

VOTE BECAUSE YOUR COMMUNITY IS WORTH IT.

VOTE BECAUSE YOU ARE WORTH IT.

WE'LL SEND YOU A REMINDER WHEN IT'S TIME TO VOTE.

MINNESOTA PARTICIPATION PROJECT
An initiative of the Minnesota Council of Nonprofits

CHAPTER FOUR

Nonprofits and the Law

Lobby Law

Not only are nonprofits legally entitled to lobby, they are expected to do so. Congress has been very clear that nonprofits have a role in society that includes being a voice on issues that matter to people, communities, and the nation. So lobby, and do it legally. Follow the laws that govern the ways in which nonprofits must report and limit their lobbying expenditures.

This chapter explains the laws that govern how much you are allowed to spend on lobbying, how to track your lobbying activity for reporting purposes, and how to report your lobbying to the Internal Revenue Service as part of your organization's annual filing of IRS Form 990.

Note: The material in this chapter describes federal and state law governing tax-exempt charitable, educational, scientific, and literary organizations under section 501(c)(3) of the Internal Revenue Code. Private foundations are subject to more stringent rules on lobbying than other organizations with 501(c)(3) status. Detailed information about the unique rules governing private-foundation lobbying is available from the Alliance for Justice and other organizations cited in Appendix B: Resources for Nonprofit Lobbying.

The 1976 Lobby Law

Before 1976, there was enormous ambiguity over the amount of lobbying that non-profits could do. The IRS rules required that tax-exempt nonprofits, 501(c)(3) organizations, could lose their tax-exempt status if they did more than an "insubstantial" amount of lobbying. This "insubstantial-lobbying test"[5] was never specifically defined in IRS rules, and individual IRS agents had no guidance in what constituted "too much lobbying." The vague guidelines were confusing to regulators and left nonprofits with great uncertainty about how much lobbying was legal.

Consult an attorney

Laws change and vary from state to state. Use the information in this book as a general guideline, but seek legal advice as well.

This early ambiguity in nonprofit lobbying law still causes some non-profits to fear that lobbying will make them vulnerable to losing their tax-exempt status. A law passed in 1976 has clarified that nonprofits *can* lobby. Be sure that your nonprofit's board and staff understand that nonprofits fall under the "insubstantial test" if they don't take steps to be covered by the "lobbying-expenditure test" established in the 1976 Lobby Law. The expenditure test is preferable for charities because it creates a clear and measurable set of guidelines for lobbying activity. Directions for how to be covered by the 1976 Lobby Law option follow.

What the Lobby Law Allows

The 1976 Lobby Law establishes clear guidelines for lobbying expenditures. These guidelines are called the "lobbying-expenditure test" and were passed under Sections 501(h) and 4911 of the Tax Reform Act of 1976. This law clarifies that 501(c)(3) nonprofits that elect to fall under these rules can spend up to a defined percentage of their budget for lobbying without threatening their tax-exempt status. In 1990, the IRS published final rules on implementing the Lobby Law. Those rules make it quite clear that nonprofits should elect to be covered by the lobbying-expenditure test and not fall under the vague insubstantial-lobbying test. It is important to note that private foundations and churches, which are 501(c)(3) organizations treated in specific ways by the IRS tax code, cannot file IRS Form 5768, the form used to file for coverage under the 1976 Lobby Law.

Be sure that your nonprofit knows that it can choose whether or not to fall under the 1976 Lobby Law. If you elect to be covered by the Lobby Law, you need to do two things:

1. Take formal steps to elect to fall under the 1976 guidelines

2. Know the lobbying limits

---

[5] This is also called the "no-substantial-part test."

1. Take formal steps to elect to fall under the 1976 guidelines

To elect to be covered by the rules, your organization must file IRS Form 5768 with the IRS. This is sometimes called the "(h) form" because it refers to Section 501(h) of the Internal Revenue Code. A copy of IRS Form 5768 is included in Appendix D: Samples on page 202. To obtain the form, download it from the IRS website, www. irs.gov, or call the IRS and ask for Form 5768, Election/Revocation of Election by an Eligible Section 501(c)(3) Organization to Make Expenditures to Influence Legislation. Despite the overwhelming title, it is a simple one-page form that can be filed at any time. The IRS has provided clear documentation to nonprofit organizations that filing this form is favored by the IRS and will not trigger an audit or any other activity that should concern you. Organizations that elect to fall under the rules have an easy way to account for their lobbying expenditures and provide clear information to the IRS. Everyone appreciates clarity on this issue.

Note that federal grants and some foundation grants place restrictions on lobbying. Review foundation grant agreements closely and be sure that you understand the specific activities for which funds can by used. Federal grants are covered by rules in OMB Circular A-122, which is available from the federal Office of Management and Budgets, and other acts. These rules are explained fully in materials available from Center for Lobbying in the Public Interest and OMB Watch. (See Appendix B: Resources for Nonprofit Lobbying.)

2. Know the lobbying limits

The 1976 Tax Reform Act divides lobbying into direct lobbying and grassroots lobbying.

Direct lobbying occurs when an organization communicates its position with regard to legislation or legislative proposals directly with legislators, legislative staff, executive branch officials, and executive staff. An example: the executive director of ABC Nonprofit informs Representative Smith about the organization's support for universal child care and urges Smith to cosponsor proposed universal-child-care legislation.

Grassroots lobbying occurs when an organization asks the public to support, oppose, or otherwise influence legislation by contacting elected and appointed officials. A grassroots lobbying effort is most frequently triggered by a "call-to-action" phrase, such as "call your congressperson today to ask them to vote YES on HF 123." Call-to-action phrases are commonly used in action alerts and press releases. An example: the executive director of ABC Nonprofit sends out an action alert to the media, public, donors, and other nonprofits, asking them to write letters to their state representatives and the governor in which they urge support of the universal-child-care legislation recently proposed.

Note: In some states, nonprofit organizations become involved in ballot initiatives and referenda. The 1976 Lobby Law does apply to ballot initiatives and referenda. Charities that have elected the lobbying-expenditure test may count their work on ballot initiatives and referenda as direct lobbying. This is an interesting detail in the tax law. Work on ballot initiatives and referenda is considered direct lobbying because, with these measures, the "people" become the "legislature," that is, the decision-making body. Therefore, in lobbying people to vote for or against such a measure, nonprofits engage in direct lobbying.

Figure 1. Lobbying Limits under the Expenditure Test shows the guidelines for lobbying expenditures.

Figure 1. Lobbying Limits under the Expenditure Test

Exempt Purpose Expenditures*	Total Lobbying	Grassroots Lobbying
Up to $500,000	20%	5%
$500,000 to $1,000,000	$100,000 + 15% of excess over $500,000	$25,000 + 3.75% of excess over $500,000
$1 million to $1.5 million	$175,000 + 10% of excess over $1 million	$43,750 + 2.5% of excess over $1 million
$1.5 million to $17 million	$225,000 + 5% of excess over $1.5 million	$56,250 + 1.25% of excess over $1.5 million
Over $17 million	$1 million	$250,000

* In reviewing this chart, note that your organization's "exempt-purpose expenditures" are all payments that you make in a year *except* investment management, unrelated businesses, and certain fundraising costs.[6]

Figure 1 makes it clear that nonprofits that elect to fall under the guidelines may comfortably expend a significant amount on lobbying, with more spending allowed on direct lobbying than on grassroots lobbying. For example, an organization that made exempt expenditures of $1.2 million could spend up to $195,000 on *all* lobbying ($175,000 plus 10% of $200,000). Of that $195,000, a maximum of $48,750 could

---

[6] "Certain fundraising costs" includes the cost of external fundraising consultants, an in-house fundraising department of two or more people who spend the majority of their time on fundraising, or any separate accounting unit that is designated as a fundraising department. (See the IRS regulations for a full description of excluded expenditures.)

be spent on grassroots lobbying ($43,750 plus 2.5% of $200,000). Take a moment to calculate your own organization's lobbying limits under these guidelines.

Exempt-purpose expenditures: _____

Total lobbying as allowed in Figure 1: _____

Grassroots lobbying allowed: _____

Why Your Organization Should Elect to Fall under the 1976 Lobby Law

The guidelines offer clear benefits to nonprofits that lobby. Consider the following:

1. Lobbying is measured by expenditures. This sets clear, specific, measurable guidelines for lobbying.

2. There are specific definitions of what activities related to legislation do not count as lobbying. For nonprofits that elect coverage under the 1976 Lobby Law, activities that do not count toward lobbying limits include

   - Contacts with elected officials or executive branch representatives about proposed regulations (as opposed to legislation).

   - Lobbying by volunteers. (No monetary value is assigned to the time volunteered.)

   - Communication with the organization's members on legislation as long as there is no call to action.

   - A nonprofit's response to written requests from a legislative body for technical advice on pending legislation.

   - Self-defense lobbying, such as lobbying on issues that affect the organization's existence relative to tax status, powers, or lobbying rights. (Lobbying for program funding *does* count as lobbying; lobbying to protect your right to lobby does not.)

   - Disseminating the results of nonprofit research and analysis if presented in a fair and full way so that the audience could form an independent opinion.

For more information . . .

You can get further information about the lobby law and the laws governing nonprofit activities in elections from:

Alliance for Justice
11 Dupont Circle NW, 2nd Floor
Washington, DC 20036
202-822-6070
www.afj.org
www.bolderadvocacy.org/navigate-the-rules

If You Choose *Not* to Fall under the Law . . .

If you take no action, your organization will be covered by the vague IRS assessment of whether or not your organization does any substantial lobbying. When the IRS applies the insubstantial-lobbying test, it decides which activities related to legislation count as lobbying and how much lobbying is acceptable. Cases are decided on an individual basis and leave nonprofits struggling with uncertainty. In addition, under the insubstantial-lobbying test, which addresses all nonprofit lobbying activity, the penalties are quite severe. Under that test, a nonprofit can lose tax-exempt status and the right to receive tax-exempt charitable donations.

If you elect to fall under the expenditure test and file IRS Form 5768, clear guidelines govern what you can expend on lobbying. In addition, only your organization's lobbying expenditures will be counted, not all lobbying activity. And the penalties for exceeding the lobbying-expenditure limits are much less severe than the failure to meet the insubstantial-lobbying test. Violations of the expenditure limits usually result in tax penalties, and a nonprofit would lose its tax-exempt status only under extraordinary circumstances.

Clearly, it is in your best interest to elect to fall under the law, and to file the proper paperwork immediately.

Reporting Lobbying Expenditures

All 501(c)(3) organizations (except churches, associations of churches, and integrated auxiliaries) *must* report lobbying expenditures to the IRS. For those nonprofits that do not elect to fall under the 1976 Lobby Law, the IRS requires detailed descriptions of a wide range of activities related to lobbying. For organizations that elect, the only requirement is to report how much was spent on lobbying and how much of the total amount for the year was spent on grassroots lobbying.

Keeping Track of Lobbying Expenditures

Whether or not you elect to fall under 1976 Lobby Law guidelines, you'll need records to back up your claims for lobbying expenditures or activity for purposes of reporting to the IRS on Form 990. One way to keep track of activity and expenses is to use a chart. This allows for ongoing assessment of whether or not your organization is coming close to lobbying limits. Note that there are distinct advantages to involving volunteers and board members in lobbying in that unpaid time does not count toward your lobbying limits. Totals are aggregated for annual reports to the IRS.

Worksheet 17: Lobbying Activity Reporting Form on page 263 helps you keep track of activity and hours. A sample is on page 158.

Create a system to keep track of your expenditures on direct and grassroots lobbying by compiling the individual employee expenditures and tallying them along with additional administrative overhead. Keep a reminder of the maximum you can spend under the 1976 Lobby Law, so you know when you're approaching the limit. Figure 2. Lobbying Limits helps you calculate your organization's maximum expenditures.

Figure 2. Lobbying Limits

Direct Lobbying		Grassroots Lobbying	
Our annual maximum direct-lobbying expenditures (from page 151)		Our annual maximum grass-roots-lobbying expenditures (from page 151)	
Total staff costs:		Total staff costs:	
+ Total expenses:		+ Total expenses:	
+ Administrative overhead:		+ Administrative overhead:	
TOTAL:		TOTAL:	

State Lobbying Laws

Be sure that you contact the office of the attorney general and the office of the secretary of state to learn about lobbyist registration and reporting requirements in your state. Most states require all lobbyists, including nonprofit lobbyists, to report lobbying expenditures and often to identify the issues on which they are active. The guidelines vary greatly from state to state.

Some states have very strict laws. They may require advance registration, as does New York State, and impose significant penalties for failure to register and comply with reporting requirements. States also may have different definitions of who is considered an official. In Michigan, nonprofits have to count interactions with appointed officials and department and agency heads to comply with the Michigan Lobbying Registration Act.

Moreover, some local governments have laws governing the lobbying activity of charities. This is true in New York City and in Suffolk County, New York, for example.

Checklist of activities

❑ Inform your board, staff, and professional consultants of the provisions of the 1976 Lobby Law.

Date accomplished:_____

❑ Propose board and executive director action to elect to file under the provisions of the law.

Date accomplished:_____

❑ File Form 5768 with the IRS if your organization has chosen to fall under the guidelines.

Date accomplished: _____

❑ Keep track of lobbying activities and expenditures.

Date system started: _____

❑ Report lobbying activity to the IRS on your 990 Part VI-A.

Date accomplished: _____

❑ File lobbyist-registration forms and reports with your state and local governments if required.

Date accomplished: _____

Some states and municipalities have enacted "gift bans" that govern lobbyists' ability to provide meals or gifts to legislators. Such ethical-practices rules also govern the limits on political contributions that lobbyists can make to elected officials. Nonprofits need to be particularly attentive to these constraints. Most states have an entity, called an "ethical-practices board" or "campaign-finance board," which can provide you with your state's rules.

Remember that 501(c)(3) nonprofits cannot engage in electioneering. Nonprofits may lobby. Nonprofits may not work to influence the outcome of an election.

Work with the regulators in your state to ensure that your nonprofit is providing information on a timely basis and meeting accountability expectations. Consider inviting a representative of the office of the attorney general, the office of the secretary of state, and even your state's entity responsible for oversight of ethical practices to meet with your organization to explain state requirements for registration and reporting of lobbying activity. Provide key staff and board members with the opportunity to attend training that covers lobbying activities and state requirements. These are sometimes provided by state associations of nonprofits or state bar associations.

The checklist on this page will help you keep track of your activities to meet IRS reporting requirements. Create a similar checklist that will allow you to comply with state and local requirements as well. Make a copy to keep in your policy guide.

Ballot Measures and the Lobby Law

Can We Take a Position on Ballot Questions?

In general, 501(c)(3) organizations properly steer clear of developing viewpoints or taking positions on decisions before voters. IRS regulations prohibit our sector from influencing the outcome of elections as they relate to candidates or parties. Within this context, many nonprofit organizations have adopted a strategy of public education related to all things on the ballot: providing information but not a viewpoint is the proper nonprofit role. But ballot questions are different. Our challenge and opportunity is to view the ballot—otherwise off-limits—as a place where we may develop and share our nonprofit view on a policy question and advocate for a particular outcome. For the most part, we need to continue to view the ballot as a place where our constituencies make their own choices, without our influence, but ballot questions present an exception to this rule.

Ballot Initiative Advocacy Is Lobbying

The reason nonprofit organizations may participate in ballot-question advocacy is that it is considered lobbying, an allowable activity for our sector. In order to make a difference in policy change, we must influence, or lobby, the decision makers. In many cases, it is a body of elected officials, but, in ballot questions, it is the general public—the voters. For this reason, since we are influencing the decision makers, it is a lobbying activity despite its placement on the ballot. In fact, any activity intended to influence the outcome of a ballot question, whether directly communicating with the public or engaging in another activity that is intended to influence the outcome (such as contributing money or in-kind staff time to a ballot-initiative campaign) is all considered lobbying. Like other lobbying, this activity has IRS regulations and reporting requirements. Organizations engaged in ballot-question advocacy require accounting systems that allow accurate tracking of expenses intended to influence the voters, reporting these expenses (with any other lobbying expenses your organization has incurred) on Form 990 in compliance with the insubstantial test or H election.

Who Cares about the Work?

In addition to regular IRS lobbying regulations and reporting requirements, often lobbying work on ballot questions is also subject to state campaign-finance regulations and reporting requirements. The reasons for these federal and state-level requirements are different. At the federal level, the IRS regulations and reporting requirements are the result of the choice we made to be a 501(c)(3) organization. Along with this designation, we gain preferential tax treatment for which we agree to certain conditions—namely, refraining from influencing the outcome of elections and adhering to lobbying limits. The regulations and reporting requirements for the IRS are intended to maintain our 501(c)(3) status and provide the public assurance that we have adhered to the standards that allow us to do so. State campaign-finance reporting is designed for the different purpose of providing public information, and possibly imposing limits, related to the flow of money that influences elections. These laws vary substantially from state to state, are much more likely than the IRS rules to change from time to time, but have in common a goal of bringing "sunshine" to elections. Typically, these rules make no reference to 501(c)(3) status and are in no way related to the IRS. But, similarly, they are likely to require accounting systems that allow for timely and accurate reporting of both fundraising and expenses related to influencing a ballot question. Check your state's campaign finance board or secretary of state's office for the campaign-finance laws that affect your activities.

Nonpartisanship and Election Law

If your organization is a 501(c)(3) public charity, the IRS has a basic rule that limits your activity. You must be nonpartisan. A nonprofit that is a public charity may do nothing to influence the outcome of an election by supporting a candidate or party. This mandate applies to both overt statements or actions that demonstrate support or more nuanced inferences or indicators of support. The mandate seems clear, but nonprofits need to be rigorous in avoiding any explicit or implicit suggestion of support for a candidate or party. The Internal Revenue Service applies a "facts-and-circumstances" test to any situation in which it is not completely clear whether or not a public charity has engaged in partisan activity. Because the facts-and-circumstances test provides no clear bright-line test, nonprofits are careful to monitor their activity. Is it helpful to use the basic question: will this statement or action be perceived to support a candidate or party in an election?

Keep in mind that your work on policy issues is not political work. Lobbying is permissible activity as discussed above. And advocacy and lobbying are nonpartisan issue work! This is true regardless of whether one political leader or party supports or opposes your position on an issue. Your work is to focus on the issue, using data, stories, and the voices of your supporters to make the case.

While nonprofits are required to be scrupulously nonpartisan, the IRS and others recognize that such organizations have a critical role to play in engaging the electorate in democratic processes. As discussed in Chapter 3, nonprofit organizations have the right and the responsibility to educate and mobilize voters in elections, and the following types of activity are permissible and important nonprofit opportunities:

- Engage in lobbying on ballot measures (Remember, this is lobbying, not political activity. Voters are the decision makers in ballot measures.)
- Conduct nonpartisan voter-registration drives
- Mobilize voters. Conduct nonpartisan Get-Out-the-Vote drives
- Educate all candidates in a race about your organization's issues
- Educate voters on the issues (without leading them to a conclusion about how to vote on candidates)
- Work with all political parties to get issues included in all party platforms
- Conduct voter-protection activities

Specifically prohibited activities include:

- Endorsing candidates for public office
- Making campaign contributions or other expenditures on behalf of candidates
- Draw attention to the difference between candidates on your issues

For a full list of activities that will enable your nonprofit to engage people in elections and maintain your nonpartisanship, review Chapter 3 and rely on other resources included in this book, especially the Alliance for Justice and Nonprofit VOTE.

Summary: It's Your Legal Right

This chapter emphasized that nonprofits are legally entitled to lobby. Moreover, you learned that nonprofits are expected to lobby in the best interests of the people they serve. You learned that the 1976 Lobby Law clarified many ambiguities about nonprofit lobbying. You may now elect to fall under that law, and, if you stay within well established guidelines, you should have no difficulties.

You also learned what forms to file with the IRS and how to set up a tracking system for direct- and grassroots-lobbying costs.

Too often, board members or organizational consultants who don't know about the 1976 Lobby Law believe that, when nonprofits lobby, they place their tax-exempt status at risk. Nothing could be further from the truth. The IRS has been clear about reporting requirements and has stated that organizations that have elected to fall under the 1976 law have a strong history of compliance. It has documented in letters to national nonprofit organizations that filing IRS Form 5768 in no way triggers an audit.

Be sure that your board knows and understands this.

WORKSHEET 17 Lobbying Activity Reporting Form

Give copies of this worksheet to all employees who may be involved in lobbying work. Collect them every two weeks to compile an ongoing record of lobbying expenditures.

Employee Timesheet

Name: **Jason**

Title: **Public Policy Coordinator**

Pay period: **2/1 - 2/8**

Multiplier (Hourly cost of wages and benefits) **$26.50**

Direct lobbying

Note: *Direct lobbying* consists of any activities (and related expenses) you undertake to directly influence legislators and their staff or to influence executive branch officials and their staff, regarding how they act on specific legislation. Direct lobbying includes asking our members, defined as anyone giving a nominal amount of time or money to our organization, to ask legislators to vote a particular way on a bill. In the chart below, describe the activity, the date, the number of hours, and any related expenses (parking, travel, and so forth).

Activity:	Date:	Hours:	Expenses: (materials, postage, travel)
Urging support for SF 721—met w/ Senators Smith, Robinson, Hou.	2/6	1.5	$4.00 (parking)
Handout for SF 721. Wrote and printed one page "Vote Yes."	2/2– 2/5	3	$240 (print 400 copies)
E-mail alert to members	2/3	2.5	

Total staff costs: (Total hours) x (Hourly wage and benefits multiplier): **$185.50**

Total expenses: **$244.00**

TOTAL direct-lobbying expenditures (staff costs plus expenses): **$429.50**

(continued)

Grassroots lobbying

Note: *Grassroots lobbying* consists of any activities (and related expenses) you undertake to ask the public to influence legislation by contacting elected and appointed officials and their staff. In the chart below, describe the activity, the date, the number of hours, and any related expenses (materials copied, phone charges, and so forth).

Activity:	**Date:**	**Hours:**	**Expenses:** (materials, postage, travel)
Wrote, produced, mailed PSA to radio stations: "Vote Yes SF 721"	2/20–2/22	18	$220 (tape production) $42 (postage)
Contract w/designer: "Vote Yes SF 721" display ad	2/20	.5	$400 (design services)
Purchase space for "Vote Yes" in neighborhood newspapers	2/27	3.5	$1,200 (ad space)

Total staff costs: (Total hours) x (Hourly wage and benefits multiplier):   <u>$583</u>

Total expenses: <u>$1,862</u>

TOTAL grassroots-lobbying expenditures (staff costs plus expenses): <u>$2,445</u>

Afterword

You've done it!

Your organization has recognized that public policy advocacy is a strategic way to fulfill your mission. You have developed a plan for integrating public policy work into your ongoing activities. The infrastructure is in place to carry out this work whenever it allows you to meet your organizational goals.

And, in many instances, you have already carried out a lobbying campaign.

For most nonprofit organizations, the commitment to including public policy work is new. For all of us in nonprofit organizations, it is increasingly important to continue to be a powerful force for change in our communities, our states, and the nation. If we do not speak out on the issues that we know best, the policy dialogue is diminished. And it is nonprofits that enable the citizens, the people, the communities we serve to be their own best voice. We are often their channel for reaching decision makers on issues that touch their lives.

Lobbying is honorable work. Nonprofit organizations, dedicated to mission and to enabling people to participate fully in democratic society, make a significant difference in how we care for one another.

Advocate with pride, conviction, and determination.

Now that you have begun this work, carry it on.

RAPID RESPONSES TO
CRISES OR OPPORTUNITIES

Emergencies happen.

With little warning, issues spring up that will harm your organization's funding. Legislators or interest groups will surprise you with measures that could weaken programs and services important to your clients. New opportunities appear. Any of these surprises can jolt your organization into action.

You need to move fast!

Most of this book focuses on thoughtful planning and careful preparation for your public policy work. Because surprises are inevitable in the public policy arena, this section describes key steps to help you act effectively under pressure and with short timelines in emergency circumstances.

There are five steps to take:

> Step 1: Form a rapid-response team
>
> Step 2: Learn everything possible about the issue
>
> Step 3: Determine your organization's position on the issue
>
> Step 4: Determine the actions you will take
>
> Step 5: Lobby through direct contact, grassroots influence, strategic alliances, and media advocacy

Step 1: Form a rapid-response team

If your organization has not yet created a rapid-response team, create a temporary one to address the immediate problem or opportunity.

The rapid-response team is responsible for coordinating your response and making decisions about actions that your nonprofit will take.

The executive director and board chair of the organization have the responsibility of appointing a rapid-response team. That team should consist of three to five board and staff members most knowledgeable about the public policy process and the issue being debated. This rapid-response team must include designated decision makers who have the authority to "sign off" on a decision. The rapid-response team must also have the authority to mobilize your organization's staff and financial resources in response to a critical issue.

Note: You need to record and report lobbying activity to the IRS. Review Chapter 4 for guidelines and forms.

Step 2: Learn everything possible about the issue

Know that, when you need to move quickly to understand the issue, formulate your plan for engagement, and engage your key audiences, most of what you need to know is available online. Governmental entities – legislatures, county boards, city councils – post the text of policy proposals. Their websites include information about the elected officials who are leading the work on the issue. In addition, those websites provide timelines and, in some cases, tutorials about how the system works and the steps in the decision-making process.

Organizations—nonprofits, business groups, local government associations, and academic institutions—that have an interest in the issue are likely to provide information and insights into the issue as well as the landscape of who supports and who opposes it. Their technology-based outreach efforts should provide everything from research and analysis to messages that they are disseminating at websites, on Facebook, at Twitter, and in blogs. The more controversial and high impact the proposal, the more chatter. As always, sort Internet-based information carefully. But use technology to get a quick start on the issue that concerns you and the policy debate.

Rely on your network. Calls to people who know the issue well, work on policy, and are willing to help give your nonprofit information and advice are a valuable resource.

Find the answers to the following questions:

- What change is being proposed?
- Why is it being proposed now?
- How will it affect our organization and the people we serve?

- Who is sponsoring, supporting, or opposing the proposal?

- Where will the issue be decided: state legislature, county commission, city council, or an administrative agency?

- What action, if any, has already been taken on the proposal? Where is it in the decision-making process?

- What are the next steps in the decision-making process?

To get the information needed to answer these questions, you can do the following:

1. Begin by getting as much information from the source that initially alerted you to the crisis or opportunity. You might learn of the issue through a call from an elected official, an article in a newspaper, or a report from someone in an organization or agency who knows your concern. Probe that source for as much information as possible.

2. Use the resources available at the arena of influence to learn about the content and status of a proposal. Contact the elected official who is reported to be the author of the issue and discuss the proposal and its intended outcomes. Use legislative information sources, including websites that allow you to track legislation via the Internet, to read any bills that have been introduced. Read reports of any action taken on the bill.

3. Find out when elected officials will act on the bill. This creates a deadline for you. You should develop your position and contact legislators as far in advance of the debates and votes as possible. You may also want to be prepared to testify at public hearings and provide comments to the press that may inform the debate.

4. Move quickly to talk to other organizations that are likely to be concerned about the issue. Some of them may have systems in place for monitoring and acting on public policy proposals. State associations of nonprofits, coalitions of groups with shared interests, and leadership groups with lobbying experience and expertise in your field of interest can be excellent resources for getting you up to speed on an issue.

5. Read materials produced by interest groups and organizations whose viewpoint opposes yours. Meet with them to learn more about their position and to explore compromises if this is appropriate. Gather as much information about opposition perspectives as possible. You will need to anticipate the arguments that opponents will offer.

6. Begin immediately to monitor the legislative process and the media. This will ensure that you track any changes in the issue as you are learning as much as you can as fast as you can.

Step 3: Determine your organization's position on the issue

Based on what the rapid-response team learns in the information-gathering phase of the work and based on its analysis of the impact that the proposal will have on your organization's constituencies, decide on your position. Decide whether you support or oppose the position and what action you want elected officials to take. You may want them to approve an idea, defeat an idea, or accept an alternative proposal that you will offer. Within your organization, the rapid-response team should recommend a position to the board and staff for discussion and adoption.

Step 4: Determine the actions you will take

Decide which of the following you will do:

- Lobby elected officials to adopt your position. Your organization's chosen representative may ask decision makers to vote for or against a proposal. Or you may ask them to consider an amendment or alternate proposal that you offer to address your concerns.

- Mobilize supporters including your clients, members, volunteers, and the general public to join in the lobbying effort by contacting legislators.

- Join with other organizations that share your position on the issue.

- Include media advocacy in your lobbying campaign.

Step 5: Lobby through direct contact, grassroots influence, strategic alliances, and media advocacy

Lobby officials directly

1. Develop a position statement that serves as the basis for discussions with elected officials and their staff. It should be a statement that you can use for posting at your website, including in your social-media outreach, and in making calls, writing letters, presenting testimony, and providing written material for them to consider while the issue is being debated. Your position statement should be attractive and compelling, It must include the problem, your positions, and the action you are requesting. (Their support! Their vote!)

2. Get information about key decision makers and how to reach them. This means getting lists of elected officials and their staff, especially members of committees that will make decisions on this issue.

3. Collect information about the administrative agencies that are working with the elected officials to shape or analyze proposals in your issue area. These are often the "experts" upon whom state and local elected officials rely. Your organization will need to know who these agencies are and educate them about your concerns and position. They can be powerful allies.

4. Communicate with legislators who will be deciding your issue. Face-to-face meetings are the best connection, when possible. Be sure to target people with power: committee chairs and members, political leaders, and your own elected representatives. Describe your organization's mission and activities briefly. State your concern about the proposal. Explain your position using data and stories that make a compelling case. Ask for their vote. If they have questions, provide or promise to get them answers . . . and do it!

5. Follow up initial contacts with materials that state and substantiate your position. If appropriate, send e-mails or write letters that summarize the discussion and thank the official for support if it has been committed. Make phone calls to thank the elected official for his or her support or to answer questions.

Mobilize grassroots supporters

1. Find out how you can contact your organization's members and clients so that legislators can be reached by their own constituents—voters in their districts— whenever possible. Rely on existing in-house databases, e-mail blasts, phone banks, and social media to reach your base of supporters.

2. Communicate with supporters as early as possible explaining the issue, your position, the timeline for legislative action, and the role that they can play. If you are asking them to contact elected officials, provide names, addresses, and key points that they should make in the conversation. *Give your supporters clear directions about what they should do to be a voice on the issue.* Appendix D: Samples includes a boilerplate flyer, Tips for Contacting Your Representative, which you can adapt for your uses.

3. Convene an informational briefing and strategy session that brings together supporters and people who will be affected by the issue. Give them information about the issue, the impact of proposed legislation, your organization's position, and the action that you want them to take. You may ask them to meet with their legislators, make phone calls, send e-mails, write personal letters, provide testimony, write letters to the editor, or attend hearings. Include a brief training session in your briefing session, giving them tips on how to communicate with legislators. (See Learn the Best Strategies for Using Grassroots Support, page 106.)

Activate your allies

1. Join with other nonprofits and entities that share your position on the issue. If no coalition exists but other groups would be interested in joining forces, take the lead and convene the meeting.

2. Work cooperatively with staff and elected officials who agree with your position and who can share information, be vehicles for communicating your ideas, and influence decision makers. No one can lobby a legislator like another legislator!

Checklist for rapid responses

When you find yourself in the position of having to leap into action, this checklist will help you be as prepared and strategic as possible:

❏ We have a rapid-response team in place to shape and orchestrate our response to the crisis or opportunity.

❏ We know who the decision makers are within our organization as we respond to this unexpected crisis or opportunity.

❏ We know the precise content of the proposal that we need to support or stop. (Be sure you have accurate, complete, and detailed information about the initiative being considered. Sometimes a single word, such as *may* instead of *shall*, can make a major difference in policy.)

❏ We have assessed the implications of this proposal for our organization, constituents, and community.

❏ We know where the proposal is in the legislative process.

❏ We have a timeline of anticipated key decision-making moments.

❏ We have a clear position on the issue and can make a compelling case for our views. (Be sure that you state your position and your rationale in a brief paper. The paper should state the *action* you are asking legislators to take: vote yes or no; amend/modify a proposal; increase appropriations.)

❏ We know who else is working on this issue, both for and against.

❏ We understand the arguments that opponents will present and are prepared to respond to them.

❏ We know our allies and are working out a shared strategy for effective lobbying.

❏ We have decided the action steps we will take to assert our position, communicate with legislators, and mobilize grassroots support. We have a list of key action steps, timed strategically so that we make compelling arguments to influence decision makers before their minds are made up and their votes are tallied.

Use the media

1. Designate one member of the rapid-response team as a spokesperson on the issue for the organization. Provide clear, accurate, reliable, and interesting information. Never invent facts or overstate your case.

2. Draw on your existing ties with the media. Urge them to print your letters to the editor, write editorials supporting your position, and feature the programs or services at stake in the debate.

3. Use the media strategically. Select the media most likely to be noticed by the people you are trying to influence. Hone your message to fit the particular medium you are working with.

Summary

A rapid-response team *can* make a difference in a legislative emergency by acting on one legislative initiative or responding to one particular, once-in-a-lifetime policy debate. But why get caught? Adopting public policy as an ongoing component of your work is likely to be more fruitful. It can be tough to enter the debate as a newcomer, late in the game, and without an established presence in the public-affairs arena. Ongoing involvement is more likely to position your organization to make a significant change in a public policy.

So, once you solve the unexpected crisis or take advantage of the sudden opportunity, use this planning guide to design your nonprofit organization's long-term public policy strategies.

Resources for Nonprofit Advocacy and Lobbying

1. **Organizations that support nonprofit advocacy, organizing, and lobbying**

The Alliance for Justice

Washington, DC

www.afj.org

202-822-6070

The Alliance for Justice offers detailed information online and through a wide variety of publications and training events. It focuses on nonprofit engagement in policy and election activity with an emphasis on laws that govern nonprofit lobbying and activities in election cycles.

Independent Sector (ID)

Washington, DC

www.independentsector.org

202-467-6100

Independent Sector is a national organization dedicated to leading, strengthening, and mobilizing the nonprofit and philanthropic communities. In addition to events and resources on governance and management, IS focuses on policy and advocacy. It addresses issues of particular interest to the sector and provides information and training in multiple formats to support nonprofits.

National Council of Nonprofits (NCN)

Washington, DC

www.councilofnonprofits.org

202-962-0322

The National Council of Nonprofits is the national organization that works with state associations across the United States. It provides resources, training, and convenings to advance the work of the sector, with a specific emphasis on advocacy. NCN also hosts the information developed by the Center for Lobbying in the Public Interest at www.clpi.org. NCN not only provides information that will support your nonprofit in building its policy plans and actions but will connect you with your state association of nonprofits, which is likely to be your best source of information about nonprofit work in your state. NCN also lists resources for further study in all aspects of nonprofit activity.

The Nonprofit Quarterly

Boston, MA

www.nonprofitquarterly.org

This national publication, online and in print, provides daily commentary and ongoing in-depth articles about issues of import to the nonprofit sector and the public. Articles often focus on policy issues and nonprofit advocacy efforts, as its tagline suggests: "Promoting an active and engaged democracy." See this as essential reading for understanding the policy context in the country in a timely way and with insights from national thought leaders.

Academic centers: Explore the universities and colleges in your state to identify departments, centers, and faculty whose work is relevant to your nonprofit's issues. Develop relationships with these potential partners and those who provide research and education on nonprofit advocacy.

2. Basic reading for nonprofit advocacy

Amidei, Nancy. *So You Want to Make a Difference: Advocacy Is the Key.* Washington, DC: OMBWatch, 1999.

> Amidie's classic work helps individuals and organizations understand the basic rationale for engaging in public policy. It provides basic information about governmental structures and processes, especially at the national level.

Avner, Marcia. "Advocacy, Lobbying, and Social Change," in David Renz, *The*

Jossey-Bass Handbook of Nonprofit Leadership and Management, Third Edition.
San Francisco, CA: Jossey-Bass, 2010. Pages 347-373.

> The chapter provides a comprehensive overview of advocacy, including defini-
> tions, the advocacy cycle as a framework for planning and building ongoing
> effective strategies. Three key areas of advocacy are discussed in detail: grassroots
> organizing, direct lobbying, and media advocacy.

Avner, Marcia. *Advocate for Impact: Policy Guide for State and Local United Ways.*
Alexandria, VA: United Way Worldwide. 2010.

> Designed for United Way organizations, this booklet guides service organiza-
> tions in developing an advocacy component of their work in order to meet
> their mission. It covers basic advocacy skills and includes examples of service
> organizations' accomplishments in advocacy.

Avner, Marcia. *The Nonprofit Board Member's Guide to Lobbying and Advocacy.*
St Paul, MN: Fieldstone Alliance, 2002.

> This companion publication to the Lobbying and Advocacy Handbooks em-
> phasizes the roles and responsibilities that are unique to a nonprofit board.
> Fieldstone Alliance publications are sold by Turner Publishing.

Bass, Gary. "Advocacy in the Public Interest," in *Essays on Excellence: Lessons from
the Georgetown Nonprofit Management Executive Certificate Program.* Washington,
DC: Georgetown University, 2009.

> Bass is the former President of OMB Watch and the Executive Director
> of the Bauman Foundation. He has written widely based on his work in
> research and advocacy on policy issues that impact the nonprofit sector
> and the role of government in our democracy. This is a valuable study of
> nonprofit advocacy.

Beyond the Cause: The Art and Science of Advocacy. Washington, DC: Independent
Sector, 2012.

> This 2012 report identifies strategies for the nonprofit and philanthropic center
> to increase its public policy impact. IS identifies a set of essentials for successful
> advocacy and presents recommendations for increasing the sector's effective-
> ness in shaping policy, primarily at the national level.

Boris, Elizabeth T., with Matthew Maronick, "Civic Participation and Advocacy,"
in Lester Salamon, *The State of Nonprofit America, Second Edition.* Washington,
DC: Brookings Institution Press, 2012. Pages 394-422.

The text provides excellent and timely information about the nonprofit sector. This chapter includes up-to-date information about the current status of nonprofit activity and challenges facing the nonprofit sector's efforts in civic engagement, advocacy, and lobbying. It looks at 501(c)(3) and 501(c)(4) organizations, levels of involvement in engagement and advocacy, and case examples of work.

Reid, Elizabeth, J., "Advocacy and the Challenges It Presents for Nonprofits," in Elizabeth T. Boris and C. Eugene Steuerle, *Nonprofits and Government, Second Edition*. Washington, DC: The Urban Institute Press, 2006. Pages 343-372.

This reading also covers the basics of the importance of nonprofit advocacy and looks at advocacy in the context of the policy environment, government funding, and a complex and ever changing regulatory framework. It explains the lobby and election laws that govern three types of nonprofits: 501(c)(3), 501(c)(4), and 527 organizations as of 2006 law.

Smucker, Bob. *The Nonprofit Lobbying Guide, 2nd ed.* Washington, DC: Independent Sector, 1999. This is available online at www.independentsector.org/lobby_guide

This classic is one of the first guides for nonprofits and presents a comprehensive view of the lobby law, the importance of lobbying, and personal stories of nonprofit successes. Smucker is recognized as a key leader in advancing nonprofit advocacy, and this work includes much of his wisdom and experience.

3 Grassroots organizing

The Center for Community Change

Washington, DC

www.communitychange.org

202-339-9300

The Center for Community Change is a leadership organization founded in 1968 and working to build the power and capacity of low-income people, support them in strengthening communities, and shape the policies and institutions that affect their lives. It is a central point for information on grassroots organizing and building social-change movements. Sign up for their updates online.

Alinsky, Saul. *Rules for Radicals.* Chicago: University of Chicago Press. 1946.

This is an American classic on community organizing and excellent background for nonprofits engaging in policy work. Alinsky's theories have served as a basis for many types of organizing that have emerged in the decades since this was written.

Ganz, Marshall. *Why David Sometimes Wins: Leadership, Organization, and Strategy in the California Farm Worker Movement.* New York: Oxford University Press, 2009.

> Ganz is a leader in the field of community organizing. This work tells the story of the Cesar Chavez and the Farm Workers movement in California and provides inspiration and insight for effective social-change organizing and movement building. It is an engaging and scholarly analysis of the struggles and strategies that are included in movement-building work.

Minieri, Joan, and Paul Getsos, *Tools for Radical Democracy: How to Organize for Power in Your Community.* San Francisco: Jossey-Bass, 2007.

> This is a step-by-step guide for nonprofits engaging in community organizing. It covers key concepts and includes skill-building exercises. A highlight of the book is the guidance that it provides in the design and implementation of an issue-based campaign. The authors emphasize the role of organizing in building leadership.

Sen, Rinku. *Stir It Up: Lessons in Community Organizing and Advocacy.* San Francisco: Jossey-Bass, 2003.

> The Ms Foundation sponsored this work, which identifies key strategies for advancing the mission of social-change organizations. It focuses on organizing in the context of the global economy and is based on Sen's own experience in organizing in women's groups for economic justice.

Wellstone Action. *Politics the Wellstone Way.* Minneapolis: University of Minnesota Press, 2005.

> Used often in conjunction with trainings, *Politics the Wellstone Way* is a guide for citizen engagement and a useful tool for trainers and organizers. It urges civic engagement and integrates strategies of policy, organizing, and politics.

There are many training centers for organizing for secular and faith-based nonprofits in the United States. Among these are the Industrial Areas Foundation www.industrialareasfoundation.org), the Gamaliel Foundation (www.gamaliel. org), PICO National Network (www.piconetwork.org), and Wellstone Action (www.wellstone.org).

4. Philanthropy and advocacy

Alliance for Justice, Investing in Change: A Funder's Guide to Supporting Advocacy. Washington, DC: Alliance for Justice. 2004

> AFJ makes the case for advocacy to foundations and, in this and other publications, provides recommendations and templates for assessing nonprofit capacity and evaluating advocacy.

Arons, David, *Power in Policy: A Funders Guide to Advocacy and Civic Participation.* St Paul, MN: Fieldstone Alliance. 2007

> Intended to demonstrate the value of investments in advocacy to foundations and expand interest in supporting policy work, *Power in Policy* makes a compelling case for funding advocacy. It includes essays and case stories by philanthropic leaders and serves as a critical work that advances the importance of advocacy in meeting the missions of nonprofits and foundations.

5. Election-related activity and civic engagement

Nonprofit VOTE

Boston, MA

www.nonprofitvote.org

617-357-8683

> Nonprofit VOTE is the source of sound information and tools for your nonprofit to use in planning and carrying out effective voter-engagement campaigns. Web-based, this center provides everything from the rationale for nonprofit voter engagement to planning guidance, state-based information resources, downloadable materials for training and campaigns, and information about resources for democracy work. It conducts research and analysis on the impact of nonprofit work, and it provides strong support for maintaining nonpartisanship while promoting voter registration, voter and candidates information, and voter mobilization.

6. Legal issues

The Alliance for Justice is recognized as a valuable resource for materials and training on nonprofit lobbying, advocacy, and civic-engagement work. See the website for information about trainings, including webinars, workshops, and other events. See online segments on rules, electoral activity, ballot measures, executive and administrative advocacy, and litigation. Review all of the publications available at their website, www.afj.org, with special attention to:

The Rules of the Game: An Election Year Guide for Nonprofit Organizations. Washington, DC. 2010.

> This is a user-friendly guide to federal tax and election laws that govern nonprofits in an election year. It explains the permissible ways to organize election activity and become involved in the political process in rigorously nonpartisan ways.

Worry Free Lobbying for Nonprofits: How to Use the 501(h) Election to Maximize Effectiveness. (Reprinted 2011 and available online)

> This basic booklet is free and important for all nonprofit staff and board members planning to do advocacy work.

Keeping Track: A Guide to Recordkeeping for Advocacy Charities (2012)

> Written by John Pomeranz, a foremost expert in the issue of nonprofit lobbying and the law, provides detailed systems for accurate accountability for lobbying expenditures and reporting

Information about State and Local Governments, Arenas for Change

The National Association of Counties

www.naco.org

NACo is the only national organization that provides essential services to the nation's 3,068 counties and advocates on their behalf. It has a "Find a County" opportunity online and descriptive information about each county's economy, demographics, structure, and history. It provides information about the elected officials at the county level, bios, and contacts.

The National Council of State Legislators

www.ncsl.org

NCSL has a great deal of information about the issues that state legislators face and provides videos, podcasts, and webinars that capture key policy experts and policy analysis on state-level issues ranging from agriculture and rural development to human services, tax policy, and election systems. It has a searchable database of state legislators.

National League of Cities

www.nlc.org

NLC works with over 1,900 cities, villages, and towns and serves as a resource and advocate for their local-government interests. It, too, has valuable policy information and will guide you to your state's associations of local governments.

Public Technology Institute

www.pti.org

PTI supports local-government executives and elected officials and is the only technology organization created to provide these services. It offers research, education, and consulting services. For nonprofits, it provides information about its many members and links to city and county websites.

State and Local Government on the Net

www.statelocalgov.net

This site serves as a directory of official state-, county-, and city-government websites and can help your organization learn about all of the entities in your service or organizing region. This allows you to remain up to date in post-election periods when new leaders take office and when there are issues that have been addressed in other locations that you want to learn about.

Subscribe to regular information provided by the governmental bodies with which you work in your advocacy efforts. Most provide online reports of current policy issues, progress on bills or ordinances, and action on policy proposals. You can sign up for everything from voter registration to e-newsletters, announcements of public meetings, and formal information about funding source, application processes, and emerging opportunities.

Because of the complex and important relationships that nonprofits have with every level of government, take the time to learn about your arenas of influence and the people of the process. The resources identified here will help you to begin the important work of building strategic working relationships with elected officials and their staff.

Legislative Process: A Guide

You can't advocate successfully without a basic understanding of the structures, systems, and people that make laws happen. The following is a basic overview—enough to get you started on the journey. You will learn the rest as you actually contact the people who get things done. Make use of the resources in Appendix B: Resources for Nonprofit Lobbying for further background information. Feel free to scan or copy this legislative guide to distribute to the planning team.

Legislative Structures

Legislatures are representative forms of government. Legislative districts are drawn based on population, and members are elected to represent the interests of their district as they tackle the larger charge of shaping public policies that set the state's priorities.

In almost all states, the legislative branch is bicameral. This means it has two bodies, a house (or assembly) and a senate. The house of representatives is usually the larger legislative body. Its members each represent fewer people than do members of the senate. The senate is most often a smaller body whose members represent a larger district than do members of the house. There is an enormous variety in the size of state legislatures and the frequency and duration of their sessions. (Note that Nebraska has a unicameral legislature: only one body to represent the state residents.)

Legislatures come in all sizes and shapes!

New Hampshire has the largest house in the United States, with 400 members. It also has one of the smallest senates, 24 members. States vary:

	House or Assembly	Senate	Total
Colorado	65	35	100
Connecticut	151	36	187
Georgia	180	56	236
Illinois	118	59	177
Minnesota	134	67	201
Mississippi	170	45	215
New Jersey	80	40	120
North Carolina	120	50	170
Add your state here:			

The average size of legislatures is 40 senators and 104 house members. In total, there are 7,424 state legislators in the United States; 1,984 senators; and 5,440 representatives in chambers usually called the "house of representatives" but sometimes called the "assembly" or "general assembly."

In states with bicameral legislatures, every citizen is represented by a member of the house and a member of the senate. *That means each person involved in your organization has two connections—one to a representative, one to a senator—to help you as you call for action on bills.* As you can see, even a small nonprofit that mobilizes its friends and allies can exercise a lot of influence.

Legislative Process: How Does an Idea Become a Law?

Each state and local government has its own unique structures and processes. Information about your state's system is available on the Internet. State websites all follow the same pattern: www.state.XX.us. Insert your state's postal initials at "XX" and you'll get the website. For example, www.state.mn.us is Minnesota's website; Florida's website is www.state.fl.us.

Local governmental legislative processes are sometimes more difficult to learn about, but if you find the right source of information, you can get everything you need. If your city or county has a website, study it for information about how the unit of government is structured, what steps a proposal moves through to become a law, and the calendar of activity. Full-time and year-round activity is more likely to be found at the local level. Most states have legislatures that are in session for only part of each year.

The basic process in state legislatures is relatively linear. It usually looks like:

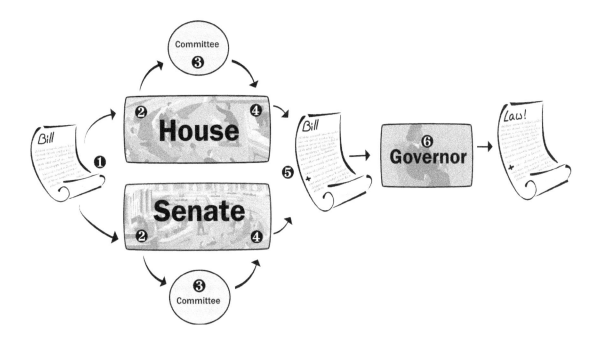

1. A bill for a proposed new law may be introduced in either the house or the senate but usually in both chambers. In some states, all appropriations bills must originate in the house. Each bill may have a number of coauthors. The first authors in the house and senate are the chief authors of the bill and are responsible for steering the bill through the legislative process. The other authors are generally chosen to demonstrate diverse political and regional support for the measure. In some states, multiples of the same bill are introduced to demonstrate widespread support.

2. After a bill is introduced to the full house or senate (or both), it is assigned to a committee that oversees the issue addressed by the bill. Child-care bills might go to a human services committee or a children and families committee. Bills that are complex or controversial are referred to multiple committees in some but not all states. For example, a bill to limit feedlots in agricultural

areas might go to an agriculture committee and then to an environment committee. Sometimes a committee refers a bill to a subcommittee for discussion. Committee chairpersons usually play a key role in determining which bills are heard and when, though some states require that every bill introduced must be heard in at least one committee. The committee hearings are open and provide an opportunity for members of the public to listen to the debate and provide testimony. Committees have their own rules and procedures for taking testimony. *It is important to know how to sign up to testify on issues of concern to your nonprofit.* The best way to find out is by calling the staff person assigned to the committee, the committee chair, or the house or senate information offices in your state. The chief author of a bill can also provide guidance.

3. The role of the committee is to decide whether to amend, approve, defeat, or table a measure. If the committee recommends approval (passage) of the bill, it recommends to the full house or senate that action to pass the bill be taken on the floor.

4. The full house or senate will take the committee recommendation, debate the bill, sometimes adopt amendments to it, and vote on the measure.

5. When there are differences between house and senate versions of a bill, states have varying formal procedures to negotiate the differences. Some states have a system of sending bills back and forth between the house and senate, attempting to get resolution. If the resolution can't be achieved that way, joint committees may be appointed to work out the differences. Other states make much more extensive use of conference committees. As soon as a difference between the house and senate versions of a bill becomes apparent, a conference committee is appointed. In some states, the conference committee report cannot be amended, making conference committees extremely important in getting your work done. Identify the process that is used in your state.

6. If both bodies approve the final bill, it is sent to the governor for a signature or veto. Each state has a rule for the period of time that the governor has to consider and veto a measure. Each state has a prescribed requirement for the number of votes needed to override a veto. If the governor signs the bill, it becomes law and goes into effect on a date identified in the bill.

7. Once your bill is passed, you can switch your attention from the legislature to the process known as "implementation," or "administrative rulemaking." Usually, the legislature enacts the basic policy but permits or requires an agency to formulate the rules to implement the changed policy. This is generally done to ensure that the policy is enacted in a way that it was intended and written by staff with expertise in the affected areas. This poses an excellent opportunity to ensure the bill is enacted in a way that will meet the purpose and mission of your hard work. Don't forget to weigh in at this stage, too!

Appendix B: Resources for Nonprofit Lobbying identifies ways that you can learn more about the arenas for change in which you are working. Use websites. Call information offices listed in the Government Offices sections of phone directories. Or stop by and visit information offices at your state capitol, county building, and city hall. Worksheet 7: The Legislative Arena on page 223 is an additional tool to help you record what you learn.

The People of the Process

While you need to know the rules and procedures for making and influencing laws, it is the *people* who count. Knowledge of who controls what decisions is critical to your success. Following is a guide to the people necessary to the lawmaking process. Worksheet 8: The People of the Process on page 229 helps you record the names and contact information for your state.

Legislative roles

Committee chairs and members

Legislative bodies carry out most of their work through committees. Each state has its own unique committee structure, but, in all states, the role of committee chair is powerful. Committee chairs usually set the agenda for committee debates and decide which issues to hear, when to hear them, and how much time to allow for testimony and debate. Your nonprofit doesn't need to know everyone in the legislature before engaging in lobbying, but you should know where your bill will be heard. For both direct and grassroots lobbying, your nonprofit needs to target committee chairs and committee members who will act on your bill. This will prepare the legislative committee to take its formal action with a good understanding of the issue, its impact, and the concerns of citizens who support your measure.

Political caucus leaders

Politics matters. Key political leaders become "speakers of the house" and "senate majority leaders" and have significant power in legislative bodies. So, although nonprofits are prohibited from engaging in any form of electioneering, you need to know the political landscape at the state and local level to understand who has the power in elected bodies.

Legislative officials from the same political party form caucuses within the house and senate. Each caucus elects its own leaders. The majority caucus, the one with the most members, chooses the person who will represent the caucus's interests in the legislature and to the public. In the house of representatives, this person would be called the speaker of the house, and, in most states, the speaker is perceived as being the most powerful legislator. The caucus leader in the senate is usually called the majority leader or sometimes the president of the senate or chair of the rules committee.

A person is also chosen to convene the caucus, work to compel members to vote for a "caucus position," and manage the caucus members' activities in floor debate. This caucus manager may carry the title of majority leader in the house. In the senate, the title is often assistant majority leader or whip. Majority caucus leaders appoint legislators to chair committees and serve on commissions and therefore have a role in deciding who has positions of power in the legislative process itself.

Minority caucuses have leadership structures as well. Minority leaders serve in a parallel way to shape caucus positions, serve as spokespersons for minority positions, work within the caucus to build loyalty and consensus on policy positions, and manage caucus action. They recommend to the majority leaders who should represent the minority on committees.

Majority and minority leaders in the house and senate are key players. They are often dealmakers on tough and complex issues. And because majority and minority caucus leaders in both the house and senate are responsible for election activities and charged with building the most strength and power they can for their party caucus, they are often tuned in to the voice of the voters. Nonprofits that can win multipartisan support for their issues from these leaders are often well-positioned for legislative success.

Many legislative bodies also have caucuses formed around issues and interests. These can include women's caucuses, minority community caucuses, children's-issues caucuses, and more. They hold regular meetings and seek information from organizations that have experience and expertise in their issue area. They often work as an effective voice on a specific set of issues and can control a block of votes.

Legislative staff

Staff are critical people in the process. As gatekeepers and facilitators of communication, they play a key role in providing access to decision makers and information. They know the process, the people, the power structures, and the schedules. Work with them as much as possible.

Staffing patterns vary widely among the states. The descriptions included here reflect general patterns. Explore how your state legislature staffs its work by contacting your legislature's general information offices or website.

Begin by learning the staff structures in the institution you are trying to influence. Refer to Worksheet 8 and your planning committee's identification of people key to the legislative process. Update the worksheet if needed to add new names and additional information.

Nonpartisan staff may provide a wide variety of functions, ranging from secretarial responsibilities to policy research and administration. They facilitate access to legislators, convey information to them, and often have significant substantive knowledge that shapes the policy discussion.

In addition to their nonpartisan staff, elected officials sometimes have political caucus staff assigned to them. In Minnesota, for instance, the House of Representatives and Senate each have caucus staff. The majority party has more staff positions available to it than does the minority party in each body. Caucus staff track votes and document them for reports to constituents, prepare information for legislators to use in responding to constituents or preparing for political events or campaigns, assist in building lists of supporters and events for political campaign use, and arrange party-related functions, including caucus meetings.

City councils, county commissions, and other forms of government have varying levels of staffing to support their work, depending on their status as a full- or part-time body, their budgets, and the degree of complexity of the system.

Get to know these staff when they are free from the rush of a legislative session or local-government peak season. Introduce yourself and your organization. Let them know your issues and that you will be asking legislators to meet with you and support your efforts. Tell them about the expertise and experience in your organization and how you can be a resource to them.

Build strong communication links with these staff by getting to know what they care about, their responsibilities, and how they like to be reached when you have a pressing need for their help. If they understand your need, find working with you to be respectful and interesting, and know how to reach you easily, they can help move your information and ideas into the center of the policy debate. And often these staff can give you information that you require as you shape your lobbying strategy. They often know who favors and opposes an issue, the schedules for meetings on your topic, and the results of analysis of your issue being carried out by research staff or state agencies. Once you have built a strong working relationship with staff, they may be willing to alert you to key changes in the debate, page you for hurriedly scheduled discussions of your topic, and find times when the legislator whom you need to see can give a few minutes.

Executive branch officials and staff

These people shape proposals presented to the legislature, recommend budgets, and often assess the merits of proposals being debated. Governors and mayors also have the power of the veto. Working with the administrative agencies involved in your issues and with the chief executive and his or her staff enables you to have your ideas and information introduced early in the process, in the planning phase. Having advocates within the administrative branch can provide support during the debate and help to avoid vetoes of measures that are passed. In addition, these are the very people who will be charged with *implementing* your proposal once the legislation has passed, and you want to be certain these staff understand the *intent* of the legislation.

The public-affairs community

This group of people cares about policies and the way in which the public and elected officials deliberate about issues. Nonprofits are an increasingly important part of this community, which comprises lobbyists, political scientists, media covering governmental affairs, researchers and policy analysts, political activists, and citizens who choose to follow and engage in the process. Though the term *special interest* has taken on a negative taint, it is essential to have groups that care about a particular issue and are involved in shaping the public dialogue about their concerns.

Being part of the public-affairs community is valuable. Knowing other participants in the process is helpful. These people will be colleagues, teachers, and perhaps opponents. Knowing their organizations, interests, power to influence the process, and willingness to support your proposals will make yours a more strategic organization.

Samples

Sample: Tips for Contacting Your Representative

Modify the tips on pages 189–191, adapted from the *Minnesota Citizens for the Arts Advocacy Handbook*,[8] and distribute them to your supporters when you want them to contact their representatives in person, via letter, or via phone—or all three. Insert your issue, position, key messages or talking points, and legislators to contact up front. Adapt the text as needed to fit your goals.

The issue:

_____

_____

_____

_____

The position:

_____

_____

_____

_____

Key messages:

_____

_____

_____

_____

_____

Whom to contact:

_____

_____

_____

_____

[8] Adapted from *Arts Advocacy Handbook*, Minnesota Citizens for the Arts, Minneapolis, MN, 1997. Used with permission.

When meeting with your representative . . .

1. **Kiss: Keep it short and simple.**

   The meeting should be brief and concise. Know why you are there, why the legislator should care, and what you want. If you are with a group of people, you may even want to designate one spokesperson. Go to the meeting with a short list of bullet points that you want to communicate.

2. **Have your facts straight.**

   Spend a few minutes reading through materials and thinking about the issue so you have familiarized yourself with it before you meet your legislator. Talk about how the legislator's constituents will benefit from the action you want. If the legislator asks you something that you don't know, don't guess; find out the information and send it later.

3. **Be on time, polite, and patient.**

   There is no quicker way to lose support for an issue than by being rude to legislators. BE NICE. Your legislator may have two committee meetings going on while he or she is supposed to be meeting with you and may be late. Don't be offended; just be glad you have gotten some of the legislator's time and make the most of it. Don't show up unannounced or assail those individuals or organizations that oppose your issue. Attacking your legislator can only hinder your efforts.

4. **If you go as a group, introduce your group members and note what connection each person may have to the legislator's district.**

   Make sure that the legislator knows your connection to his or her district: whether you are a constituent living in the district, a person working in the district, a person affected by the issue under consideration, and so forth.

5. **Make the issue personal.**

   How does the issue affect children in your area? Senior citizens? The community? Your organization? You? Tell stories about how the issue affects the people in the legislator's district.

6. **Be a resource.**

   Leave a one-page fact sheet with your representative covering your key messages. Include contact information so that the legislator or staff member can reach you with questions or notice that the issue is going to come up for action. If your legislator needs more information than you have with you, offer to obtain it. Be sure to follow up.

7. **Before you leave, say "Thank you" again.**

   Leave some information for the legislator to read but keep that information simple, too. Be direct by asking at the end of the meeting, "Will you support my cause?" His or her answer will determine your future efforts.

8. **Make a note about what happened in your meeting and bring your report back to your organization.**

   It's important for you to share what you learn with your organization. Take a few minutes to jot down your impressions and any specific statements of support or opposition that the legislator made. Did the legislator give you any advice or display knowledge related to your issue?

9. **Continue your relationship with your legislator.**

   When you get home, promptly send a note thanking your legislator for his or her time and giving other information about you or your organization that may be of interest. Invite the legislator to any events involving your organization or the issue that he or she may enjoy, learn from, or otherwise benefit from attending.

10. **Provide opportunities for positive publicity.** (Photo opportunities, events, occasions to meet people) Invite your legislator to

    - Your annual meeting
    - A public announcement of your season's activities
    - Opening-night gatherings
    - Parades
    - Any open houses or other events sponsored by your organization
    - Grand openings
    - Chamber of commerce or service club meetings

When writing to your representative or executive . . .

1. **Use the correct address and salutation**.

   For example, Dear Senator (name), or Dear Representative (name), or Dear Governor (name).

2. **Type or write your letter clearly.**

   If your letter is not easy to read, it could be discarded. Be sure to include your return address on the letter.

3. **Use your own words and stationery.**

   Legislators feel that personal letters, rather than form letters, show greater personal commitment on the part of the writer and therefore carry greater weight.

4. **Keep your message focused.**

   Avoid writing a "laundry list" of issues. Your most important message may get lost in a crowd of other issues.

5. **Be brief.**

   Choose a few bullet points that are direct and succinct. However, include enough information to explain why you are writing.

6. **Be specific.**

   If possible, give an example of how the issue affects your district.

7. **Know your facts.**

   It is important to be accurate and honest in your letter. You can seriously hurt your credibility by offering inaccurate or misleading information.

8. **If you can, find out how your legislator voted on this issue or similar issues in the past.**

   Personalizing your letter to reflect the viewpoint of your legislator can be very effective. If the legislator has voted in favor of your issue in the past, express your thanks.

9. **Be timely.**

   Contact your legislator while there is enough time for him or her to consider and act on your request.

10. **Be persistent.**

    Do not be satisfied with responding letters that give a status report on the bill, promise to "keep your views in mind," or otherwise skirt the issue. Without being rude, write back and ask for a more specific response.

11. **Say "Thank you."**

    Like everyone else, legislators appreciate a pat on the back. If, however, your legislator did not support your position, let him or her know that you are aware of that and explain why you think he or she should have decided differently. It might make a difference next time.

12. **DON'T use a negative, condescending, threatening, or intimidating tone.**

    You will only alienate your legislator and cause bad feelings that might hurt your case. Be nice!

When calling your representative...

Calling is a very effective way to contact your legislator when you must get your message across quickly. When calling your legislator,

1. **Ask to speak with the aide handling your issue.**

   The aides have the legislator's ear and are often very knowledgeable about the details of your issue. Be sure to take down the name of the aide with whom you spoke so that you will have a contact person in case you need to contact the legislator again. You will also have the name of another person to thank.

2. **Know what you want to say and BE BRIEF.**

   It is a good idea to have notes or other information in front of you, to help you be brief and concise. Don't keep the aide or legislator on the phone for more than five minutes unless he or she prolongs the conversation; a lot goes on in a legislator's office, and aides and legislators will have many other people vying for their time. Use your time wisely and get your main points covered as close to the beginning of the conversation as possible.

3. **Leave your name, address, and telephone number (as well as e-mail and fax, if you have them).**

   This will enable the aide to get back to you with information on the legislator's position. Let him or her know that you want a reply.

4. **Follow up your phone call with a brief note of thanks for the conversation, a concise summary of your position, and additional information if it has been requested.**

5. **DON'T bluff.**

   If the legislator or aide asks you a question that you cannot answer, say that you will get back to him or her and then do the appropriate follow-up.

Finally, don't forget the governor

The governor presents the first draft of the state budget and also signs or vetoes bills. Send letters to the governor just as you do to your legislators. The governor's address and phone number are [List them here.]

_____

_____

_____

_____

_____

_____

_____

_____

Annotated Samples: From Concept Presentation through Final Passage

The following section presents materials used by the POWER Campaign, a coalition of consumer, labor, and environmental groups working to promote clean, renewable sources of power in Minnesota.[9] Following are just some of the many print and electronic materials used by the POWER Campaign.

---

[9] Used with permission. The author is grateful to the POWER Campaign for its contribution to this book.

Exhibit 1: POWER Campaign letterhead and poster

The POWER Campaign is a coalition of diverse groups with a shared interest in environmentally friendly energy. Note how its letterhead names the members of the coalition, which helps other supporters see the broad-based support for the coalition's work. The letterhead reinforces the "lightbulb" symbol chosen by the coalition, as well as its slogan "Energy we can live with."

The coalition also created a reproducible poster (at right of the letterhead). The poster emphasizes the group's name, its symbol, its slogan, and the three key messages of its proposed bill: "reliable, affordable, clean." It also promotes the coalition's website.

Exhibit 2: Proposal outline and one-page summary

The POWER Campaign developed an in-depth outline of its proposed bill, dubbed "The Energy Reliability and Affordability Act of 2001," to submit to potential authors. This four-page document lists the various articles within the bill. The coalition also created a one-page summary, to remind potential authors of the key points within the bill.

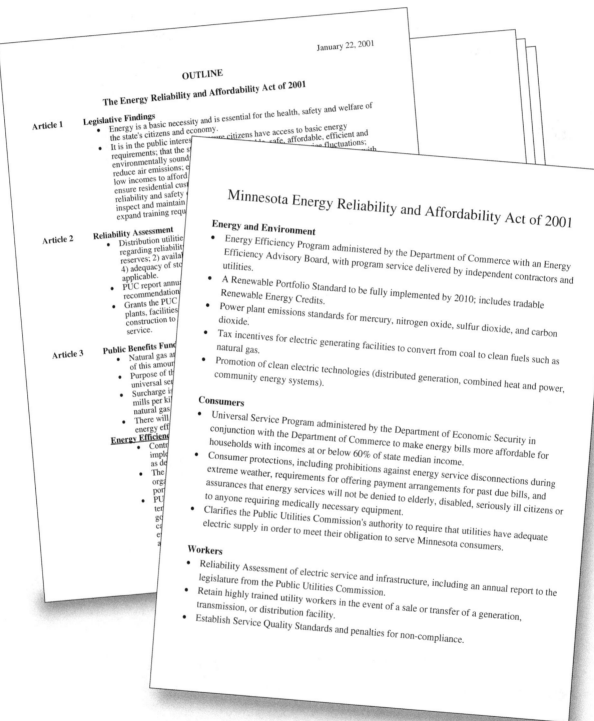

January 22, 2001

OUTLINE
The Energy Reliability and Affordability Act of 2001

Article 1   **Legislative Findings**
• Energy is a basic necessity and is essential for the health, safety and welfare of the state's citizens and economy.
• It is in the public interest that the state's citizens have access to basic energy requirements; that the s... to safe, affordable, efficient and environmentally sound... ...ee fluctuations; ...with reduce air emissions; e... low incomes to afford... ensure residential cus... reliability and safety... inspect and maintain... expand training requ...

Article 2   **Reliability Assessment**
• Distribution utilitie... regarding reliabilit... reserves; 2) availa... 4) adequacy of st... applicable.
• PUC report annu... recommendation...
• Grants the PUC... plants, facilities... construction to... service.

Article 3   **Public Benefits Fund**
• Natural gas a... of this amoun...
• Purpose of th... universal se...
• Surcharge is... mills per ki... natural gas...
• There will... energy eff...

Energy Efficienc...
• Contr... imple... as de...
• The... org... po...
• PU... ter... g... c... e... a...

Minnesota Energy Reliability and Affordability Act of 2001

Energy and Environment
• Energy Efficiency Program administered by the Department of Commerce with an Energy Efficiency Advisory Board, with program service delivered by independent contractors and utilities.
• A Renewable Portfolio Standard to be fully implemented by 2010; includes tradable Renewable Energy Credits.
• Power plant emissions standards for mercury, nitrogen oxide, sulfur dioxide, and carbon dioxide.
• Tax incentives for electric generating facilities to convert from coal to clean fuels such as natural gas.
• Promotion of clean electric technologies (distributed generation, combined heat and power, community energy systems).

Consumers
• Universal Service Program administered by the Department of Economic Security in conjunction with the Department of Commerce to make energy bills more affordable for households with incomes at or below 60% of state median income.
• Consumer protections, including prohibitions against energy service disconnections during extreme weather, requirements for offering payment arrangements for past due bills, and assurances that energy services will not be denied to elderly, disabled, seriously ill citizens or to anyone requiring medically necessary equipment.
• Clarifies the Public Utilities Commission's authority to require that utilities have adequate electric supply in order to meet their obligation to serve Minnesota consumers.

Workers
• Reliability Assessment of electric service and infrastructure, including an annual report to the legislature from the Public Utilities Commission.
• Retain highly trained utility workers in the event of a sale or transfer of a generation, transmission, or distribution facility.
• Establish Service Quality Standards and penalties for non-compliance.

Exhibit 3: POWER Campaign summary sheet

Using its letterhead, the POWER Campaign created a one-page, quick-reading summary of the bill's goals. This sheet can be used with legislators, media representatives, and grassroots supporters, among others. Note how the summary reinforces the key messages "reliable, affordable, clean," both in its headline and in the subheads.

Energy we can live with

AARP, Minnesota State Legislative Committee

American Wind Energy Association

Clean Water Action Alliance

Energy CENTS Coalition

International Brotherhood of Electrical Workers (IBEW)

IUE-CWA Local 1140

Izaak Walton League

Legal Services Advocacy Project

Minnesota Alliance for Progressive Action (MAPA)

Minnesota Community Action Association

Minnesotans for an Energy-Efficient Economy (ME3)

Minnesota Project

Minnesota Public Interest Research Group (MPIRG)

Minnesota Senior Federation

Minnesota Wind Energy Association

North American Water Office

Prairie Island Coalition

Sierra Club North Star Chapter

Southwest Regional Development Commission

Union of Concerned Scientists

Windustry

POWER Campaign
Energy that is
Reliable, Affordable, Clean

Environmental, consumer, and utility worker organizations have joined together in the POWER Campaign (People Organizing for Workers, the Environment and Ratepayers) to improve Minnesota's energy policy. The POWER Campaign is advancing legislation in the 2001 legislative session that promotes a **reliable, affordable and clean** supply of electricity.

POWER calls for a sensible energy policy that encourages cleaner fuel sources and conservation, increases reliability and affordability, protects jobs and worker safety, improves air quality, enhances public health, and ensures consumer protection. POWER members believe that deregulation poses serious threats to workers, consumers and the environment.

Goals for the POWER Campaign include:

Reliable
- Enact worker protections, power safety standards and reliability standards
- Establish and enforce service quality standards
- Require an annual reliability assessment of electric service and infrastructure

Affordable
- Fund low-income bill payment and conservation assistance
- Protect against loss of utility service during extreme weather conditions

Clean
- Increase energy efficiency and conservation
- Meet more of our electricity needs from renewables — at least 10% by 2010
- Promote cleaner energy technologies
- Reduce air emissions from old coal plants

During the 2001 Session, members of the POWER Campaign urge all legislators to plug in to the energy debate and support an energy legacy that keeps the lights on with reliable, affordable and clean energy we can live with.

Exhibit 4: Fact sheets in support of key points

Fact sheets, available from the POWER Campaign's website, build extra support for the campaign. Note that one fact sheet focuses on adequate, reliable energy; another supports affordability; and a third supports cleaner air and enhanced public health. These are the "longhand" versions of the coalition's key messages, "reliable, affordable, clean."

Exhibit 5: Testimonials

To strengthen the legitimacy of its goals and build momentum, the POWER Campaign assembled a collection of quotes from various stakeholder groups, including legislators, coalition members, consumer agencies, labor, health, economic development, and the environment. Testimony from "like minds" can help persuade others to join the cause.

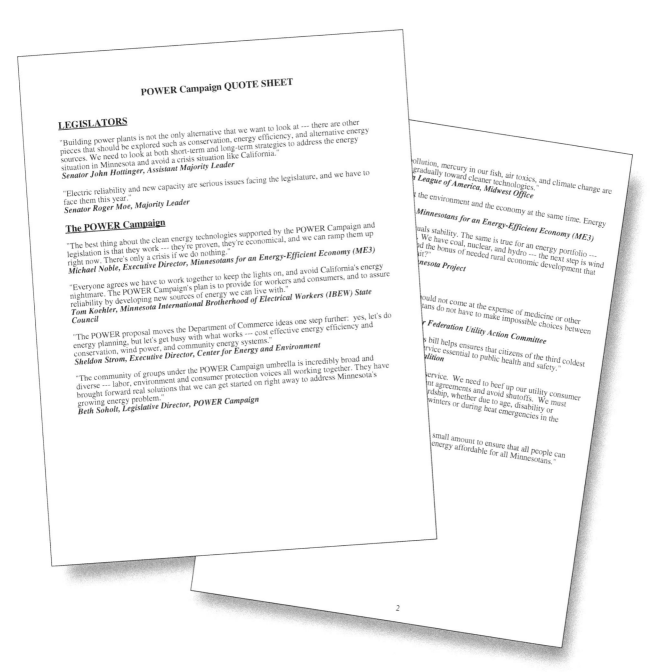

Exhibit 6: Energy Lobby Day

The coalition sponsored a Citizen's Energy "Lobby Day" at the capitol. Supporters were invited to bring others with them (including children). All attending received "talking points" highlighting arguments effective with legislators: "the bill crosses class lines and has proven solutions to real problems"; "energy is unaffordable to 25% of Minnesota's population . . . the costs and the risks to public health and safety are far greater than the costs required to ensure that everyone can maintain continuous energy service"; "I support choosing clean, renewable technologies for the power we need." On the reverse side of the talking points, supporters received tips for writing to legislators and writing letters to the editor.

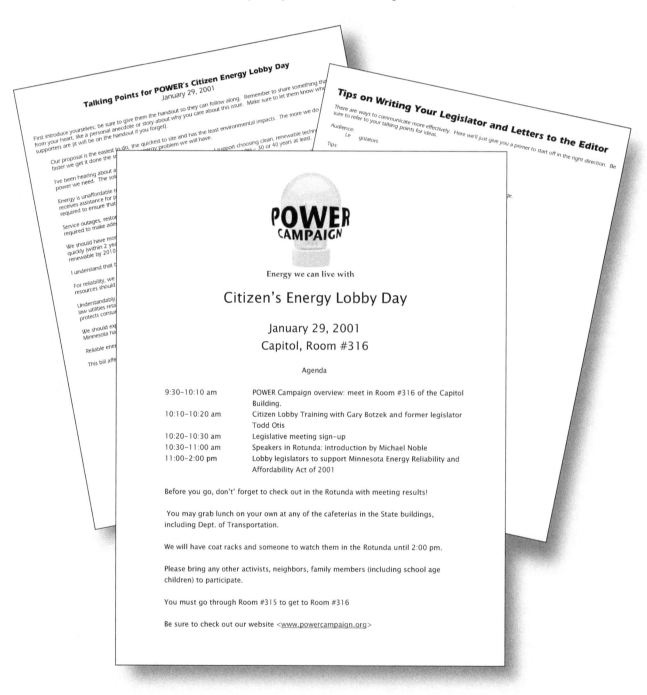

Exhibit 7: Website

The POWER Campaign's website (www.powercampaign.org) provides pages and pages of information, including background, information on coalition members, and updates on recent energy-policy news. Especially helpful are pages to help supporters locate their representative; a supporter can even point-and-click to send an e-mail to a representative. Another page provides a sign-up form for website visitors who want to become actively involved in support of the bill.

Exhibit 8: Media advocacy

The POWER Campaign effectively uses the media to forward its goals. Shown here are a news release and prepared comments for a press conference, and a collection of resulting coverage in both news and opinion sections of Minnesota papers.

NEWS RELEASE

Contact:
Ross Bennett
Communications Coordinator
(651) 645-6159, ext. 25

For Immediate Release

Monday, Jan. 22, 2001

POWER Campaign Announces Legislative Initiative

A major legislative initiative was announced Tuesday by the People Organized for Workers, the Environment and Ratepayers (POWER) Campaign at a State Capitol news conference. The legislative initiative, proposed by a coalition of consumer, labor and environmental groups, calls for a sensible energy policy that promotes a reliable, affordable, clean supply of electricity.

Components of the Energy Reliability and Affordability Act of 2001 include:
- Annual reliability assessment of electric service and infrastructure
- A Universal Service Program to provide bill payment and energy conservation assistance to income eligible consumers
- Tax incentives for electric generating facilities to convert from co cleaner fuels
- Energy Efficiency Program (replaces current CIP program)
- Promotion of clean electric technologies (distributed generation, combined heat and power, community energy sy
- A renewable portfolio standard includin

POWER CAMPAIGN

Energy we can live with

AARP, Minnesota State Legislative Committee

American Wind Energy Association

Clean Water Action Alliance

Energy CENTS Coalition

International Brotherhood of Electrical Workers (IBEW)

IUE-CWA Local 1140

Isaak Walton League

Legal Services Advocacy Project

Minnesota Alliance for Progressive Action (MAPA)

Minnesota Community Action Association

Minnesotans for an Energy-Efficient Economy (ME3)

Minnesota Project

...ve Director, POWER Campaign

...the POWER Campaign News Conference. My name is Beth Soholt and I am the Legislative Director for the

...onored to have several Senators and Representatives in attendance to say a few words about the POWER ...ve Ken Wolf, Senator Jim Metzen, Representative Bill Hilty, and Senator Steve Kelley. We are also pleased ...m the Department of Commerce here.

...out other members of the POWER community who are in attendance today:
...r, ME3
... Center for Energy and Environment
...egal Services Advocacy Project
... Minnesota Senior Federation
...Minnesota State Legislative Committee

...POWER Campaign will be available for comments following the news conference.

...gy has moved to the top of the public policy concerns all across America. Californians can directly attest ...n the reliability of the electric grid is jeopardized, blackouts roll across neighborhoods, and prices ...as prices across the country have sent consumers reeling and energy had become the number one public ...ust realize that we are not immune to these problems. In fact, current projections are that within this ...rt by 2000-3000 megawatts, or enough power for 300,000 households.

...he footsteps of California and we don't have to. In fact, in testimony before the Senate ...and Utilities Committee, State Commerce. Commissioner Bernstein recently stated that what ...ctric reliability, affordability and protection from price spikes. In order to provide reliable, affordable ...ion now, before Minnesota is in the midst of a crisis. The good news I that we have some time, not a .... get started on things we know we can implement

---

Metro/State

TUESDAY, JANUARY 23 ♦ 2001

DAILY LEGISLATIVE REPORT
Coalition hopes to head off power shortage

Advocates want to increase Minnesota energy supplies without building new power plants.

By Robert Whereatt
Star Tribune Staff Writer

A coalition of consumer, labor and environmental groups declared its support Monday for legislation that it said would increase the state's energy supply without new electricity-generating plants.

The groups' representatives said their goal is to make up an expected shortage of 2,000 to 3,000 megawatts — power for about 300,000 homes — within 10 years through energy efficiency, conservation, use of renewable fuels, new technology and the upgrading of existing powe

> Promote the use of solar, wind and hydroelectric power.
> ...security to workers

...plants.
"We
the fo
we do
holt, I
Orga
ronn
POW
ing
sho

aff
tai
Se

effectively has control over which measure eventually passes from his committee and goes to the House floor.

...representatives on
...few power

...bbyist for
...he Legisla-
...uthorizing
...ating facili-
...lines.
...ht it could
...without new
...They were

...his company
...into the ener-
...at to produce
...00 megawatts
...ting plants are
...the power out-
...e Island nucle-
...ng, Minn.
...an be contacted
...rtribune.com

...a future
...ing Northern
...lity on the
...e in south-

Our perspective

Power shortage
Minnesota has time for study

For people who never think twice about flipping on a light switch, this winter has become an unnerving time. California's power grid is about to blow a fuse. A new forecast says that Minnesota could experience electricity shortages within five or six years — less than the time required to build a new power plant. There is even agitation, despite California's example, for Minnesota to join the free-market bandwagon and consider electricity deregulation in the current legislative session.

Gov. Jesse Ventura's advisers are urging a slower course — a year of study, producing recommendations for the 2002 Legislature — and they have it about right. Never mind California. There are too many questions about the *other* 25 states that have tried electricity deregulation for Minnesota to rush into the breach.

Commerce Commissioner James Bernstein has had his staff studying electricity policy in other states for some months. There are lots of lessons

Consumers and economists are still trying to figure out if the deregulation of airlines and long-distance phone service — now 20 years old — worked as well as it should have.

and attractive ways to deliver it to homeowners and businesses.

But there's often a gulf between theory and execution. Consumers and economists are still trying to figure out if the deregulation of airlines and long-distance phone service — now 20 years old — worked as well as it should have. Economist Paul Krugman observes that some industries really are natural monopolies — a single provider is most efficient, or barriers

---

MINNESOTA

Minnesota wind farm is ...up as tourist attraction

...ment activities in the region," Jaunich said.

The facility began taking shape in February seven miles south of Hendricks along Lincoln County Road 1.

Although construction has not been completed, many already have visited the site to catch a glimpse of the unique facility and wind farms nearby.

"Iowa, North and South Dakota, Minnesota, Wisconsin, Illinois, Nebraska, they come from all over, all the surrounding states, even from Canada," Jaunich said. "Even though it's still not completed, they have been taking tours."

To help make it a tourist attraction, the company is planning to lay out native prairie grasses and develop walking trail paths around the facility.

"At some point, we would like to see buffalo on the property," said Mark Hanson, the area manager of the company. "It's just an idea. We don't know how feasible it's going to be."

The company hopes to open the facility to the general public this winter, offering ...rs of the facility and the wind farms, guest rooms and interpretive information on wind energy production.

...e are in the process of planning how ...ve," Jaunich said. "We are going to ...ourselves before we open it to the ...public."

Northern Alternative Energy is one of the wind energy development companies that construct wind turbines along the Buffalo Ridge. For a wind-generated electricity purchase agreement with Xcel Energy Inc., the company is developing

...DRICKS, MINN.
...visitor cen-
...wind-swept,
...Ridge.
...in Minne-
...the Mid-
...the fa-
...rporate
...e base
...rporate

...we
...reg
...ny,
...a

Exhibit 9: PowerPoint presentation

To make its case to the legislature, the POWER Campaign prepared a PowerPoint presentation. Three leaders from organizations in the coalition, each representative of a different type of constituency, delivered the presentation. Note how the campaign's logo, slogan, and key messages are reinforced.

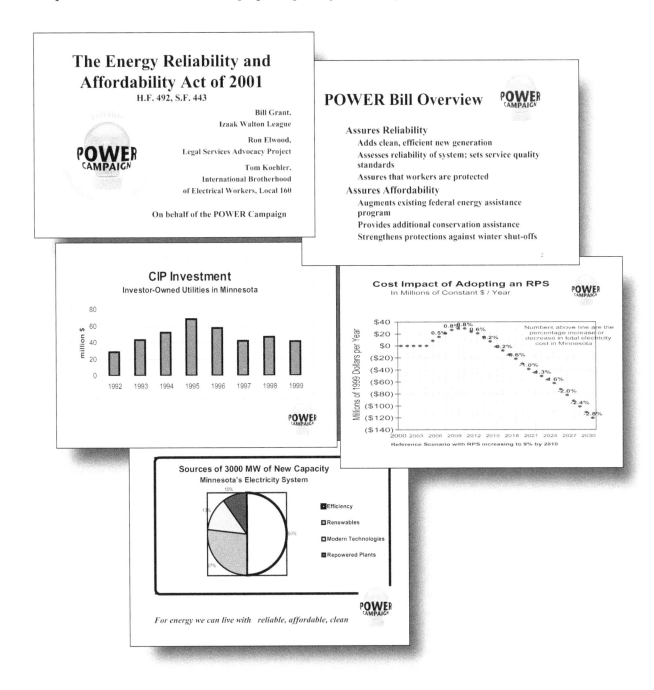

IRS Form 5768

File IRS Form 5768 to be covered by lobbying guidelines in the 1976 Tax Reform Act. Remember that filing this form, often called the "(h) election" because it refers to Section 501(h) of the IRS code, gives your organization clear guidelines for how much lobbying you are allowed to do if you are a 501(c)(3) organization. The IRS has provided clear indication to nonprofits that it favors use of this form.

Form **5768**

(Rev. December 2004)

Department of the Treasury
Internal Revenue Service

Election/Revocation of Election by an Eligible Section 501(c)(3) Organization To Make Expenditures To Influence Legislation

(Under Section 501(h) of the Internal Revenue Code)

For IRS Use Only ▶

Name of organization

Employer identification number

Number and street (or P.O. box no., if mail is not delivered to street address)

Room/suite

City, town or post office, and state

ZIP + 4

1 **Election**—As an eligible organization, we hereby elect to have the provisions of section 501(h) of the Code, relating to expenditures to influence legislation, apply to our tax year ending...and all subsequent tax years until revoked. *(Month, day, and year)*

   Note: *This election must be signed and postmarked within the first taxable year to which it applies.*

2 **Revocation**—As an eligible organization, we hereby revoke our election to have the provisions of section 501(h) of the Code, relating to expenditures to influence legislation, apply to our tax year ending... *(Month, day, and year)*

   Note: *This revocation must be signed and postmarked before the first day of the tax year to which it applies.*

Under penalties of perjury, I declare that I am authorized to make this (check applicable box) ▶ ☐ election ☐ revocation on behalf of the above named organization.

(Signature of officer or trustee)   (Type or print name and title)   (Date)

General Instructions

Section references are to the Internal Revenue Code.

Section 501(c)(3) states that an organization exempt under that section will lose its tax-exempt status and its qualification to receive deductible charitable contributions if a substantial part of its activities are carried on to influence legislation. Section 501(h), however, permits certain eligible 501(c)(3) organizations to elect to make limited expenditures to influence legislation. An organization making the election will, however, be subject to an excise tax under section 4911 if it spends more than the amounts permitted by that section. Also, the organization may lose its exempt status if its lobbying expenditures exceed the permitted amounts by more than 50% over a 4-year period. For any tax year in which an election under section 501(h) is in effect, an electing organization must report the actual and permitted amounts of its lobbying expenditures and grass roots expenditures (as defined in section 4911(c)) on its annual return required under section 6033. See Schedule A (Form 990 or Form 990-EZ). Each electing member of an affiliated group must report these amounts for both itself and the affiliated group as a whole.

To make or revoke the election, enter the ending date of the tax year to which the election or revocation applies in item **1** or **2**, as applicable, and sign and date the form in the spaces provided.

Eligible Organizations.—A section 501(c)(3) organization is permitted to make the election if it is not a disqualified organization (see below) and is described in:

1. Section 170(b)(1)(A)(ii) (relating to educational institutions),
2. Section 170(b)(1)(A)(iii) (relating to hospitals and medical research organizations),
3. Section 170(b)(1)(A)(iv) (relating to organizations supporting government schools),
4. Section 170(b)(1)(A)(vi) (relating to organizations publicly supported by charitable contributions),
5. Section 509(a)(2) (relating to organizations publicly supported by admissions, sales, etc.), or
6. Section 509(a)(3) (relating to organizations supporting certain types of public charities other than those section 509(a)(3) organizations that support section 501(c)(4), (5), or (6) organizations).

Disqualified Organizations.—The following types of organizations are not permitted to make the election:

a. Section 170(b)(1)(A)(i) organizations (relating to churches),

b. An integrated auxiliary of a church or of a convention or association of churches, or

c. A member of an affiliated group of organizations if one or more members of such group is described in **a** or **b** of this paragraph.

Affiliated Organizations.—Organizations are members of an affiliated group of organizations only if **(1)** the governing instrument of one such organization requires it to be bound by the decisions of the other organization on legislative issues, or **(2)** the governing board of one such organization includes persons (i) who are specifically designated representatives of another such organization or are members of the governing board, officers, or paid executive staff members of such other organization, and (ii) who, by aggregating their votes, have sufficient voting power to cause or prevent action on legislative issues by the first such organization.

For more details, see section 4911 and section 501(h).

Note: *A private foundation (including a private operating foundation) is not an eligible organization.*

Where To File.—Mail Form 5768 to the Internal Revenue Service Center, Ogden, UT 84201-0027.

Cat. No. 12125M   Form **5768** (Rev. 12-2004)

Worksheets

Worksheets are also available online to purchasers of this book. To use the online worksheets, visit http://www.turnerpublishing.com/lobbying-and-advocacy-handbook-worksheets.

After completing this checklist, circulate it to all members of the planning team prior to the first meeting.

1. Identify members of the planning team.

2. Set a schedule of meetings.

Meeting 1:

Meeting 2:

Meeting 3:

Meeting 4:

Meeting 5:

Meeting 6:

3. Write the "charge" or "job description" for the planning team.

*There are two parts to this assessment. **Part A** looks at the substance of your organization's public policy objectives. **Part B** looks at your organization's current capacity to do the work.*

Use this assessment to create a public policy readiness profile. This profile will help you to see how prepared you are to do this work effectively and examine your capacity to do the work. Refer to it as you complete planning and assess your first months of policy work. Mark your progress along the way. Remember that your response marks a starting point. Consider this a tool to inspire a sense of direction.

Part A: Public Policy Objectives

1. What are your issues?

In the context of our mission, goals, and existing work, we have identified issues and objectives that can be furthered by engaging in debates about public policy and specific legislation.

            YES   NO   IN PROGRESS

Our public policy issues are:

2. What are you already doing to address these issues?

We have organizational involvement and expertise in the public policy areas we most want to influence.

            YES   NO   DEVELOPING

Expertise and experience are demonstrated in

Programs:

(continued)

Services:

Research:

Education, awareness, community outreach:

Advocacy:

Lobbying:

3. Where are your issues decided and debated?

    ❏ Congress   ❏ Court

    ❏ State Legislature   ❏ Don't know

    ❏ County Board   ❏ Other:_____

    ❏ City Council

    ❏ State Administrative Agency

    ❏ City or County Agency

(continued)

Arenas for influence where we have an interest in shaping policy decisions are:

4. What policy changes do you want?

We know the actions or changes that are needed in legislation to address the problems and opportunities that we have identified in our priority issue areas.

YES   NO   SOME

Desired changes in laws, ordinances, or budget and tax policy are:

5. Will you be reactive or proactive?

We will be proposing policy changes and need to prepare a campaign to introduce and lobby for a new idea.

YES   NO

We will be responding to an existing legislative proposal or another group's efforts by supporting it.

YES   NO

(continued)

We will be lobbying to stop a measure that we think will have negative impact on our community or the people we serve.

        YES   NO

6. Will you be lobbying onetime only, or are you in it for the long haul?

        ONETIME ONLY   ONGOING COMPONENT

Check the approaches compatible with your organization's strengths and objectives:

- ❏ Background research and information gathering to "make the case"
- ❏ Public education and awareness
- ❏ Responding to issue alerts by organizations taking the lead on issues
- ❏ Direct lobbying of elected officials
- ❏ Mobilizing grassroots support
- ❏ Working with other organizations in a coalition or an informal alliance
- ❏ Media advocacy
- ❏ Other: _____

Part B: Organizational Capacity for Public Policy Work

1. Who is the organizational champion of public policy work, and how deep is the organization's commitment?

The persons serving as key conveners of the discussions about policy work and the stewards of organizational readiness for policy work are

Name: _____ Title: _____

Name: _____ Title: _____

Name: _____ Title: _____

We have begun the organizational discussion about why and how to do policy work.

        YES   NO   IN THE SEEDING PHASE

The board of directors has made a commitment to policy work.

        YES   NO   IN DISCUSSION

Our organization's staff share a commitment to policy work.

        YES   NO   A FEW SKEPTICS

(continued)

Members, clients, stakeholders, and other supporters are ready to go.

YES   NO   NEED TO TALK TO THEM

2. Do you have a public policy plan?

Our organization is engaging in a planning process to decide how to incorporate public policy work into our organizational strategy and work plan.

YES   NO   PLAN TO

3. Who's doing what and when?

We have designated a person to coordinate our policy planning and work.

YES   NO   RECRUITING

The role of the board is clear.

YES   NO   WORKING ON IT

Staff roles are clear.

YES   NO   WORKING ON IT

We have a "rapid response" team ready to make decisions and set the course for action when we are in the midst of fast-moving policy action.

YES   NO   WORKING ON IT

We have decided to form an ongoing public policy advisory committee and its role has been defined.

YES   NO

4. Where is the voice of the community?

We have systems in place to educate, inform, and mobilize our members and our constituencies in support of our issues.

YES   NO   WORKING ON IT

(continued)

5. Do you understand legislative processes and structures?

We know how our state (or local) government moves an idea through the legislative process to become law.

YES   NO   LEARNING

We know the key structures (house, assembly, commission, committee, political caucuses) and the players (leadership, members, staff) whom we will need to influence.

YES   NO   LEARNING

6. What are you prepared to do now?

We are ready to

❑   Compile and present the information that makes the case for our position
❑   Identify legislative proposals that affect our issues
❑   Identify decision makers and our supporters who are their constituents
❑   Monitor the introduction and progress of bills
❑   Record all of our action on our issues
❑   Inform all interested people as the debate progresses
❑   Issue calls to action to people ready to act
❑   Record all press coverage of our issue
❑   Maintain a record of our activity

7. The best things are not always free. What resources will you commit to policy work?

We have budgeted for staff time, materials development, and information dissemination.

YES   NO   PLANNING FOR NEXT YEAR

8. Media matters. Are you camera-ready?

We have included a media-advocacy component to our lobbying plan.

YES   NO   WORKING ON IT

9. Nonprofits can and should lobby, but do you know the rules?

We understand the IRS rules governing 501(c)(3) lobbying and reporting.

YES   NO   WORKING ON IT

We understand the registration and reporting requirements our state has in place.

YES   NO   WORKING ON IT

Record your mission statement. Then brainstorm a public policy vision and related goals for the organization. What will change in three to five years as a result of your public policy efforts? What broad goals will get you there?

Your mission statement:

Your vision statement for public policy work:

Your broad public policy goals:

Issues and priorities will change as the policy landscape changes from year to year, sometimes from day to day. Identify the criteria that your organization will use to decide whether or not to advocate on an issue. Be sure that your criteria keep you close to the core of your mission and goals.

Based on our mission and goals, we will select public policy issues and action strategies that address the following principles:

On the table below, list those issues currently in discussion, those anticipated over the next year, and those you wish to initiate. Then place a check (✓) if the issue fits with your mission, goals, and criteria.

	Serves mission	Fits goals	Consistent with criteria	Ranking priorities
Issues already in discussion				
Issues to anticipate				
Issues to initiate				

List in priority order your selected issues, policy objectives, and positions.

Issues	Policy objectives	Positions

For each issue identified in Worksheet 5, note the arenas of influence where your lobbying efforts will occur. Also note any actions you've taken so far.

Issue	Arena of current debate (or likely arena for new initiatives)	Action to date

This worksheet will help you gain an overview of the legislative arena. Keep it as a record of sources of information.

1. Locate information resources.

Identify resources provided by the information offices at the state legislature, county commission, or city council:

Website: _____

Explore the website to find:

1) How to find your legislative district

2) The composition of the legislative bodies, house and senate: numbers, political parties

3) Ways to access information about and contacts for each legislator

4) How to follow a bill

5) How the house and senate committees are structured

6) How to sign up for schedules of committee hearings and floor sessions

7) How to subscribe to information and updates from the house and senate or specific committees

8) How to find the rules that govern the process

9) Maps of the capitol complex (and parking!)

10) All of the information sources available at the legislature

11) Protocol for providing testimony

12) How to access live coverage and archives of meetings online or on TV

(continued)

Keep a record of bulletins and alerts: What information is available on a regular basis to provide updates on schedules and legislative activity, and how do you get it?

Title: _____

Topic: _____

How to subscribe: _____

Title: _____

Topic: _____

How to subscribe: _____

Title: _____

Topic: _____

How to subscribe: _____

Webcast, televised (cable/closed circuit), or archived coverage of hearings and meetings: Does it exist, where are schedules posted, how and where can it be viewed?

_____

_____

_____

Contact office for TV and other media services:

_____

_____

_____

_____

Ombudsperson or clerk who provides information to the public:

Name: _____

Contact information: _____

Name: _____

Contact information: _____

(continued)

2. Understand the legislative process.

Use this portion of the worksheet to create a working record of your state's legislative process, powers, and budget. The work you do now can be handed on to others who join the advocacy efforts at a later date.

a. How does an idea or a bill get introduced? Describe the specific steps in the process. (For example, a bill is introduced, then it goes to a policy committee for debate, then it goes to a finance committee if costs are involved, and so on.)

b. What are the committees in your selected arenas of influence?

c. When are the opportunities in the process for public hearings and comments?

d. Are all meetings open to the public? If not, which meetings are open?

e. What are the key decision-making points in the process?

(continued)

3. Understand legislative powers.

    a. Where are the centers of power in this legislative body? Who has power and at what stages in the process are key decisions made?

    b. How important is the policy committee? The committee chair?

    c. How important are the political leaders of the house and senate?

    d. How much can be changed by the full house or senate after a bill passes through committees?

    e. What influence does the executive or administrative agency have?

(continued)

4. Understand the budget.

    a. How are budgets set?

    b. What is the role of administrative agencies and the governor in making budget recommendations to the legislature?

    c. What are the steps in the budget process? (Staff recommends budget? Governor proposes budget? Legislators present budget options? Sequence of committee hearings? Public hearings?)

5. Know the legislative calendar.

(continued)

Finally, find out and record the dates for legislative activity. You'll need these when you begin creating a work plan.

a. Date session begins: _____

b. Schedule of committee meetings:

    _____

    _____

    _____

    _____

    _____

    _____

    _____

c. Deadlines for bills to be introduced: _____

d. Timeline for budget issues to be decided: _____

e. Deadlines for committees to hear bills: _____

f. Timelines for public testimony: _____

g. Planned recesses, vacation: _____

h. Veto timelines: _____

i. Date of adjournment: _____

Record the names of the people in the following roles for the current legislative year. Update as new officials take office. Keep this information in a public policy guide for your organization.

State legislature

House or assembly speaker: _____

House or assembly minority leader: _____

Senate majority leader: _____

Senate minority leader: _____

Record and maintain a list of chairpersons and key members of committees that will vote on your legislative issues. List the name of the committee, the chairperson, the committee staff, and the committee members.

State agency directors and key managers

These are the people who provide information to legislators, make rules, administer contracts and grants, and propose legislation that nonprofits care about.

(continued)

Local government

County board chair: _____

County board members:

County agency directors and key staff:

City council chair:_____

City council members:

Read and discuss the following strategies. Select those that best fit your issues, objectives, and positions within the arenas you want to influence.

Direct lobbying strategies and tactics

Build positive relationships and trust with elected officials.

❏ Learn more about them, including their official responsibilities and policy priorities.

❏ Give them literature about your organization and policy objectives.

❏ Meet with them to tell them about your organization, your programs and services, your areas of expertise, and your policy positions.

❏ Put them on your e-mail and mailing lists to receive news and updates.

❏ Invite them to your site to see your work and meet your supporters.

❏ Give awards to honor the work that they do.

❏ Other ideas:

Monitor the legislative process and identify activities that affect your issues.

❏ Read materials produced by the legislative body to track bill introductions and action on bills.

❏ Monitor online reports of bill introductions, committee hearings scheduled, and committee and floor action.

❏ Have a person present in committee meetings to track the debate if feasible or watch webcast and archived committee hearings.

❏ Join existing coalitions or other organizations that are monitoring the issues that you care about.

❏ Monitor media coverage of legislative issues.

❏ Other ideas:

Provide expertise to elected officials.

❏ Provide solid research and background information on the need or opportunity that you want to address.

❏ Help propose legislation. Verbally and in writing, present ideas for legislation to elected officials. Make the case for the idea. Include the desired changes in the existing or proposed law, the rationale for the change, and the desired outcomes.

❏ Provide research that supports the position you have taken on new legislation or on an existing proposal.

❏ Brief elected officials in person at their offices with information that you have.

❏ Be available to elected officials to provide expertise as the bill is developed and as they present their positions in committee meetings, caucus meetings, and floor debates.

(continued)

❑ Conduct additional research as requested by elected officials.

❑ Identify nonprofit allies and work with them in efforts ranging from coordinated lobbying campaigns to formal coalitions to provide information on a shared priority.

❑ Research opposing viewpoints and be prepared to present the other side's view to elected officials so that they can anticipate the points that will be raised in a debate.

❑ Testify in legislative hearings as expert witnesses.

❑ Work with legislators throughout the legislative process to amend proposals and find compromise positions that are reasonable and further your cause.

❑ Other ideas:

Persuade legislators to support your position.

❑ Carry out a strategy that will gain media coverage of your issue and positive messages in support of your position.

❑ Write e-mails and letters and make phone calls to key decision makers.

❑ Attend hearings and testify in support of your position.

❑ Involve people who are affected by the issue being debated; ask them to offer their stories and perspective in formal legislative testimony.

❑ Meet with legislators—first, committee members and leaders and, eventually, all members of the legislature—to persuade them to adopt your position based on the merits of the case and its importance to the people you serve.

❑ Other ideas:

Grassroots mobilizing strategies and tactics

Build your base of supporters.

❑ Identify constituencies that will be affected by decisions about your issues.

❑ Build lists of potential supporters, both individuals and organizations.

❑ Educate potential supporters about the issue through

    ❑ Informational briefings

    ❑ Newsletter articles

    ❑ Web postings

    ❑ Social media

    ❑ Individual conversations

    ❑ Other:

❑ Invite potential supporters to sign on to your effort; as they do so, identify the actions they will take, such as making calls, sending e-mails, meeting with legislators, writing letters to the newspaper, testifying, and participating in rallies.

❑ Other ideas:

(continued)

Mobilize your supporters.

- ❏ Create an ongoing flow of information and updates on the progress of your policy efforts through, e-mail, social media, or website postings. Include calls to action as appropriate.

- ❏ Maintain a system for asking supporters to act. Use phone calls, e-mail, social media, and other alerts that explain which decision makers to contact, how to reach them, when to contact them, and what to say.

- ❏ Provide training for supporters in effective lobbying tactics.

- ❏ Create events that allow supporters to contact elected officials easily, such as "Day on the Hill" events or rallies.

- ❏ Ask supporters to allow reporters to interview them and use their experiences and concerns in media coverage of the issue.

- ❏ Other ideas:

Remember, executive branch officials have extraordinary powers to both influence and ultimately implement legislative initiatives. You do not want to leave these players out of your advocacy efforts.

Strategy	Yes	No	To Be Developed
I have familiarized myself with the Governor's political agenda and can articulate how our policy piece supports the executive branch's vision and goals.			
I know the name of the staff person in the Governor's office who has expertise in our issue area.			
I have met face-to-face with the Governor's policy aide assigned to our issue area.			
I have provided research, data, and stories regarding our issue to the Governor's staff.			
I have identified legislative champions on our issue who will have influence with the Governor.			
I understand which state agency has jurisdiction over our issue area.			
I have provided written information and/or asked to meet with state agency staff responsible for implementing rules related to our issue area.			
I have offered to provide testimony on our issue when it supports state-agency priorities or have offered to work with state staff to seek common ground when it doesn't.			
I have explored opportunities to serve on state boards, commissions, and task forces related to our issue and area of expertise.			
I have sought out the technical knowledge needed to assist state rulemaking staff in writing regulations that ensure meeting the intended purpose and enforcement of passed legislation.			

The goal of this exercise is to identify the most effective media to use to reach each of your audiences. Identify and write your message goal and the audience you want to reach with that specific message. Then circle the media vehicles that are mostly likely to reach the specific audience. For example, when you want to reach your own board, staff, clients, and donors with your position on an issue and the rationale for taking the position, you might reach that targeted and affiliated audience with a phone call, and/or at a board meeting, and/or with an e-mail. To reach the media and a broader public-affairs community, you might use phone calls, a press release, meetings, website postings, e-mail, and social media. Use the sample below as a guideline but adapt it for your issue campaign.

Organizational Assessment:

❑ Does your organization have a media strategy?

❑ Is the media plan discussed as part of the overall lobbying plan?

❑ Do you revise the media plan on a regular basis as your lobbying campaign evolves?

Organizational Infrastructure:

❑ Do you have a staff person who is responsible for carrying out the media plan and coordinating all the media efforts in your organization?

❑ Do you have a planning calendar of key lobbying events? Are media goals and plans included in the lobbying planning calendar?

❑ Has your organization identified its primary, formal spokespersons?

❑ Do your spokespersons need media training and preparation? Have you determined how they will get it?

❑ Have your board and staff prepared a plan for "rapid response" to an opportunity or a crisis that presents itself with little warning? Is there a "team" that can respond quickly?

❑ Is the chain of decision making for media statements clearly designated and understood by everyone within the organization?

❑ Does your public policy budget have a media component?

Media Systems:

❑ Are your media lists up to date, complete with names of editors, reporters, or producers for all media outlets you plan to use?

❑ Do you know deadlines, work hours, and preferred communications modes for key people who work on your public policy issues?

❑ Do your lists distinguish types of coverage: news, feature, editorial, columns, calendars?

❑ Do you have a file for keeping all relevant media coverage and for a complete record of coverage of your organization's work?

❑ Are you in regular contact with the editor and reporters you have designated as key contacts?

(continued)

Is your information media ready?

❑ Do you have accurate, concise, interesting information about your organization: its mission, history, programs, and services?

❑ Have you shaped a clear message and talking points for the policy issue you plan to raise?

❑ Have you held introductory meetings with members of the press who are likely to cover your organization and issues?

❑ Do you maintain an information base that is a valuable resource to the press, including data, stories, and a portfolio of real people who are willing to talk to the press?

(continued)

State your message. Identify the audience you aim to reach. Circle the ways to reach them. What media do they use?

Message	Mode of Communication	Audience
Position on an issue and the rationale	Newsletter Direct mail Phone call Meeting Report on issue Press release Press conference Street theater Website posting E-mail Blog Social-media posting Paid media advertising Other	Organization's board, staff, clients, and donors
Making the case and building public support for your position on an issue	Newsletter Direct mail Phone call Meeting Report on issue Press release Press conference Street theater Website posting E-mail Blog Social-media posting Paid media advertising Other	Opinion shapers: journalists, academic experts, and other community leaders
Outreach on the issue to engage supporters who will work with you to influence decision makers	Newsletter Direct mail Phone call Meeting Report on issue Press release Press conference Street theater Website posting E-mail Blog Social-media posting Paid media advertising Other	Potential allies: organizations in the nonprofit sector

(continued)

Outreach on the issue to engage supporters who will work with you to influence decision makers	Newsletter Direct mail Phone call Meeting Report on issue Press release Press conference Street theater Website posting E-mail Blog Social-media posting Paid media advertising Other	Potential allies: governmental agencies
Fundraising request to support your advocacy capacity	Newsletter Direct mail Phone call Meeting Report on issue Press release Press conference Street theater Website posting E-mail Blog Social-media posting Paid media advertising Other	Individual donors, foundations
Request to an elected official to support your policy position on a specific piece of legislation	Newsletter Direct mail Phone call Meeting Report on issue Press release Press conference Street theater Website posting E-mail Blog Social-media posting Paid media advertising Other	Elected officials, staff

(continued)

Outreach to the media with dates and stories to support your policy position	Newsletter Direct mail Phone call Meeting Report on issue Press release Press conference Street theater Website posting E-mail Blog Social-media posting Paid media advertising Other	Newspapers, radio, TV
Request direction on a proposed amendment to your position during legislative debates	Newsletter Direct mail Phone call Meeting Report on issue Press release Press conference Street theater Website posting E-mail Blog Social-media posting Paid media advertising Other	Rapid-response team, board
Update supporters on outcomes of a legislative hearing Respond to an attack by opponents to strengthen support for your position and clarify facts Call for action by supporters Other	Newsletter Direct mail Phone call Meeting Report on issue Press release Press conference Street theater Website posting E-mail Blog Social-media posting Paid media advertising Other	Supporters, board, staff, allies Board, staff, supporters, journalists, general public Organized base of supporters who have been prepared to act Other

(continued)

Respond to an attack by opponents to strengthen support for your position and clarify facts	Newsletter Direct mail Phone call Meeting Report on issue Press release Press conference Street theater Website posting E-mail Blog Social-media posting Paid media advertising Other	Board, staff, supporters, journalists, general public
Call for action by supporters	Newsletter Direct mail Phone call Meeting Report on issue Press release Press conference Street theater Website posting E-mail Blog Social-media posting Paid media advertising Other	Organized base of supporters who have been prepared to act
Other	Newsletter Direct mail Phone call Meeting Report on issue Press release Press conference Street theater Website posting E-mail Blog Social-media posting Paid media advertising Other	Other

Record below the positions you will create, the individuals who will fill those positions, and their responsibilities. Remember, in most organizations, the positions are incorporated into existing jobs.

Position	Person/title	Job description/Role in public policy
Board Chair		
Board		
Executive Director		

(continued)

Position	Person/title	Job description/Role in public policy
Public Policy Advisory Committee		
Public Policy Coordinator		
Lobbyist		

(continued)

Position	Person/title	Job description/Role in public policy
Organizer		
Communications and Media Specialist		
Rapid-Response Team		

(continued)

Position	Person/title	Job description/Role in public policy
Spokesperson(s) for the organization on public policy issues		
Other staff (researcher, support staff, program staff with lead responsibility in key issue areas)		

Record below the individuals who have key responsibilities for decisions in your organization. This information will become essential in the fast-changing legislative environment. Keep it as part of your public policy guide.

Decisions to be made	Key decision makers
Adopt the organization's policy goals and strategies	
Shape the organization's policy agenda	
Set the organization's formal policy priorities	
Assign responsibilities to board	
Assign responsibilities to staff	
Allocate financial resources	
Manage organizational activity in carrying out public policy activities	
Approve public statements about the organization's position	
Approve positions in negotiations with elected officials when issues are in hurried stages of debate	
Other:	
Other:	
Other:	

Create a preliminary budget for your policy work. Determine the amount of time that each staff person will dedicate to public policy work and budget the required amount of salary and benefits. Plan for all related program activities, such as printing, postage, travel, and meetings. Don't forget administrative costs.

Item	Cost
Personnel: Salaries	
Executive director (% of time x salary) _____	_____
Public policy coordinator (% of time x salary) _____	_____
Lobbyist (% of time x salary, or contract fee) _____	_____
Support staff (% of time x salary) _____	_____
Other as determined by roles identified in your nonprofit_____	_____
Personnel: Benefits (% your nonprofit applies)_____	_____
Total Personnel Costs _____	_____
Public Policy Program Activities	
Technology: hardware and software, as determined by plans to reach elected officials and mobilize supporters _____	_____
Website _____	_____
Social media _____	_____
E-mail _____	_____
Telephone _____	_____
Printing, as determined by plans for educational materials and alerts _____	_____
Postage _____	_____
Travel	
Board and public policy advisory committee travel to meetings _____	_____
Staff travel _____	_____
Public policy advisory committee meetings (space, food) _____	_____
Events (Day on the Hill, policy training, briefings) _____	_____
Administrative (% of organizational administrative budget as determined by % of overall work that is public policy)_____	_____
Other_____	_____
Total Program Costs _____	_____
_____ **TOTAL**	

Gather together Worksheets 1 through 12. Compile and edit them into the format in this worksheet. Route the draft to the rest of the planning team, rewrite as necessary, then seek the team's approval to send the plan to the board for approval. Save this as part of your public policy guide.

I.   Organizational mission

II.   Public policy vision and goals

A. Vision

In three years, as a result of our public policy efforts:

(continued)

B. Goals

We have the following public policy goals:

III. Issues

For each issue, state the objective, the arena of influence where that issue can be addressed, and how the organization will lobby. Identify the roles and responsibilities of staff, board, and volunteers in carrying out those lobbying activities.

Many organizations choose a single issue for their primary focus. Often, this is the best approach, especially for an organization just beginning its policy efforts. In your plan, focus on just the one issue that will dominate your work in the next year. If you plan to address multiple issues, indicate which ones will get the emphasis in your work and which you might simply monitor.

Issue 1

Objective:

(continued)

Arenas of influence:

Issue 1 work schedule:

Tasks/Activities	Who	By when

(continued)

Issue 1 work schedule *(continued)*:

Tasks/Activities	Who	By when

(continued)

Issue 2

Objective:

Arenas of influence:

(continued)

Issue 2 work schedule:

Tasks/Activities	Who	By when

(continued)

Issue 3

Objective:

Arenas of influence:

(continued)

Issue 3 work schedule:

Tasks/Activities	Who	By when

(continued)

IV. Organizational infrastructure

A. Roles and responsibilities

Insert and edit your completed Worksheet 12: Roles and Responsibilities.

B. Decision-making authority

Insert and edit your completed Worksheet 13: Decision Making. (An organizational chart for your public policy work could be included here to illustrate the roles and responsibilities of the people involved and the lines of decision-making authority.)

C. Resources needed

Insert and edit your completed Worksheet 14: Identify Resources.

In the work plan, include Worksheets 12, 13, and 14 and conclude with a narrative explanation of how the organization can proceed to accept the work plan, assign responsibilities outlined in the plan, and launch the effort.

V. Conclusion

Use this checklist to keep track of your progress in implementing your public policy work plan.

Task	Done	By whom
Roles assigned		
Roles for board and staff are defined and assigned as identified in Worksheets 10 and 11.		
Public policy advisory committee activated		
Training events		
Board, staff, and volunteer briefing		
Potential lobbyists trained		
Other training events (list):		
Systems established		
Outreach systems		
Supporters database		
Officials database, including biographies		
Key audience contact systems		
Social media		
E-mail		
Website		
Other audience contact systems (list):		

(continued)

Task	Done	By whom
Files of your lobbying materials for past, current, and anticipated issues		
Position papers		
Research reports		
Action alerts		
Files on legislative activity		
News releases		
Press-coverage clippings		
Correspondence		
Records of meetings with elected officials and staff		
Other files (list):		
Organization has public policy folders well organized, built into company system, and accessible to all policy staff		
Systems for tracking external information on legislation and issues		
Helpful websites bookmarked		
Subscriptions in place for informational resources from government		
Subscriptions in place for alerts from other organizations		
Reference materials		
Financial resources		
Need identified		
Resources secured		
Plans for additional resources		

Give copies of this worksheet to all employees who may be involved in lobbying work. Collect them every two weeks to compile an ongoing record of lobbying expenditures.

Employee Timesheet

Name: _____

Title:_____

Pay period:_____

Multiplier (Hourly cost of wages and benefits):_____

Direct lobbying

Note: *Direct lobbying* consists of any activities (and related expenses) you undertake to directly influence legislators and their staff or to influence executive branch officials and their staff, regarding how they act on specific legislation. Direct lobbying includes asking our members, defined as anyone giving a nominal amount of time or money to our organization, to ask legislators to vote a particular way on a bill. In the chart below, describe the activity, the date, the number of hours, and any related expenses (parking, travel, and so forth).

Activity:	Date:	Hours:	Expenses: (materials, postage, travel)

Total staff costs: (Total hours) x (Hourly wage and benefits multiplier): _____

Total expenses: _____

TOTAL direct-lobbying expenditures (staff costs plus expenses): _____

(continued)

Grassroots lobbying

Note: *Grassroots lobbying* consists of any activities (and related expenses) you undertake to ask the public to influence legislation by contacting elected and appointed officials and their staff. In the chart below, describe the activity, the date, the number of hours, and any related expenses (materials copied, phone charges, and so forth).

Activity:	Date:	Hours:	Expenses: (materials, postage, travel)

Total staff costs: (Total hours) x (Hourly wage and benefits multiplier): _____

Total expenses: _____

TOTAL grassroots-lobbying expenditures (staff costs plus expenses): _____

Evaluating Nonprofit Advocacy

As nonprofit advocacy becomes a component of many organizations' mission-related work, board members, program managers, donors, and other stakeholders need to understand what works well. Accountability is important in all nonprofit program work. While evaluating advocacy presents some unique challenges, it is important to the development of best practices and policy impact. Set goals and objectives, measure progress, analyze lessons to be learned from your findings, and use evaluation to shape and improve the next cycle of policy advocacy.

Evaluating advocacy requires attention to two key aspects of your organization's work: policy and process. Nonprofit's need to ask: Did we advance our policy objectives? Did we meet our objectives for how we actually did the work of building our capacity for policy work, organizing, advocating, and engaging in media advocacy? The questions about capacity and process are most important to long-term engagement in policy. Winning is good, and we always want to achieve the desired policy outcomes. Nevertheless, in assessing policy, whether or not the legislation that you support or oppose is resolved in the way that you desire is not always the best measure of your accomplishment. There are too many external factors that impact the outcome of a policy debate. These include the fiscal landscape. Your proposal may simply cost too much to be funded in this cycle. Or you may be seeking support that is not timely.

Many state legislatures specify the time during which certain kinds of issues can be passed. Bonding proposals, for instance, may be done every other year. And many states have budget periods longer or shorter than one year. If you have a proposal that isn't supposed to get passed during the current time period, you still can consider yourself a winner if you get the right language and right sponsors behind your idea so it can pass when the right time comes. Other external factors include the political landscape. If the majority of those who are voting on your measure in the house and or senate are loyal to an agenda, partisan or other, that does not favor your position, you may not be able to get the votes needed for passage. Many groups are seeing this factor limit their ability to support increased revenue or election reforms. In instances in which you have legislative support, a governor may oppose your position and exercise veto power.

You get the point: whether or not your measure passes or fails is not the only or best measure of your organizing, media, or lobbying strengths.

So what should you measure?

All nonprofits, and the boards and donors who hold them accountable, should focus on measurable objectives in two key areas:

1. **Capacity building.** Did your organizations build its capacity to advocate effectively in a sustained way? Set objectives each legislative cycle for your internal growth in each of the areas addressed in this book in Worksheet 1: Public Policy Readiness Inventory. That document lays out goals to aim for in building capacity and doing advocacy and organizing well. Measure growth (or loss) in:

   - your board's commitment to policy work
   - board participation in the process
   - thoughtfulness and use of planning for advocacy
   - whether you follow your established processes for setting a policy agenda
   - the development of your internal and external communications systems
   - meeting objectives for use of social media
   - engagement of members, constituents, and targeted partners
   - completion and quality of planned research
   - management of lists and information-dissemination tools
   - quality and participation in training
   - ability to follow policies for organizational decision making about advocacy actions

Identify specific and measurable ways in which you want to ramp up your work in each area that is important to your advocacy infrastructure and base your evaluation on how close you are to meeting each objective.

2. **Advocacy actions.** Again, begin each cycle of work with a plan that includes measurable objectives. You may set out to form a coalition of nonprofits that share your concern on an issue, or you may intend to add value to an existing collabora-

tive effort. You can then assess how close to your objective you have come. Some of the components of advocacy for which you can set objectives include:

- number of contacts you have to recruit, update, and engage supporters
- number of allies whose support and action have been part of your issue campaign
- number of people engaged in activities that you host—from lobby trainings to issue briefings to a Day on the Hill
- number of contacts with elected officials and staff
- number of elected officials who are reached by a constituent
- number of elected officials who respect and use the information that you provide
- number and quality of social-media–based outreach and responses
- numbers and nature of media stories about your issue, organization, and campaign

Your evaluation work must, of necessity, be both quantitative and qualitative in nature.

The measurable objectives suggested above and others that are pertinent to your particular work can be addressed quantitatively, for the most part. You can identify that your organization has officially adopted a policy plan, that your board members have participated in the process, that you have a written plan for your issue campaign, that you had increasing numbers of supporters at events and exceeded your expectations.

But much of policy work—effectiveness of communications; the development of good working relationships with partners, elected officials and their staff, the media; the satisfaction levels of your supporters and partners with your strategy and efforts; the wisdom of your strategy—requires qualitative assessments. This work can be done with interviews, surveys, and focus groups, and this is often the most helpful information for building on your experience.

To gain the deepest understanding of your achievements and shortcomings, be intentional and dedicate time to qualitative studies. Begin with your own internal assessment of key elements of your work. Then seek honest input from those with whom you worked: partner organizations, individual supporters, members of the press, elected officials (especially your champions who counted on your partnership), and your members or constituencies who are invested in your success.

Issue campaigns grow out of the strength of your capacity, the intelligence of your strategy, the efficacy of your organizing, and your ability to be a trusted resource to elected officials. How the campaign advances is a story, and many organizations find it useful to tell the story of a campaign, to create a case story. If your story is well-told, it will capture for your internal use, your external audiences, and your next round of planning all of the key lessons to be learned and used in the future.

Evaluating advocacy is an emerging field of work. For specific tools to evaluate advocacy, consult with national intermediary organizations that support nonprofit advocacy, e.g., The Alliance for Justice. Work with academic institutions in your state to use the evaluative tools that may be developed there for nonprofit-advocacy evaluation. Ask your professional and sector associations to share tools and examples that already have been developed for similar issue campaigns and organizational capacity-building efforts. However you choose to build evaluation into your plans, do it and allow it to drive future efforts.

Index

More results-oriented books from the Fieldstone Alliance

Lobbying & Advocacy

The Lobbying and Advocacy Handbook for Nonprofit Organizations
Shaping Public Policy at the State and Local Level
by Marcia Avner

The Lobbying and Advocacy Handbook is a planning guide and resource for nonprofit organizations that want to influence issues that matter to them. This book will help you decide whether to lobby and then put plans in place to make it work.

240 pages, softcover   9780940069268

The Nonprofit Board Member's Guide to Lobbying and Advocacy
by Marcia Avner

Written specifically for board members, this guide helps organizations increase their impact on policy decisions. It reveals how board members can be involved in planning for and implementing successful lobbying efforts.

96 pages, softcover   9780940069398

Collaboration

Collaboration Handbook
Creating, Sustaining, and Enjoying the Journey
by Michael Winer and Karen Ray

Shows you how to get a collaboration going, set goals, determine everyone's roles, create an action plan, and evaluate the results. Includes a case study of one collaboration from start to finish, helpful tips on how to avoid pitfalls, and worksheets to keep everyone on track.

192 pages, softcover   9780940069039

Collaboration: What Makes It Work, 2nd Ed.
by Paul Mattessich, PhD, Marta Murray-Close, BA, and Barbara Monsey, MPH

An in-depth review of current collaboration research. Major findings are summarized, critical conclusions are drawn, and 20 key factors influencing successful collaborations are identified. Includes The Wilder Collaboration Factors Inventory, which groups can use to assess their collaboration.

104 pages, softcover   9780940069329

A Fieldstone Nonprofit Guide to Forming Alliances
by Linda Hoskins and Emil Angelica

Helps you understand the wide range of ways that they can work with others—focusing on alliances that work at a lower level of intensity. It shows how to plan and start an alliance that fits a nonprofit's circumstances and needs.

112 pages, softcover   9780940069466

The Nimble Collaboration
Fine-Tuning Your Collaboration for Lasting Success
by Karen Ray

Shows you ways to make your existing collaboration more responsive, flexible, and productive. Provides three key strategies to help your collaboration respond quickly to changing environments and participants.

136 pages, softcover   9780940069282

Funder's Guides

Community Visions, Community Solutions
Grantmaking for Comprehensive Impact
by Joseph A. Connor and Stephanie Kadel-Taras

Helps foundations, community funds, government agencies, and other grantmakers uncover a community's highest aspiration for itself, and support and sustain strategic efforts to get to workable solutions.

128 pages, softcover   9780940069305

A Funder's Guide to Evaluation: Leveraging Evaluation to Improve Nonprofit Effectiveness
by Peter York

More and more funders and nonprofit leaders are shifting away from proving something to someone else, and toward *im*proving what they do so they can achieve their mission and share how they succeeded with others. This book includes strategies and tools to help grantmakers support and use evaluation as a nonprofit organizational capacity-building tool.

160 pages, softcover   9780940069480

A Funder's Guide to Organizational Assessment
Tools, Processes, and Their Use in Building Capacity
by GEO

In this book, funders, grantees, and consultants will understand how organizational assessment can be used to build the capacity of nonprofits, enhance grantmaking, impact organizational systems, and measure foundation effectiveness.

216 pages,   9780940069534

Strengthening Nonprofit Performance
A Funder's Guide to Capacity Building
Paul Connolly and Carol Lukas

This practical guide synthesizes the most recent capacity-building practice and research into a collection of strategies, steps, and examples that you can use to get started on or improve funding to strengthen nonprofit organizations.

176 pages, softcover   9780940069374

Management & Planning

The Accidental Techie
Supporting, Managing, and Maximizing Your Nonprofit's Technology
by Sue Bennett

How to support and manage technology on a day-to-day basis, including setting up a help desk, developing a technology budget, working with consultants, handling security, creating a backup system, purchasing hardware and software, using donated hardware, creating a useful database, and more.

176 pages, softcover   9780940069497

Benchmarking for Nonprofits
How to Measure, Manage, and Improve Results
by Jason Saul

This book defines a systematic and reliable way to benchmark (the ongoing process of measuring your organization against leaders)—from preparing your organization to measuring performance and implementing best practices.

128 pages, softcover   9780940069435

The Best of the Board Café
Hands-on Solutions for Nonprofit Boards
by Jan Masaoka, CompassPoint Nonprofit Services

Gathers the most requested articles from the e-newsletter *Board Café*. You'll find a lively menu of ideas, information, opinions, news, and resources to help board members give and get the most out of their board service.

232 pages, softcover   9780940069794

Bookkeeping Basics
What Every Nonprofit Bookkeeper Needs to Know
by Debra L. Ruegg and Lisa M. Venkatrathnam

Complete with step-by-step instructions, a glossary of accounting terms, detailed examples, and handy reproducible forms, this book will enable you to successfully meet the basic bookkeeping requirements of your nonprofit organization—even if you have little or no formal accounting training.

128 pages, softcover   9780940069299

Consulting with Nonprofits: A Practitioner's Guide
by Carol A. Lukas

A step-by-step, comprehensive guide for consultants. Addresses the art of consulting, how to run your business, and much more. Also includes tips and anecdotes from 30 skilled consultants.

240 pages, softcover   9780940069176

The Fieldstone Nonprofit Guide to
Crafting Effective Mission and Vision Statements
by Emil Angelica

Guides you through two six-step processes that result in a mission statement, vision statement, or both. Shows how a clarified mission and vision lead to more effective leadership, decisions, fundraising, and management. Includes tips, sample statements, and worksheets.

88 pages, softcover   9780940069275

The Fieldstone Nonprofit Guide to
Developing Effective Teams
by Beth Gilbertsen and Vijit Ramchandani

Helps you understand, start, and maintain a team. Provides tools and techniques for writing a mission statement, setting goals, conducting effective meetings, creating ground rules to manage team dynamics, making decisions in teams, creating project plans, and developing team spirit.

80 pages, softcover   9780940069206

Financial Leadership for Nonprofit Executives
Guiding Your Organization to Long-term Success
by Jeanne Peters and Elizabeth Schaffer

Provides executives with a practical guide to protecting and growing the assets of their organizations and with accomplishing as much mission as possible with those resources.

144 pages, softcover   9780940069442

The Five Life Stages of Nonprofit Organizations
Where You Are, Where You're Going, and What to Expect When You Get There
by Judith Sharken Simon with J. Terence Donovan

Shows you what's "normal" for each development stage that helps you plan for transitions, stay on track, and avoid unnecessary struggles. This guide also includes The Wilder Nonprofit Life Stage Assessment to plot and understand your organization's progress in seven arenas of organization development.

128 pages, softcover   9780940069220

The Manager's Guide to Program Evaluation:
Planning, Contracting, and Managing for Useful Results
by Paul W. Mattessich, Ph.D.

Explains how to plan and manage an evaluation that will help identify your organization's successes, share information with key audiences, and improve services.

96 pages, softcover   9780940069381

The Nonprofit Mergers Workbook
The Leader's Guide to Considering, Negotiating, and Executing a Merger
by David La Piana

A merger can be a daunting and complex process. Save time, money, and untold frustration with this highly practical guide that makes the process manageable and controllable. Includes case studies, decision trees, 22 worksheets, checklists, tips, and complete step-by-step guidance from seeking partners to writing the merger agreement, and more.

240 pages, softcover   9780940069725

The Nonprofit Mergers Workbook Part II
Unifying the Organization after a Merger
by La Piana Associates

Once the merger agreement is signed, the question becomes: How do we make this merger work? *Part II* helps you create a comprehensive plan to achieve *integration*—bringing together people, programs, processes, and systems from two (or more) organizations into a single, unified whole.

248 pages   9780940069411

Resolving Conflict in Nonprofit Organizations
The Leader's Guide to Finding Constructive Solutions
by Marion Peters Angelica

Helps you identify conflict, decide whether to intervene, uncover and deal with the true issues, and design and conduct a conflict-resolution process. Includes exercises to learn and practice conflict-resolution skills, guidance on handling unique conflicts such as harassment and discrimination, and when (and where) to seek outside help with litigation, arbitration, and mediation.

192 pages, softcover   9780940069169

Strategic Planning Workbook for Nonprofit Organizations, Revised and Updated
by Bryan Barry

Chart a wise course for your nonprofit's future. This time-tested workbook gives you practical step-by-step guidance, real-life examples, one nonprofit's complete strategic plan, and easy-to-use worksheets.

144 pages, softcover   9780940069077

Marketing & Fundraising

The Fieldstone Nonprofit Guide to Conducting Successful Focus Groups
by Judith Sharken Simon

Shows how to collect valuable information without a lot of money or special expertise. Using this proven technique, you'll get essential opinions and feedback to help you check out your assumptions, do better strategic planning, improve services or products, and more.

80 pages, softcover   9780940069190

Coping with Cutbacks:
The Nonprofit Guide to Success When Times Are Tight
by Emil Angelica and Vincent Hyman

Shows you practical ways to involve business, government, and other nonprofits to solve problems together. Also includes 185 cutback strategies you can put to use right away.

128 pages, softcover   9780940069091

Marketing Workbook for Nonprofit Organizations Volume I: Develop the Plan
by Gary J. Stern

Don't just wish for results—get them! Here's how to create a straightforward, usable marketing plan. Includes the six Ps of Marketing, how to use them effectively, a sample marketing plan, tips on using the Internet, and worksheets.

208 pages, softcover   9780940069251

Marketing Workbook for Nonprofit Organizations Volume II: Mobilize People for Marketing Success
by Gary J. Stern

Put together a successful promotional campaign based on the most persuasive tool of all: personal contact. Learn how to mobilize your entire organization, its staff, volunteers, and supporters in a focused, one-to-one marketing campaign. Comes with *Pocket Guide for Marketing Representatives*, where representatives can record key campaign messages and find motivational reminders.

192 pages, softcover   9780940069107

Venture Forth! The Essential Guide to Starting a Moneymaking Business in Your Nonprofit Organization
by Rolfe Larson

The most complete guide on nonprofit business development. Building on the experience of dozens of organizations, this handbook gives you a time-tested approach for finding, testing, and launching a successful nonprofit business venture.

272 pages, softcover   9780940069244

Vital Communities

Community Building: What Makes It Work
by Wilder Research Center

Reveals 28 keys to help you build community more effectively. Includes detailed descriptions of each factor, case examples of how they play out, and practical questions to assess your work.

112 pages, softcover   9780940069121

Community Economic Development Handbook
by Mihailo Temali

A concrete, practical handbook to turning any neighborhood around. It explains how to start a community economic-development organization and then lays out the steps of four proven and powerful strategies for revitalizing inner-city neighborhoods.

288 pages, softcover   9780940069367

The Community Leadership Handbook
Framing Ideas, Building Relationships, and Mobilizing Resources
by Jim Krile

Based on the best of Blandin Foundation's 20-year experience in developing community leaders, this book gives community members 14 tools to bring people together to make change.

240 pages, softcover   9780940069541

The Fieldstone Nonprofit Guide to Conducting Community Forums
by Carol Lukas and Linda Hoskins

Provides step-by-step instruction to plan and carry out exciting, successful community forums that will educate the public, build consensus, focus action, or influence policy.

128 pages, softcover   9780940069312

The Creative Community Builder's Handbook
How to Transform Communities
Using Local Assets, Art, and Culture
by Tom Borrup

Creative community building is about bringing community development, arts and culture, planning and design, and citizen participation together to create sustainable communities. This book provides examples and tools to help community builders utilize human cultures and the creativity in everyone.

280 pages, softcover   9780940069473

Violence Prevention & Intervention

The Little Book of Peace

Designed and illustrated by Kelly O. Finnerty

A pocket-size guide to help people think about violence and talk about it with their families and friends. You may download a free copy of *The Little Book of Peace* from our web site at www.wilder.org/pubs.

24 pages
Also available in Spanish and Hmong language editions.

Journey Beyond Abuse: A Step-by-Step Guide to Facilitating Women's Domestic Abuse Groups

by Kay-Laurel Fischer, MA, LP,
and Michael F. McGrane, LICSW

Create a program where women increase their understanding of the dynamics of abuse, feel less alone and isolated, and have a greater awareness of channels to safety. This book includes 21 group activities that you can combine to create groups of differing length and focus.

208 pages, softcover   9780940069145

Moving Beyond Abuse: Stories and Questions for Women Who Have Lived with Abuse

(Companion-guided journal to *Journey Beyond Abuse*)

A series of stories and questions that can be used in coordination with the sessions provided in the facilitator's guide or with the guidance of a counselor in other forms of support.

88 pages, softcover   9780940069152

Foundations for Violence-Free Living: A Step-by-Step Guide to Facilitating Men's Domestic Abuse Groups

by David J. Mathews, MA, LICSW

A complete guide to facilitating a men's domestic-abuse program. Includes 29 activities, detailed guidelines for presenting each activity, and a discussion of psychological issues that may arise out of each activity.

240 pages, softcover   9780940069053

On the Level

(Participant's workbook to *Foundations for Violence-Free Living*)

Contains 49 worksheets, including midterm and final evaluations. Men can record their progress.

160 pages, softcover   9780940069060

What Works in Preventing Rural Violence

by Wilder Research Center

An in-depth review of 88 effective strategies you can use to prevent and intervene in violent behaviors, improve services for victims, and reduce repeat offenses. This report also includes a Community Report Card with step-by-step directions on how you can collect, record, and use information about violence in your community.

94 pages, softcover   9780940069046

CPSIA information can be obtained
at www.ICGtesting.com
Printed in the USA
BVHW01*1543030918
526377BV00013B/281/P